In this book Mark Rupert argues that American global power was shaped by the ways in which mass production was institutionalized in the USA, and by the political and ideological struggles integral to this process. The production of an unprecedented volume of goods propelled the United States to the apex of the global division of labor, ensuring victory in World War II and enabling postwar reconstruction under American leadership. He describes an "historic bloc" of American statesmen, capitalists and labor leaders who fostered a productivity-oriented political consensus within the USA, and sought to generalize their vision of liberal capitalism around the globe. Through a study of the Ford Motor Company, he focuses on the incorporation of industrial labor as a junior partner in this hegemonic bloc, and argues that the recent erosion of its position under the pressures of transnational competition and the political forces of right-wing reaction may open up new possibilities for transformative politics.

CAMBRIDGE STUDIES IN INTERNATIONAL RELATIONS: 38

Producing hegemony

Cambridge Studies in International Relations is a joint initiative of Cambridge University Press and the British International Studies Association (BISA). The series will include a wide range of material, from undergraduate textbooks and surveys to research-based monographs and collaborative volumes. The aim of the series is to publish the best new scholarship in International Studies from Europe, North America and the rest of the world.

Series list continues after index

This book is dedicated to my brother Eric, whose love of history was an inspiration; and my daughter Anna Elise, who brings with her renewed hope for the future.

Producing hegemony

The politics of mass production and American global power

Mark Rupert

Department of Political Science
Syracuse University

 CAMBRIDGE
UNIVERSITY PRESS

Published by the Press Syndicate of the University of Cambridge
The Pitt Building, Trumpington Street, Cambridge CB2 1RP
40 West 20th Street, New York, 10011–4211, USA
10 Stamford Road, Oakleigh, Melbourne 3166, Australia

© Cambridge University Press 1995

First published 1995

Printed in Great Britain at the University Press, Cambridge

A catalogue record for this book is available from the British Library

Library of Congress cataloguing in publication data
Rupert, Mark.
Producing hegemony: the politics of mass production and American
global power / Mark Rupert.
p.   cm. – (Cambridge studies in international relations: 38)
Includes bibliographical references.
ISBN 0 521 46112 X. – ISBN 0 521 46650 4 (pbk.)
1. Technological innovations – Economic aspects – United States –
History – 20th century.
2. Mass production – United States – History – 20th century.
3. United States – Foreign relations – 20th century.
4. International economic relations.
I. Title.   II. Series.
HC110.T4R87   1995
338'.064'0973–dc20   94–28827   CIP

ISBN 0 521 46112 X hardback
ISBN 0 521 46650 4 paperback

CE

Contents

Figures

Tables

Acknowledgements

This project evolved over a period of years, and in its course I have accumulated a great many debts, large and small. While I cannot acknowledge all of these in particular, I shall express my gratitude in general terms to everyone who has lent a hand, or provided constructive criticism, or given me moral support as I struggled with this. As my sixth grade teacher used to say (albeit with rather different implications), "you know who you are."

I owe very special debts indeed to Bill Thompson and David Rapkin, teachers and friends who started me on the path of studying IPE, and allowed me the freedom to explore routes that they themselves would not have chosen. I am also happy to express my appreciation to my graduate school comrades, Suzanne Frederick, Sandy and Dwayne Dawson, and Bridgett Chandler, partners in crime without whom I might never have survived graduate school.

The members of the political science department at Syracuse University, my home since 1987, have been supportive in a variety of ways and I would like to express my gratitude to them collectively. Individual friends and colleagues have also provided invaluable support. Although we have met only once, the work of Robert Cox has had a profound influence on my thinking. Over the last several years, Craig Murphy and Stephen Gill have been very helpful and supportive. John Agnew has with good cheer and amazing perspicacity read and commented on everything I ever gave him, and each time I have learned something important. Naeem Inayatullah has, with his own characteristically dialectical combination of friendliness and antagonism, provoked and challenged and stimulated my thinking since the first day I met him.

During the writing of this book, my partner Margot Clark has been tolerant of my preoccupation and moodiness, my domestic delinquency, and the amplification of all my manifold character flaws and unpleasant tendencies. Her unconditional love and support have made it possible for me to finish this project and, I hope, to grow along the way. Margot, who is a librarian and indexer, also compiled the index for this book

Research for this book was supported by a grant from the Syracuse University Faculty Senate and another from the Henry J. Kaiser Family Foundation. This funding made it possible for me to spend time working in the Archive of Labor and Urban Affairs at Wayne State University's Reuther Library, and at the Henry Ford Museum in Dearborn, Michigan. At ALUA, Ray Boryczka, Tom Featherstone and the archive staff patiently helped this neophyte to get his bearings and accomplish his goals in the limited time available. At the Ford Archive, I was ably assisted by Cathy Latendresse and the staff. I am also grateful to Dorcas MacDonald and the staff of the interlibrary loan office at Syracuse University's Bird Library, who cheerfully scoured the nation's libraries so that I might write this book.

Lastly, I want to thank John Haslam of Cambridge University Press, and Trevor Horwood my copy editor, for guiding me through the publication process with patience and good humour, as well as good advice.

An earlier version of the argument developed in this book was published in article form in *International Studies Quarterly*, 34, 4. Parts of that article are reproduced in various parts of this book.

1   Introduction

This study investigates the production of global social power in the twentieth century, social processes which made possible an American global hegemony. It seeks to integrate theoretical argument and historical interpretation in order to address gaps in the literatures of international relations and International Political Economy. A central contention of the study is that the "neorealist" orthodoxy of International Political Economy, and to a significant extent even its radical critics, have in their studies of global power neglected crucial processes through which power has been produced, and the conflicting social relations which at once underlie and make possible that production, and which also make problematic its long-term reproduction.

The historical interpretation which I construct differs in significant ways from existing accounts of hegemony in the twentieth-century world. Understandings of global hegemony produced by "neorealist" scholars such as Robert Gilpin, Robert Keohane, and Stephen Krasner have focused upon state power and the creation of international regimes for the coordination of policy and the facilitation of cooperation among otherwise rivalrous states. The conception of hegemony central to Immanuel Wallerstein's world-system theory has emphasized the role of hegemonic states in creating a poltical structure to sustain global exploitation and accumulation, without imposing upon the world-economy as a whole the overwhelming overhead costs of world-empire. For Wallerstein, hegemony arises from one state's productive preeminence in the global division of labor, and the commercial, financial, and ultimately military–political powers which are seen to emerge from that structural predominance. Previous Gramscian studies by scholars such as Kees van der Pijl and Stephen Gill have highlighted coalitions among fractions of the capitalist class, and the transnational networks of power which these coalitions have constructed in the postwar world. The account developed here suggests these various aspects of global hegemony were made possible by an underlying process which has yet to be adequately understood by scholars of International Political Economy.

In contrast to these approaches, the central working hypothesis of this project is that the exercise of US global power was shaped by the historically specific ways in which mass production was institutionalized, and by the political, cultural, and ideological aspects of this process at home and abroad. This complex process involved the deliberate fostering by American statesmen, capitalists, and labor leaders of a centrist, productivity-oriented political consensus in the core countries of the world economy – especially France, Italy, Germany, Japan, as well as at home in the USA. This, in turn, entailed narrowing the possible political horizons of labor movements and the incorporation of more "moderate" elements of organized labor as junior partners in the historic bloc underlying the new hegemonic world order. The anticommunism of the Cold War, and a more widespread prosperity based upon securing for organized industrial labor a somewhat larger share of the fruits of the mass production economy, helped to cement together the elements of this bloc. A major theme of this study, then, is the direct relevance of "domestic" production politics to "international" relations, and vice versa.

The stakes involved in this reinterpretation are both practical and academic. In recent decades, as the problematic underpinnings of this globally predominant historic bloc have reasserted themselves, the American working class has received an economic and political battering unprecedented in postwar experience. Their wages have been depressed, their working conditions transformed, and their unions attacked without apology or pretense. Among the results of these tendencies have been dramatic increases in inequality of income and wealth, along with spreading and deepening poverty, and a political disaffection evidenced in the popular appeal of such a charismatic and putatively apolitical figure as Ross Perot. The process which has produced such painful and disorienting consequences – the disintegration of the hegemonic historic bloc – has been integrally related to world order formation and degeneration; yet the predominant theoretical traditions in the field of International Political Economy have been unable to apprehend the politics of class which have been central to

2

this process. The major goal of this project was to begin to redress this systematic imbalance.

The crisis of International Political Economy

International Political Economy (IPE) emerged as an important sub-field of the academic study of international relations (IR) during the 1970s, a period of unsettling change in the global political economy. Twenty years after the emergence of the field, IPE finds itself in crisis. Under the pressure of a barrage of scholarly critiques and in the face of global social change, the prevailing theoretical orientations in IPE – neorealism and world-system theory – have begun to reveal their limitations as modes of social self-understanding appropriate to the late twentieth century. I will argue here that both schools of thought embody relatively static theories of politics which emphasize distributional struggles within a given field of social relations. Corresponding to these limited conceptions of politics are abstract and essentially ahistorical conceptions of the state. Neither theory sees politics as an open-ended process of social self-production, and therefore neither directs inquiry toward historical, contextual, and hence contingent variations in state–society relations and in state powers grounded in these relations. Concrete political struggles which could be seen as essential to the historical formation of "state–society complexes"[1] and the production of state powers are largely submerged in the formal explanatory accounts produced by these research traditions. As a consequence of the limited conceptions of politics which characterize both neorealism and world-system theory, I contend that the major currents of contemporary IPE inquiry are largely unable to understand processes of transformation which characterize the late twentieth-century world, and that both theories entail fundamentally conservative implications which derive from their ahistorical presuppositions. In order to flesh out this contention, I will briefly discuss each school of thought.

Neorealism: the contradictions of orthodoxy

For almost two decades now, the predominant school of thought within the mainstream of IPE inquiry has been neorealism. By "neo-realism" I mean to refer not to the works of any one author or to any particular theory, but to a family of arguments related by a common set of fundamental, if often unspoken, commitments. In particular, I

3

follow Robert Cox, Richard Ashley, and Alex Wendt in identifying neorealism with presuppositions of atomistic ontology and empiricist epistemology in the construction of IR–IPE arguments.[2] In its various incarnations, neorealist IPE has been primarily concerned to explain the emergence of political order among competing states, an order which makes possible regularized international economic relations.

In framing this explanatory problem, neorealist IPE has taken as its theoretical point of departure a metaphor of Hobbesian inspiration in which states are understood as pre-constituted individuals, struggling for security in a lawless and amoral world. This represents, in Hayward Alker's words, a "presumption of anarchy in world politics."[3] At the core of neorealism, then, is an implicit commitment to a vision of the social world cast in terms of *abstract individualism*. Steven Lukes has described as follows this fundamental vision and the analytic strategy which it entails:

> According to this conception, individuals [or, for neorealism, sovereign states] are pictured abstractly as given, with given interests, wants, purposes, needs, etc.; while society and the state [or, for IPE, cooperation and order among states] are pictured as sets of actual or possible social arrangements which respond more or less adequately to those individuals' requirements. Social and political rules and institutions are, on this view, regarded collectively as an artifice, a modifiable instrument, a means of fulfilling independently given individual objectives; the means and the end are distinct. The crucial point about this conception is that the relevant features of individuals determining the ends which social arrangements are held ... to fulfill, whether these features are called instincts, faculties, needs, desires, rights, etc., are assumed as given, independently of a social context.[4]

In light of this conception of the social universe, politics is understood in terms of competition among primordial "individuals" – in this case, states – over relative shares of resources which confer power and wealth, and which may be instrumentally deployed in interactions with other such individuals. Accordingly, the fundamental analytical problem for neorealist theorists has been to explain the emergence of cooperation and order in the context of such an anarchic, competitive system of individual states: "In a world of conflicting nation-states," Robert Gilpin asked in a classic formulation, "how does one explain the existence of an interdependent international economy?"[5]

Early attempts at solving this theoretical puzzle used the metaphor of "public goods" to suggest that a single, politically and economically

4

preponderant state – a systemic leader or "hegemon" – might be a necessary (if not sufficient) condition for the construction of order in the international system.[6] According to this line of reasoning, only such an extraordinarily powerful state could and would undertake to organize provision of the public good of international order, overcoming endemic free-rider problems in the international system by virtue of its disproportionate stake in the construction and maintenance of a more liberal international order. As a consequence of its systemic preponderance, a hegemonic state would also have a preponderant interest in constructing a global system of order and would be more willing to assume an asymmetrical share of the costs of that order. In several studies this general framework – which came to be known as "hegemonic stability" theory – demonstrated some ability to make sense of macro-historical fluctuations in the degree of "order" which characterized the international system over the past two centuries, albeit with some significant explanatory limitations which suggested the need to incorporate factors from other (sub-systemic) levels of analysis.[7]

Subsequently, a cluster of historical and theoretical critiques from within the mainstream of IPE suggested that hegemonic stability theory overstated the extent to which leading states actually used their extraordinary power to compel others to cooperate in the construction of an encompassing, systemic order. Further, it was argued that the metaphor of public goods was not an entirely apt one insofar as it overstated the "jointness" and "non-excludability" which characterize international regimes, and understated the extent to which distributive issues and strategic bargaining among a relatively small group of actors are relevant to the problem of cooperation under anarchy. Hence, it was argued, game theoretic models such as prisoner's dilemma might be more appropriate than a public goods approach as the analytic core of neorealist IPE theory. Finally, critics disputed the extent to which the current situation could be adequately described in terms of hegemonic decline and a corresponding increase in international disorder.[8] Yet, despite the vigor of these arguments, the characteristic neorealist definition of the central analytical problem of IPE was not fundamentally challenged in these intramural debates. Viewing the world in terms of abstract individualism, neorealist scholars continue to be preoccupied with the conditions under which sovereign states in an anarchic environment will engage in cooperative behavior towards one another.[9]

The atomistic presuppositions upon which this theoretical problematic rests have, however, been directly attacked by critical theorists representing various orientations toward social inquiry.[10] Common to these critiques has been the charge that neorealism embodies a deep conservatism, at once cognitive and political, insofar as its guiding vision of the social universe *presumes* the existence of sovereign states as individual actors in an environment of anarchy and in so doing simultaneously valorizes the sovereign state and abstracts it from its socio-historical context. The social bases of state power, the historically specific ideologies and socially productive practices which sustain it, are placed outside the scope of inquiry, supplanted by formal calculations of interest and comparative assessments of the putatively power-bearing resources possessed by states. In the paragraphs which follow, I amplify this critique of neorealism, drawing upon insights which derive from the Marxian–Gramscian perspective which I will develop more fully in the next chapter.

The model of the state which appears to underlie much neorealist thinking is based upon an appropriation of the mercantilist view, characteristic of the early modern age of absolutism and the rise of commercial capitalism. Indeed it may seem natural, in light of neorealism's abstract individualism and its attendant vision of politics as distributive competition, for neorealists to embrace as a central axiom of their political economy Jacob Viner's classic interpretation of mercantilist thought, stressing the long-run harmony between wealth and power as instruments and "proper ultimate ends" of state policy.[11] If wealth and power were interdependent in the era of commercial capitalism, the reasoning goes, it must be all the more important for states to be able to influence or control the location of wealth-producing activities in the era of industrial capitalism and high technology. Thus neorealist scholars may confound a static mercantilist social cosmology with a Smithian view of wealth as socially produced value, and discuss modern state–society complexes in terms more appropriate for pre-industrial absolutist states.

In modern capitalist social formations, however, where economics and politics are conceived as separate spheres of social activity, where wealth is produced in the private sphere of individual self-interest while political community is to be exclusively expressed in the public, I would suggest that the premises of classical mercantilism are singularly ill-suited to an adequate understanding of states, state powers, and their historically contingent grounding in state–society relations.

In adopting the statist view of social reality characteristic of classical mercantilism, neorealist scholars collapse the potentially antagonistic relationship between the political and economic aspects of modern state–society complexes into a single, abstract unity, and so they are able to assert *a priori* a long-term complementarity between wealth and power as means–ends of such abstract national communities. Acceptance of this mercantilist perspective at face value has the effect of exempting from systematic inquiry the historically specific social relations and political struggles which underlie the state, the processes by which wealth and power resources are produced and accumulated, and the pursuit of these as seemingly "proper ultimate ends" of political community. As a consequence, the explanatory accounts of neorealist political economy are historically one-sided and entail quite conservative political implications.

Furthermore, the empirical claims of neorealist analyses can starkly contradict the basic mercantilist presupposition of long-run harmony between wealth and power as means–ends of national policy. Thus, one of the major conclusions of Gilpin's pioneering study strongly suggests that a primary factor underlying the diffusion of American productive capacities, and the consequent long-term political-economic decline of the United States, is a fundamental disjuncture between the political and the economic aspects of social organization – that is, between the realms of public and private activity (as these are understood in capitalist states–societies): "from the perspective of the home economy the benefits of direct foreign investment are private; the *costs* (and they are substantial) are public. Such investment benefits the owners of capital to the overall disadvantage of other groups and the economy as a whole."[12]

The fundamental implications of such conflicts have not been recognized by neorealist scholars, and hence this contradictory form of argumentation is often simply reproduced. Thus, nearly a decade after the publication of Gilpin's seminal work, Robert Keohane could write with apparent confidence that "Reflection on wealth and power as state objectives soon yields the conclusion that they are complementary. For contemporary statesmen, as for the mercantilists of the seventeenth and eighteenth centuries, power is a necessary condition for plenty, and vice versa."[13] And this despite the argument of his own study that the complementarity of public and private pursuits is subject to chronic tensions which can inhibit their harmonization over the long run:

The key tradeoffs for the United States in the 1980s, as for mercantilist statesmen in the seventeenth century and American leaders in the late 1940s, are not between power and wealth but between the long-term power–wealth interests of the state and the partial interests of individual merchants, workers, or manufacturers on the one hand or short-term interests of the society on the other. The United States is not the only country that has been unable to formulate long-term goals without making concessions to partial economic interests.[14]

Indeed, this latter generalization would seem to raise questions about the socio-historical conditions under which private economic interests are able to come into conflict with public policy goals as defined by the state. Yet, as a consequence of its basic commitment to abstract individualism, and the mercantilist conception of the state which it resurrects upon that basis, neorealism is precluded from explicitly addressing such questions. In order to do so, it would seem necessary to develop some systematic conception of the historical relationship between the state and capitalism. Immanuel Wallerstein's theory of the capitalist world-economy offers one possible alternative to the neorealist cul-de-sac.

World-system theory: a radical alternative?

In a sustained effort to construct an alternative, critical and historical political economy, Immanuel Wallerstein has posited a radical disjuncture between the economic and political aspects of social life at the global level. It is perhaps ironic, then, that he too ends up with a highly abstract and one-sided understanding of states, their historical grounding in state–society relations, and the politics of these in the modern world.[15]

Motivated initially by a professed desire to avoid the abstraction of national societies from the larger context of social relations in which they are embedded, and from the historical evolution of these global social relations, Wallerstein recast his central concept of a social system:

We take the defining characteristic of a social system to be the existence within it of a division of labor, such that the various sectors or areas within are dependent upon economic exchange with others for the smooth and continuous provisioning of the needs of the area. Such economic exchange can clearly exist without a common political structure and even more obviously without sharing the same culture.[16]

8

These are the characteristics in terms of which Wallerstein identifies the modern (c. 1500) world-system as an historical social system. It is, he asserts, a "world-economy," an integrated production system with a single division of labor encompassing multiple political units and cultures. Moreover, since production within this structure is carried out for the purpose of profitable market exchange, it is a "capitalist" world-economy.

The unique strength of this system and the key to its longevity is that capitalism operates on a scale larger than that which any juridically defined political unit can control. This allows capitalists a significant degree of flexibility in their dealings with political forces of nation, class, and state. On the one hand, their global mobility allows them the freedom to evade such onerous political controls as might be placed on the accumulation process if the geographical scope of the division of labor were coextensive with that of territorial political authority. On the other hand, however, when it suits their purposes the capitalists of a particular state can use the political machinery of that state to intervene in world markets to gain advantage in their competitions with the capitalists of other states. Further, within the parameters of these structural constants, periodic "hegemonies" have provided the low-overhead political organization required for more intensive spells of global accumulation.[17]

The capitalist world-economy, then, is the only self-contained "social system" of the modern world and hence encompasses all other social relations, including political loci such as classes, ethnic/national groups, and states. Indeed, Wallerstein repeatedly asserts, the structurally preeminent world-economy has so fundamentally shaped the development of these political structures that it may be said to have *called them into being* as subordinate or secondary relations.

> [T]here emerged within the world-economy a division of labor ... and along with this specialization went differing forms of labor control and differing patterns of stratification which in turn had different political consequences for the "states", that is, the arenas of *political* action.[18]

> The development of the capitalist world-economy has involved the creation of all the major institutions of the modern world: classes, ethnic/national groups, households – and the "states." All of these structures postdate, not antedate capitalism; all are consequence, not cause.[19]

9

For Wallerstein, the political character of these subsidiary structures is determined by the imperatives of accumulation on a world scale. Classes are understood as being constituted within the capitalist world-economy and they, in turn, have constructed state machineries as they have sought to institutionalize their class power and their ability to intervene in world markets.[20] Structures of class and state which might otherwise be viewed as embodying irreducible political relations instead become expressions of the world-system. In Wallerstein's theoretical arguments, explicitly political action is, in effect, delimited within these secondary structures while capital accumulation proceeds unhindered at the level of the world-system. Concrete struggles among and between class and state actors are thus reduced to secondary importance, subordinated to the structurally preeminent world-economy.

Through his identification of states with dominant classes and their world-market interests, Wallerstein collapses potentially contradictory state–society relations into an ahistorical, abstract unity no less than do the neorealists. As a consequence of these reifications, interpretation of *how* particular state–society complexes were historically constructed cannot play a central role in the explanatory accounts of either neorealism or world-system theory. I will argue in subsequent chapters that such an interpretation – inaccessible in terms of either of the approaches reviewed above – reveals much about the distinctly neo-liberal character of state–society relations in the USA, about the world order which those relations helped to foster, and about possibilities for change in the late twentieth century.

The plan of this study

Dissatisfaction with both neorealism and world-system theory constitutes the point of departure for this study. However, the study also seeks to address specific lacunae in the literature of critical International Political Economy. Over the last decade, scholars seeking to overcome the cognitive and political limitations of mainstream approaches have created alternative research projects formulated in terms of a wide variety of heterodox theoretical positions. Among these a prominent tendency has been the work of Gramscian-inspired scholars. In chapter 2, I argue that these pioneering Gramscian analyses represent a "progressive" development in both a scientific and a political sense. Yet, while I find reason to be encouraged by this growing literature, I have been troubled by significant omissions which this study attempts to remedy.

The Gramscian tendency in IPE has not yet produced an historical analysis of the role of the American working class in the construction of hegemony. Nor has it generated an explicit interpretation of the relationship of Gramsci to Marx, the fundamental vision of human social life which they may have shared, and the relationship of any such Marxian–Gramscian social ontology to the theory and practice of IPE. These connections remain largely implicit in this literature. A goal of this project, then, is to sketch the broad outlines of an alternative social ontology, in order to make clear and explicit just how a Marxian–Gramscian vision of IPE diverges from the mainstream, as well as from such putatively radical frameworks as world-system theory. Chapter 2 outlines such an alternative vision of IPE based upon an interpretation of the classic works of Karl Marx and Antonio Gramsci.

This more explicit formulation of a Marxian–Gramscian social ontology also serves to frame the critical analysis of global power relations which the remainder of the project seeks to develop. After outlining this relational vision of IPE, I then proceed to develop an historical interpretation which interweaves struggles and processes at multiple levels of analysis: from world order, to state–society relations, to industrial regimes and ideological struggles within particular workplaces. Chapter 3 initiates this reinterpretation by synthesizing several convergent, if heterodox, currents in the literatures of international political economy, as well as diplomatic and social history, in order to construct a vision of the broad contours of a global complex of social power relations which was in place by the mid-twentieth century. At the core of this complex of relations was the institutionalization of mass production and consumption, and the hegemony of a modified form of liberalism which, following Robert Cox, I will call "neoliberalism". Neoliberalism sought to fuse into an organic and harmonious whole such elements as (1) an emphasis on the importance of industrial productivity and economic growth as conditions of political stability, and a corresponding toleration of limited political intervention into market processes in order to secure the conditions of growth; (2) the incorporation of "moderate", economically oriented industrial unions into the mainstream of liberal democratic capitalism; and (3) a more liberal and open world economic order which could provide the widest possible market for mass produced commodities, while still affording some scope for macroeconomic policies which encourage economic growth.

Some of the preconditions of the rise of neoliberalism – the emergence of mass production in America, and the early internationalization of associated productive practices and managerial ideologies through the first decades of the century – are traced in chapter 4. Chapter 5 presents an historical overview of the institutionalization of mass production in the USA and the formation of an "historic bloc" to serve as a vehicle for neoliberal hegemony. I argue that the neoliberal accommodation was made possible by, and in turn shaped, the politics of private power in the sites of capitalist production. I then focus, with somewhat higher resolution, upon the relationship between production politics, ideological struggle and union organization during the decades when mass production was being institutionalized in the USA. More specifically, chapters 6 and 7 examine the Ford Motor Company in the years between the creation of the moving line system of production (1913–1914) and the Cold War consolidation of a social consensus on the preeminence of American-style liberal capitalism among the world's social systems, and its suitability as a universal model for other states–societies to emulate (c. 1952). These chapters develop an interpretation of the ideological struggles between Ford management and industrial unionists, both attempting to win the allegiance of rank and file auto workers through languages and symbols of "Americanism." The unionization struggles at Ford, and the ideological theme of "Americanism vs. Fordism" which both facilitated and constrained the triumph of unionism, is interpreted as a representative aspect of the ideological struggles which ultimately generated the postwar cultural consensus.

Finally, chapter 8 examines the historical degeneration of the postwar hegemonic framework and its global infrastructure, and situates the decline of unionism in America within that historical context. I argue that what we are now witnessing is not so much the penultimate stage of a national trajectory of rise and decline, as some scholars have suggested, but rather the process of degeneration of the historic bloc which underlay the postwar hegemonic world order. This transnational process has important ramifications for American society and foreign policy insofar as it involves the exclusion of those elements of organized industrial labor which had formerly been included in the hegemonic bloc, and a tendency to discipline labor through increasingly coercive, rather than consensual, means. Absent a hegemonic social consensus at home, modes of political action which had been marginalized or foreclosed may surface. This widening of political possibilities could take the form of a redefinition of "Americanism" in a more cosmopolitan culture of resistance within global capitalism, or it could emerge in a xenophobic or racist reaction to global restructuring which blames workers in other countries, or those perceived as others within the USA, for taking "American" industrial jobs. Beginning to sketch out possible paths for the theory and practice of International Political Economy at the close of the twentieth century is the last major task of the volume.

2 Marx, Gramsci, and possibilities for radical renewal in IPE

IPE and the politics of contending ontologies

As I suggested in the previous chapter, IPE is a field of inquiry which is in a kind of crisis. Our dominant research programs no longer enjoy the status of "normal science," and IPE is now actively contested at the most fundamental levels. A central aspect of this contest involves debates over the fundamental object(s) of inquiry which constitute IPE as a field. Should IPE concern itself with an understanding of an atomistic universe of sovereign states – in which competition for wealth and power among individual states is presumed to be the norm, and cooperation and order become extraordinary phenomena requiring explanation? Or should it be concerned with the social organization of production and exchange on a world scale – such that globally structured dominance relations and the fundamentally unequal constitution of global actors assume central importance? Are we to understand the global relationship between politics and economics by viewing it from the perspective of sovereign states, or from that of the capitalist world-economy?[1] What is at stake in the contest of social ontologies is the manner in which the human world is reproduced in thought and action. It is as much a political issue as a theoretical one; and it is, in every sense, vital.

Among its other effects, the crisis of IPE has helped to open up space for alternative world views. In recent years, there have been a growing number of creative and promising efforts to develop such alternatives. Prominent among these are Gramscian-inspired approaches to the analysis of IPE. The pioneering work of Robert Cox has been followed by major contributions aimed at applying insights of Gramsci to analyses of the postwar hegemony of a transnational capitalist historic bloc,

and of the implications of North–South struggle for the global hegemony of American-style capitalism and its characteristic culture.[2]

Taken together, these contributions mark the emergence of a new
research program in IPE which may be said the be "progressive" in
both a scientific and a political sense. In its scientific aspect, this
research program directs attention to social relations and processes
systematically neglected by mainstream neorealism as well as world-
system theory, and has provided substantial empirical support for its
major arguments. Politically, this body of research provides a critical
perspective on the contradictory nature of the social relations it
investigates, uncovering multifaceted relations of domination
embodied in these relations, and pointing toward concrete possibilities
for their transformation. In general, then, I find reason to be encouraged by this growing literature and the interests and aspirations which
it voices. The crisis of IPE, it seems, has not been all bad.

However, my enthusiasm for the emergent Gramscian research
program is tempered by a sense of caution. In attempting to work
within this new tendency, I have been struck by the absence of an
explicit interpretation of the relationship of Gramsci to Marx, the
fundamental vision of human social life which they may have shared,
and the relationship of any such Marxian–Gramscian social ontology
to the theory and practice of IPE. These connections remain largely
implicit in this literature. This chapter represents my attempt to make
these relationships clear and explicit.

I will argue that it is possible to understand both the system of
sovereign states and the capitalist world economy in non-reductionist
ways if the theory of IPE is reconstructed on the basis of a Marxian–
Gramscian social ontology. Toward this end, the next section of the
chapter presents an interpretation of the radicalized historical ontology characteristic of Marx and Gramsci. The final section then argues
that this kind of approach could serve as the basis of a critical and
non-reductionist reconstruction of IPE. Building upon such a foundation, the chapter will suggest an interpretation of the *political* relations which underlie the capitalist organization of production, as well
as the interstate system, and which allow us to understand the historical construction of these relations without *a priori* reducing one to
the other. Viewed from such a Marxian–Gramscian perspective, relations among sovereign states can be critically understood as relations
of *alienation* historically constructed among political communities
(states–societies) which are themselves constructed on the basis of

relations of alienation (i.e., the corresponding separations of the producer from the means of production, of political from economic relations, etc.). On this view, then, IPE should be critically concerned with the broadly political processes by which these relations of alienation are historically constructed and reproduced among and within the alienated political communities of the modern world.

In order to construct such an argument, however, it is first necessary to make clear and explicit the interpretation of Marx and of Gramsci upon which it will be based. This is the task of the next section. It implies that the dilemma of ontological starting points reflected in the intellectual crisis of IPE – i.e., whether the primitive unit should be states as individual agents or the world economy as generative structure – is resolvable in terms of a radicalized, historical ontology. Such a view would eschew the designation of any fixed, ontologically privileged starting point, or, for that matter, any *a priori* relation between agents and structures such as that posited by "structuration" theories. Instead, it would seek an active understanding of the concrete historical processes through which socially situated human beings produce and reproduce their world.

Marx, Gramsci, and radicalized social ontology

Marx and Gramsci may be said to have shared a common political commitment which permeated their practices of social inquiry and which constitutes, for me, their primary legacy. Both were engaged in a practice of *critique* which aimed at uncovering and making explicit a social ontology – a process of social self-creation – which underlies and makes possible the capitalist mode of production, but which is systematically distorted and hidden from view by the characteristic institutional forms and social practices of capitalism. In the process of constructing this critique of capitalist social reality, ontology itself is radicalized; no longer viewed *a priori*, i.e., as prior to and constitutive of the reality which we can know, it becomes instead an ongoing social product, historically concrete and contestable.

In the two subsections below, I attempt to reconstruct the radicalized social ontologies of Marx and Gramsci, and to situate these in their socio-political context of critique. The point here is not to account for all the myriad nuances and contradictions of their lives' work or to recover the system of meanings within which each author constructed his texts. Rather, the interpretation which follows represents an appropriation and reconstruction of the texts of Marx and Gramsci which is explicitly motivated by particular interests in the present. The purpose is to provide a basis on which to pose the central question of this chapter: how might a vision of the Marxian tradition (viewed here through what might be called a Gramscian reading of Marx and a Marxian reading of Gramsci) inform a critical understanding of IPE at the end of the twentieth century? This question will be addressed more directly in the final section of the chapter, after the interpretive foundations have been laid in this section.

Marx: nature, human social life, and the critique of alienation

From the perspective of a radicalized Marxian ontology, the historically developing *internal relation*[3] of society and nature is central to a critical understanding of human social life under capitalism and its unrealized possibilities. Instead of conceiving nature and society as discrete entities, related to one another only externally, Marx understood them as two aspects of a single process, a mediated unity. For Marx, nature and society are continually mediated through the characteristically human practice of *objectification*: the conscious creation of a world of objects through socially organized productive activity in which human beings, their social lives and their natural environment are together transformed. In this process, at once social and natural, human beings develop manifold needs and sensibilities as well as new productive powers. Hence, through productive activity human beings socially objectify themselves and may consciously transform their own "human nature" along with their social and natural circumstances. Stressing the essential connection and ongoing interchange between human social life and a natural environment which is apparently separate from and external to human beings, Marx refers to nature as "man's inorganic body." The process of objectification and the continual reconstruction of the nature–society relation are for Marx ontologically primary and account for the nature of human social beings in any given historical epoch.[4]

At the most general level of abstraction from our own historical experience, Marx suggested that social interaction with nature (i.e., objectification, the labor process) is a necessary condition for the reproduction of all human life.

> The labor process ... is purposeful activity aimed at the production of use-values. It is an appropriation of what exists in nature for the purposes of man. It is the universal condition for the metabolic

17

interaction between man and nature, the everlasting nature-imposed condition of human existence, and it is therefore independent of every form of that existence, or rather it is common to all forms of society in which human beings live.[5]

While productive activity is a necessary aspect of any form of human social life, the *ways* in which this activity is organized and carried out cannot be determined *a priori*. The social conditions of productive activity are variable – continually being reproduced or transformed in the productive practices of human beings – and thus can only be understood *historically*. The organization of productive activity is historically specific, enmeshed in particular forms of social life and the kinds of practices which they support.

It is on this basis that Marx criticizes the representation of social relations which are specific to capitalism as if they were immediately natural and universal, rather than viewing them as the product of the active mediation of human social relations and nature through productive activity, i.e., as socially produced and historically mutable. In the representation of (capitalist) social reality as if it were natural and universal, Marx sees a self-limiting form of human understanding in which objects – human social products – are abstracted from the process of their creation, and thus are attributed an autonomy and an effective power over human social life which they have by no intrinsic nature. To the extent that human beings envision their products as taking on a life of their own, humans surrender their own social powers of objectification and are increasingly "subjected to the violence of things." Human social life is then governed by the objects it has created, and the mystified forms in which it understands those objects. Social life can take on the appearance of the objective, insofar as human beings are subordinated to the objects they have produced, and in that sense are themselves objectified. Marx refers to this distorted, inverse relation of objectification in terms of "alienation" or "fetishism."[6]

Not reducible to simple cognitive error or misperception, alienation and fetishism are rooted in the material practices of capitalist social life. Under the *specific historical conditions* of capitalism, the ontologically central process of objectification takes the form of alienation. The necessary and ongoing process of mediating human beings and nature is itself mediated by the social organization of capitalist production in such a way that the internal relations between human beings and their natural and social circumstances appear as external relations of opposition: human needs and powers, nature and society, are practically separated from individualized human producers and confront them as alien and hostile forces. It is in terms of this "alien mediator" that capitalism becomes the main object of Marx's critique.[7]

The means of production (instruments, raw materials and other objective requirements for the objectification of labor) are privately owned under capitalism. Historically separated from the necessary means of production, workers must contract with someone who owns the means of production (a capitalist) in order to produce anything. The worker is forced to sell his or her capacity to work (in the language of *Capital*, "labor-power") to a capitalist in order to secure the means simply to survive, i.e., a wage. As part of this bargain, the product of the worker's labor becomes the property of the capitalist. This process of alienated labor formed the central vantage point for Marx's critical analysis of capitalism. A multifaceted relation, several aspects of estranged labor are explicitly distinguished by Marx.[8]

First, insofar as the product of alienated labor belongs not to its producer but to the capitalist, and serves only to increase the mass of capital which the worker must confront in the process of labor, "the object that labor produces, its product, stands opposed to it as *something alien*, as a *power independent* of the producer."[9] The process of alienated labor thus entails the estrangement of the producer from his or her product, from the world of objects created by labor, and therefore from "the sensuous external world," i.e., nature itself. Just as capitalism generates vast new wealth through the ever increasing mastery of nature, workers are excluded from the objective world their labor has created insofar as it becomes the private property of another.

A second aspect of alienated labor is the estrangement of the worker from his or her own life-activity, the process of self-objectification. "So if the product of labor is alienation, production itself must be active alienation, the alienation of activity, the activity of alienation."[10] Productive activity which could be intrinsically satisfying, a process of self-development, an end in itself, becomes little more than a means to the minimal end of physical survival. Instead of being an activity of self-affirmation and self-realization, the worker's labors belong to another whose purposes are alien and antagonistic to the worker. Work, then, amounts to a continuing loss of self for the worker, self-estrangement. In the very process of developing unprecedented social powers of production, workers contribute to the accumulation of capital, reproduce the capital–labor relation to which they are subordinated, and thereby actively estrange themselves from themselves.

Another major aspect of Marx's concept of estranged labor involves the alienation of human beings from one another, and of the individual from the species. For the worker, productive activity is reduced to a mere means to secure from the capitalist the necessities of survival. Under such conditions, other humans appear externally related to the worker and to the activity of work. As capitalism brings people increasingly into a single division of labor and a world market, human relations which could be self-consciously cooperative and socially creative instead become individually instrumental and thus negate the sociality of productive activity and of human life. Rather than calling forth the free development of social powers of production and a richness of sensibilities, human needs become an individual vulnerability which can be instrumentally manipulated by others.

So, within the process of alienated labor, the internal relation of human beings, society and nature – mediated through the process of objectification – is reproduced in a form which appears to those involved as an *external* relation of opposition. The mediation of society and nature continues, but in a distorted form in which producers understand themselves as individuals separate from both society and nature, and therefore do not recognize their own activity as the active production of themselves and their world. The fundamental relations of objectification which underlie and make possible production in its capitalist form are submerged and hidden from view, as the "alien mediator" of capitalism is taken for a natural necessity, a universal human condition. Capitalist production assumes the appearance of production as such, and real historical possibilities for social self-production remain latent within the present social organization of production.

This critique of alienation, as I understand it, is not based on abstract moral principles or some transhistorical conception of essential human nature which is violated by capitalism; rather, Marx's critique is aimed at the contradiction between the *historical possibilities* and the *historical actuality* which capitalism has brought into being. It is in this sense an immanent critique of the historical irony of capitalist social life, stressing the real possibilities which are latent within it, but which present themselves to us in distorted, mystified and self-limiting form. The critical leverage of Marx's theory, then, comes from the contradictory existence *within the same historical reality* of objectification – the ontologically primary and open-ended mediation of human social beings and nature – and alienation (the second order mediation, i.e., the self-limiting form of objectification through the "alien mediator" of capital) – implying that it is concretely possible to actualize the former by transcending the latter.

To summarize, then, Marx's radicalized social ontology makes possible a critical understanding of the historically specific organization of productive activity (i.e., the particular form in which the internal relation of society and nature is reproduced) in order to make explicit the possibilities for change which are latent in the social relations and practices of the present. His philosophy of internal relations allows him to view capitalism as "a system [and historical process] contained relationally in each of its parts."[11] Thus he can abstract the relation of estranged labor from the whole of capitalist social reality in order to view that whole from the vantage point of objectification–alienation. This allows him to be critical of the class-based organization of production under capitalism, and to point toward real possibilities for its transformation. While this is Marx's primary vantage point for the analysis of capitalism, it does not exhaust the possibilities of his critical method. Another vantage point from which Marx viewed capitalism was that of the relation of state and civil society, or of politics and economics.

The separation of politics and economics has an important role to play in the historically specific mode of exploitation under capitalism, for it allows this exploitation to take on a distinctively "economic" semblance. In the historical development of capitalism, the "formal subsumption of labor under capital" represents a crucial point of transition for Marx. At this point, labor is simultaneously "freed" from its feudal integuments (relations of serfdom or guild) and separated from the means of production, and hence must enter into an "economic" relationship with capital in order to secure the means of physical survival. With this development, the labor process (objectification) is subordinated to the accumulation of capital (the "valorization process," entailing manifold relations of alienation). Surplus labor is now extracted from the producers through the purchase of their labor-power in the market (and its subsequent employment in the labor process which is controlled and directed by the capitalist class, owing to their ownership of the means of production). No explicitly political coercion need enter directly into the capitalist exploitation of labor, for it appears as a simple exchange of commodi-

21

ties in the market: labor-power is exchanged for a wage.[12] "Extra-economic coercion" of the sort wielded by feudal ruling classes is unnecessary because producers are no longer in possession of the means of production. They are therefore compelled to sell their labor-power in order to gain access to those means of production and thus acquire the means to purchase the necessities of life. The dominance of capital is mediated through the "impersonal forces of the market," and appears to the individual producer as the ineluctable operation of "natural" economic laws.[13] To the extent that capitalism is supported by an explicitly coercive power, that power is situated in the putatively communal sphere occupied by the state, and appears as law and order enforced in the public interest.

This is not to say that state power or capitalist class power have no effective presence in the economy. Both are important, but neither has an explicitly "political" presence in the routine functioning of the capitalist economy. (1) Capitalist class power – "economically" based in the ability of this class to control access to the necessary means of production – plays a direct role in the labor process. Here the variable amount of surplus value is continually at issue, and the degree of capitalist control over the labor process is an object of ongoing struggle. (2) The state defines the juridical conditions of private property, contract and exchange, thus entering implicitly into the constitution and reproduction of the economic sphere, as well as the class powers which reside in that sphere. Further, the state itself can be a terrain of political class struggle and may be explicitly recognized as such. To the extent that class struggles come to be understood in explicitly political terms and encompass the state as well as the economy, they call into question the reproduction of the reified politics–economics dichotomy which is central to capitalism. In this sense, explicitly political class struggle has potentially transformative implications.

Reproduction of capitalist social relations and the process of exploitation peculiar to these relations thus presupposes the formal separation of politics and economics, so that the two spheres seem to be only externally related, and their internal relation is submerged and hidden from view. Marx clearly implies this in the following description of the formal subsumption of labor under capital:

> it dissolves the relationship between the owners of the conditions of labor and the workers into a *relationship of sale and purchase, a purely financial relationship*. In consequence the process of exploitation is

22

stripped of every patriarchal, political or even religious cloak. It remains true, of course, that the *relations of production* themselves create a new relation of *supremacy and subordination* (and this also has a *political* expression).[14]

Complementary to, but far less well developed than, Marx's analysis of the labor–capital relation is his critique the modern "political" state, in which he suggested that this form of state was premised upon capitalism's abstraction of politics from the real material life of the community (objectification), and the implicit domination of politics by the class which controls that material life.[15]

As a system centered upon the commodification and alienation of labor and, correspondingly, upon the private ownership of the means of production and appropriation of its product, capitalism presupposes the creation of a social space in which the individual's right to own and to alienate property can reside, a space in which capital and labor can meet as buyers and sellers of commodities. The creation of such a space entailed a two-fold historical development in which feudalism's characteristic fusion of economic and political relations was sundered. On the one hand, the emergence of capitalism involved the historical creation of a "private" sphere in which individuals could be understood in abstraction from the society in which they were embedded, and thus be enabled to conceive and pursue their own selfish economic interests.[16] Following Hegel, Marx referred to this sphere of apparently isolated, egoistic individuals as "civil society". The economy (in its modern sense) is situated within the individualistic realm of civil society. Corresponding to this private sphere is a public one in which the communal lives of capitalism's abstract individuals can be expressed (typically through formal procedures and systems of legal order). The same process of abstraction which separated the individual and his private property from the community, and thus created civil society as an intelligible social space, also generated the possibility of a communal space distinct from civil society. The modern political state, with all its Weberian institutional trappings, is distinguished precisely by its historical construction within this public sphere. So, as Derek Sayer stresses, "Formation of the political state and de-politicization of civil society are two sides of the same coin." In this sense, the state is internally related to the class-based organization of production in civil society: they are complementary aspects of the same historical social reality.

> This point is of capital importance, for it implies that the state is emphatically a *historical category*, in other words the concept is not a synonym for any and all forms of government (or ways in which ruling classes rule) but describes a definite and historically delimited *social form*: the social form, specifically, of *bourgeois* class rule.[17]

The modern political state developed within and is integral to a political–economic system of class rule – a state–society complex in which property is assigned to the private sphere as a primordial individual right, and hence is exempted from ongoing political dialogue in the public sphere. In a fully developed bourgeois republic, explicit class relations are banished from the public sphere, as all citizens are recognized for political purposes to be formally equal individuals. Further, insofar as the modern state presupposes the very separation of politics and economics upon which bourgeois property depends, it cannot fundamentally challenge that separation without undermining the preconditions of its own existence. Thus insulated from explicitly communal and political concerns, the "private" powers of capital are ensconced in the sanctuary of civil society, and from there implicitly permeate the public sphere, rendering it a partial, distorted and self-limiting form of community. From a Marxian perspective, then, state power and bourgeois class power are in some real historical sense interdependent. Marx and Engels summarize this relation in the following terms: "Through the emancipation of private property from the community, the state has become a separate entity, beside and outside civil society; but it is nothing more than the form of organization which the bourgeois necessarily adopt both for internal and external purposes, for the mutual guarantee of their property and interests."[18]

To the extent that the modern political state is historically embedded in, and internally related to, the manifold relations of alienation which underlie capitalism, the state itself may be said to embody alienation, to be its specifically political form. In general, capitalist alienation involves the creation of new social powers at the same time that it individualizes human beings, estranging them from their own social powers and precluding the self-conscious social control of those powers. As the political expression of this estrangement, the state may aggregate individual preferences and interests but it cannot transcend them: it becomes the instrument of some particular interests and an externally imposed obstacle to others. It can neither overcome the fundamental isolation of individuals under capitalism, nor serve as a

vehicle for the communal control of the new social powers of production which capitalism creates. The very existence of the state as a
specialized political entity testifies to the estrangement of community
and communal powers from the daily lives and productive activities of
people within capitalist social reality. The politics expressed in the
modern state is impoverished by its abstraction from the *whole* process
of social reproduction, including those aspects which are situated in
the economy; and it is perverted by the concentrations of "private"
power which exist outside the domain of "politics" as it is understood
in capitalist societies. In these senses, then, the modern political state is
premised upon, is integral to, and contains within itself relations of
alienation.

In sum, Marx's radical social ontology allows us to interpret as
historically specific instances of alienation, not just the capitalist
"economy," but the whole complex of social relations in which it is
embedded, including the formal separations of public–private,
politics–economics, and state–society. His critique implies that these
alienated relations are fundamentally contradictory, in the sense that
they bring into being the preconditions for their own transcendence. It
was precisely the theoretical and practical transcendence of these
historical relations of alienation – especially the related dichotomies of
state and society, of dominant class and subordinate groups – which
preoccupied Antonio Gramsci, and which draws my attention to his
work.

Gramsci: philosophy of praxis, hegemony and historic bloc

Gramsci's Marxism emerged out of his critique of the idealist currents
in Italian philosophy as well as the crudely materialist, positivistic, and
mechanically economistic interpretations of Marxism then widespread
in the international socialist movement. Explicitly preoccupied with
the unification of theory and practice, Gramsci reconstructed Marx's
radicalized social ontology and developed within the context of this
reactivated "philosophy of praxis" an understanding of revolutionary
political action in the advanced capitalism of the twentieth-century
West. Integral to this project was a "dual perspective" on social politics
encompassing state and society, coercive and consensual forms of
power, military and cultural aspects of struggle.[19]

In his *Prison Notebooks*, Gramsci sketches a radical social ontology
strikingly similar to that in terms of which I have tried to understand
Marx. As did Marx, Gramsci insists that human beings must not be

thought of as monads isolated from society and nature, nor as having any fixed or transhistorical essence. Rather, he consistently argues for a more empowering self-understanding in which humans are actively self-constitutive in the process of consciously reconstructing their internal relation with society and nature:

> one must conceive of man as a series of active relationships (a process) in which individuality, though perhaps the most important, is not, however, the only element to be taken into account. The humanity which is reflected in each individuality is composed of various elements: (1) the individual; (2) other men; (3) the natural world. But the latter two elements are not as simple as they might appear. The individual does not enter into relations with other men by juxtaposition, but organically, in as much, that is, as he belongs to organic entities which range from the simplest to the most complex. Thus man does not enter into relations with the natural world just by being himself part of the natural world, but actively, by means of work and technique. Further: these relations are not mechanical. They are active and conscious. They correspond to the greater or lesser degree of understanding that each man has of them. So one could say that each one of us changes himself, modifies himself to the extent that he changes and modifies the complex relations of which he is the hub.[20]

> The discovery that the relations between the social and natural order are mediated by work, by man's theoretical and practical activity, creates the first elements of an intuition of the world free from all magic and superstition. It provides a basis for the subsequent development of an historical, dialectical conception of the world, which understands movement and change ... and which conceives the contemporary world as a synthesis of the past, of all past generations, which projects itself into the future.[21]

So, much like Marx's concept of objectification, Gramsci holds that "reality is a product of the application of human will to the society of things," and that this process of producing reality entails the historical transformation of human beings and their social lives, as well as nature. Further, humans are potentially capable of self-consciously guiding this activity and thus can determine their own process of becoming.[22]

This process cannot take place in a vacuum of abstraction, however, but only in specific historical circumstances. For Gramsci, historically concrete struggles to determine the social process of becoming are the essence of politics. As did Marx, Gramsci stresses the contradictory relation of historical actuality and latent possibilities which together constitute the nexus in which political praxis can occur.

> The active politician is a creator, an initiator; but he neither creates from nothing nor does he move in the turbid void of his own desires and dreams. He bases himself on effective reality, but what is effective reality? Is it something static and immobile, or is it not rather a relation of forces in continuous motion and shift of equilibrium? If one applies one's will to the creation of a new equilibrium among the forces which really exist and are operative – basing oneself on the particular force which one believes to be progressive and strengthening it to help it to victory – one still moves on the terrain of effective reality, but does so in order to dominate and transcend it (or to contribute to this). What "ought to be" is therefore concrete; indeed it is the only realistic and historicist interpretation of reality, it alone is history in the making and philosophy in the making, it alone is politics.[23]

The conflict of historical forces, the fluid political reality with which Gramsci is chiefly concerned, is the political and ideological struggle in the advanced capitalist societies of the West – where civil society is highly developed and capitalist class power has permeated and shaped the cultural institutions of society as well as residing, ultimately, in the political state and its coercive apparatus.[24]

It is important to note at this juncture that Gramsci used such key concepts as "ideology," "civil society," and "state" in ways somewhat different than did Marx. Expanding beyond Marx's predominantly negative images of ideology as the distorted, inverted and self-limiting forms of consciousness which characterize capitalist social relations, Gramsci's vision entailed explicitly positive and enabling aspects of ideology as a potentially revolutionary terrain of struggle.[25] In accordance with his "dual perspective," centering on the internal relation of coercion and consent in the political struggles of advanced capitalism, Gramsci understands "civil society" as internally related to "political society." Whereas the latter designates the coercive apparatus of the state more narrowly understood (i.e., what we would recognize as its classically Weberian aspect), the former represents the realm of cultural institutions and practices in which the hegemony of a class may be constructed or challenged. Gramsci uses civil society to designate an area of cultural and ideological linkage between class relations in the economy and the explicitly political aspect of the state. Civil society would then include parties, unions, churches, education, journalism,

27

art and literature, etc. Together, political society and civil society constitute Gramsci's *extended* or *integral state,* the unified site in which Western bourgeois classes may have established their social power as "hegemony protected by the armour of coercion." In this broader (integral) sense, then, "the State is the entire complex of practical and theoretical activities with which the ruling class not only justifies and maintains its dominance, but manages to win the active consent of those over whom it rules."[26] Gramsci's apparently idiosyncratic usage of such concepts as these must be understood in the context of his comprehensive vision of social politics in the capitalist societies of the twentieth-century West, and his strategy for the transformation of such societies through "war of position" and the construction of a proletarian counter-hegemony.[27]

His main political objective is to bring about a transformative process, a unification of theory and practice, which will transcend the division of capitalist society into rulers and ruled, dominant classes and subaltern groups, state and society.[28] While such a struggle – eventuating in a "regulated society," that is, socialism – will necessarily entail the transformation of the capitalist economy, it is neither determined by "causes" originating in that economy, nor are its implications limited to economic changes.[29] Gramsci's radical politics envisions a comprehensive transformation of social reality through the creation of an effective counter-culture, an alternative world view and a new form of political organization in whose participatory and consensual practices that world view is concretely realized. Ultimately, Gramscian politics aims to produce a qualitatively new form of "state," a genuinely self-determining community bearing little resemblance to the self-limiting and coercive "political" state integral to capitalist social reality. In this vision of revolutionary political practice, the whole of advanced capitalist society becomes a terrain of struggle on which subordinate groups can challenge bourgeois predominance and, in the process, begin to actualize real historical possibilities for communal self-determination which have been systematically obscured by capitalist social relations and practices. Central to this process are the cultural institutions of civil society which Western capitalist societies have developed to an unprecedented degree, and which represent latent possibilities for effective mass participation in public life.

Thus I would suggest that Gramsci shares with Marx a common focus on the contradiction between historical actuality and historical possibilities *within capitalist social reality*. In that sense, it may be said that Gramsci, too, was concerned with alienation, even though he did not use that term.[30] I interpret in this light Gramsci's critique of such historically self-limiting forms of theory–practice as "economism" and "statolatry," as well as his arguments about "contradictory conscious-ness" and fragmentary "common sense" among the masses of people in capitalist society and the possibility for them to develop a more critical and coherent self-understanding and thus to actualize their capacities as practical philosophers, self-consciously determining their own economic–political–cultural relations and practices.[31] It is pre-cisely this task of critical education – enabling full and active participa-tion of the masses in all spheres of social life – which distinguishes Gramsci's transformative party and its hegemonic project from the politics of the bourgeoisie.

Gramsci's moral-political project involves the creation of a new "historic bloc" in which proletarian leadership of the various classes and groups subordinated under capitalism can be organized and expressed. The construction of an historic bloc is a precondition for the exercise of hegemony in the Gramscian sense, and entails a reconstruc-tion of state–society relations through organically related processes of political, economic and cultural change. Gramsci's concept of historic bloc holds the potential to bridge the structured separations of state–society and politics–economics in capitalist social formations, insofar as the ideological leadership of the working class can unify various groups subordinated under capitalism and provide a measure of coherence to their apparently disparate social practices. While stress-ing that changes in the organization of productive practices and class domination are organic to the consolidation of such an historic bloc, Gramsci consistently and rigorously maintains that neither political nor cultural practices are reducible to "economic" forces or interests.[32] Indeed, a necessary condition for the attainment of hegemony by a class or class fraction is the supersession of their narrow, economic interests (what Gramsci called the "economic-corporate") by a more universal social vision or ideology, and the concrete coordination of the interests of other groups with those of the leading class or fraction in the process of securing their participation in its social vision.[33]

For Gramsci, then, an historic bloc is more than a simple alliance of classes or class fractions, each instrumentally pursuing its own selfish interests. Rather, it encompasses political, cultural, and economic aspects of a particular social formation, uniting these in historically specific ways to form a complex, politically contestable and dynamic ensemble of social relations.[34] An historic bloc articulates a world view, grounded in historically specific socio-political conditions and production relations, which lends substance and ideological coherence to its social power. It follows, then, that hegemonies and historic blocs have specific qualities relating to particular social constellations, their fundamental class forces, and productive relations. They can be predominantly bourgeois or proletarian, conservative or transformative.

Bourgeois hegemony presupposes the dichotomy of leaders and led, of dominant and subordinate classes, and strives to reproduce this condition in the economy, in the political state, and in the cultural institutions of civil society. Under conditions of bourgeois hegemony, the leading ideology serves to unify secondary groups into an historic bloc with a fundamentally capitalist world view, while it enters the consciousness of the masses as part of their confounded and fragmentary "common sense," and acts to preclude the development of a mass basis for coherent alternatives to the leading world view.[35] Where its hegemonic leadership is weak or insecure, the bourgeoisie may attempt to sustain their social supremacy through the negative strategy of "passive revolution" in which the dominant group takes the initiative in making limited concessions (of a strictly "economic-corporate" type) to subordinate classes, hoping to co-opt their leading elements and forestall more comprehensive counter-hegemonic challenges.[36] Such a reformist strategy of passive revolution may serve to disable transformative praxis on the part of subaltern groups and hence to reproduce the conditions of capitalist domination.

Working-class hegemony, on the other hand, strives toward the dissolution of the dichotomy of leaders and led (as well as the reified separations of politics–economics, state–society, etc.) through the active participation of all subordinate groups within a unified revolutionary movement. This means that the hegemony of the working class cannot be based on piecemeal economic-corporate concessions to other subordinate groups, but entails a transformative process through which these various groups are enabled to participate actively and directly in the reconstruction of the social world. The fundamental project of the working class – building a participatory community in which social powers of self-production are commonly and consensually regulated – cannot proceed without them for, were it to do so, it would simply reproduce the dichotomy of leaders–led. Ultimately, the political party of the philosophy of praxis will be self-liquidating insofar as it succeeds in helping the masses to become masters of their own collective destiny, and hence eliminates the need for leadership organized in a political party, or for a specialized coercive state.[37]

In this sense, the class forces, political organization and historical objectives of an historic bloc are all internally related. It is this broader conception of *social politics* encompassing the state, the economy, and cultural spheres of a social formation which distinguishes Gramsci from more positivistic and economistic theorists of Marxism, and which directs inquiry toward the processes of socio-political struggle through which historic blocs and their hegemonies are constructed in states–societies.

I conclude this interpretive exercise by suggesting that both Gramsci and Marx understood the separations of politics–economics and state–society to be historically real; but not to be an essential part of human social existence, i.e., not to be real in any transhistorical sense. These oppositions were seen to have been historically produced – and open to historical transcendence – through social processes of objectification. An integral part of this social transformation, although by no means the whole of it, will involve the elimination of the capitalist organization of production which is internally related to these distinctly modern antinomies. In the next section of the chapter, I will sketch the implications which I believe this Marxian–Gramscian approach may hold for contemporary IPE.

Alienation and the critique of IPE

Marxian analysis has traditionally been on the margin of IR–IPE, and is widely seen as incapable of adequately conceptualizing the realities of a system of autonomous, power-wielding, fundamentally coercive administrative organizations such as sovereign states. In this vein, Gilpin simply equates Marxism with economism; and Keohane suggests that Marxist writers often resort to the implicit use of "realist" concepts in attempting to come to grips with the international, and thereby demonstrate not just the shortcomings of Marxian analysis but also the superior analytical power and basic validity the realist model of IR.[38] In this section, I will sketch the outlines of an argument grounding the Marxian–Gramscian analysis of IPE in a distinctively Marxian social ontology and philosophy of praxis. In the process, I hope to raise in the minds of readers some doubt about whether the issue of Marxism's relevance for IR–IPE is indeed closed.

What I want to argue is not so much that the method of critique can be applied to the field of IPE, but rather that the Marxian–Gramscian project of critique and transformation *encompasses, entails,* the critique of IPE. Both the system of sovereign states and the global division of labor – taken as ontologically primitive units by neorealism and world-system theory, respectively – may instead be understood as aspects of the historically specific social organization of productive activity under capitalism, as embodying relations of alienation, and as potentially transcendable.

In order to construct a radical critique of IPE and its relation to productive activity as it is organized under capitalism, it is first necessary to broaden our conception of world politics so as to accommodate a meaningful notion of transformative practice. Accordingly, it will be necessary to abandon the characteristic neorealist premise that the fundamental reality of world politics – everywhere and always – is power struggle among autonomous states in a context of anarchy. Here I do not wish to be understood as suggesting that the neorealist vision of world politics is simply wrong, that it is an illusion of "false consciousness". Rather, it is an historically real and effective but nonetheless self-limiting form of theory–practice. Neorealism, like any ideology, is grounded in practical experience and hence must have some measure of what Derek Sayer refers to as "practical adequacy" – "It must, in other words, allow men and women to conduct and make sense of their everyday activity."[39] But the way in which it allows them to make sense of their world also has the effect of portraying as natural and universal a set of social relations which are historically specific and socially mutable. It does this by abstracting these relations from the processes which produced them and through which they may be transformed. While analytical distinctions may be made between the "global" and "domestic," neorealism's reification of these "levels of analysis" fragments the field of political action, disabling critique and transformative practice. Alternatively, national and international should be construed as two aspects of an internally related whole, a whole which is in some sense capitalist and alienated. In place of the neorealist "presumption of anarchy," a Marxian–Gramscian critique would take as its point of departure the proposition that international politics as we know it is historically embedded in, and internally related to, capitalist social relations.

Insofar as the formal separations of state and society, of public and private, of the political and the economic aspects of life, are integral to the historical reality of capitalism, we may say that capitalism and its manifold relations of alienation are the necessary context within which the historical construction of sovereign states – understood in the modern sense as functionally specialized administrative–coercive, "political," organizations – becomes possible. The very existence of the kind of states portrayed by neorealist IPE presupposes relations of alienation in which "politics" assumes an identity distinct from "economics" and attains its own institutional form of expression. The alienation of the individual from the community and the abstraction of politics from individualized productive life are conditions of possibility for *both* capitalist production and the modern political state.

International politics may then be critically understood as a kind of second order alienation. That is, international politics concerns itself with the mutual estrangement of political communities which are themselves constructed within relations of alienation.[40] The first-order alienation occurs as the modern political state mediates between, on the one hand, capitalist objectification, i.e., the productive life of the community as lived in the civil society of individuals, and on the other hand, its explicitly communal life in the public sphere. The state is situated as an alien mediator between society as a collection of self-interested individuals, and society as a potentially self-determining political community. It mediates, that is, between capitalist society and itself, its own alienated political life. But the modern political state also mediates between that alienated community and other historically constructed communities. In this sense – i.e., viewed critically from within capitalist social reality – the system of states which emerged historically along with capitalist production represents another facet of the complex of social relations which embody alienation, and must therefore be part of any concrete political strategy aimed at overcoming those relations of alienation. I believe this is what Gramsci had in mind when he wrote:

> according to the philosophy of praxis (as it manifests itself politically) ... the international situation should be considered in its national aspect. In reality, the internal relations of any nation are the result of a combination which is "original" and (in a certain sense) unique: these relations must be understood and conceived in their originality and uniqueness if one wishes to dominate them and direct them. To be sure, the line of development is toward internationalism, but the point of departure is "national" – and it is from this point of departure that one must begin. Yet the perspective is international and cannot be otherwise.[41]

33

But doesn't this amount to a confession that historical materialism is indeed guilty of the crimes of reductionism and economism, and is therefore entirely unsuited for the analysis of world politics? I think not. In the following passage, Gramsci sketches his vision of how socio-political and economic relations within a nation-state are related to international phenomena:

> Do international relations precede or follow (logically) fundamental social relations? There can be no doubt that they follow. Any organic innovation in the social structure, through its technical-military expressions, modifies organically absolute and relative relations in the international field too. Even the geographical position of a national State does not precede but follows (logically) structural changes, although it reacts back upon them to a certain extent (to the extent precisely to which superstructures react upon the structure, politics on economics, etc.). However, international relations react both passively and actively on political relations (of hegemony among the parties).[42]

Clearly, in both passages Gramsci assigns an active priority to those aspects of capitalist social reality which are produced within the bounds of the "national" political community. But followers of Gilpin and Waltz should not be too quick in their condemnations; for this is no one-way causality, no crude and ahistorical economistic reduction. Instead, Gramsci is arguing that a dialectical approach must understand international politics from the perspective of the production and reproduction of social life, and that such a practical understanding cannot proceed in abstraction from specific constellations of factors – the interaction of local and global – which have shaped the historical production of particular states and the relations among them. He is clearly indicating in the second passage quoted above that IR shapes "both passively and actively" the development of socio-political relations within particular states. He reaffirms this when, in the heart of his discussion of how historic blocs and hegemonies are constructed, Gramsci reminds us that "It is also necessary to take into account that international relations intertwine with these internal relations of nation-states, creating new, unique and historically concrete combinations."[43] A Marxian–Gramscian vision of IR, I want to suggest, entails a critical reconstruction of the *historical interplay* between socio-political processes within particular states, and global relations and processes.

From this general perspective, it appears that relations of alienation

34

permeate social reality at the global level as well. In particular, the system of political states has reproduced institutions and practices which abstract politics from productive life, and hence preclude explicit communal self-determination directly within productive activity. Instead, productive activity is organized in a world "economy," a global division of labor governed by world market forces and seemingly beyond the reach of any form of communal control. Correspondingly, "politics" is understood in terms of the instrumental interactions of individualized political actors, struggling to exert some control over their social and economic circumstances. The extension of Marx's notion of alienation to encompass global social relations helps to explain the common preoccupation of neorealism and world-system theory (each from its own point of view) with the construction of political hierarchies superimposed upon the world economy. The perspectives of both neorealism and world-system theory are produced by abstracting one or the other aspect of this alienated relation of politics–economics, and then constructing abstract causal explanations in terms of this favored primitive unit.

Instead of beginning with sovereign states or the world-system as a theoretical point of departure, Marx and Gramsci can be interpreted as suggesting another vantage point from which to view IPE. From this perspective, IPE can be understood in terms of the process of objectification as it is organized under capitalism, i.e., as capitalism's global aspect. Viewing IPE as integral to capitalist social relations should not be confused with economism. In no way does this imply that political dynamics are wholly understandable in terms of "economic" causes. Rather, it implies that all social relations – including the system of states and the world economy – are historically produced and politically contestable. Such contests are fought out among various historically specific social forces and actors (e.g., functionaries of the political state, classes or class fractions, historic blocs, subaltern groups). The particular form taken by the relation of politics–economics or national–international is then seen as being determined by the outcomes of these historical struggles. Thus, for example, it is entirely consistent with this perspective to argue that interstate competition and warfare have had historically significant effects on the relation of capital and labor in the sphere of production, as well as upon state–society relations. Indeed I will argue in chapters 5–7 that this was the case in the United States during both world wars, as well as the Cold War. The point, then, is not to attribute universal

35

causal efficacy to "economic" forces or "domestic" factors, but to understand how the processes of capitalist objectification (global as well as domestic, political as well as economic) have produced contemporary social reality, and how the relations of alienation which inhere in that reality may be overcome.

This raises the question of transformative practice at the level of global social relations. How can we think about an emancipatory project which is global in its scope? It is certainly not easy to be optimistic here: for example, Berki and Wallerstein both suggest that a class-based emancipatory project will be contained within national boundaries, and will therefore be unable to address more global aspects of alienation. Once again, however, Gramsci's novel theoretical contributions may help us to conceptualize this difficult problem in new and enabling ways; for Gramsci's emancipatory project, his notions of civil society and of the hegemony which may be constructed in that site, are not necessarily circumscribed by the boundaries of nation-states. A progressive historic bloc aims at the construction of a participatory movement in which the dichotomies of leaders–led, etc., are dissolved. This process entails the dissolution of the bourgeois state in which the coercive power of the dominant class is institutionalized. Thus, for Gramsci, transformative practice need not stop at the border of the state, for the state itself is being transformed as the new hegemony is being constructed and new ways of organizing social relations are being learned. "Every relationship of 'hegemony' is necessarily an educational relationship and occurs not only within a nation, between the various forces of which the nation is composed, but in the international and world-wide field, between complexes of national and continental civilizations."[44] What is implied here is a radical political strategy which overturns the hegemony of state-based conceptions of politics, mediates between various "national" groups whose political practices had been contained within such conceptions, and enables their active participation in the construction of a global political community. What is implied here is a transformative practice of IPE.

All this may well seem utopian. What grounds do we have for believing that such a project is historically possible? In this century, the reorganization of capitalist production on a global scale, and the socio-political developments associated with this transformation, could together make possible new kinds of practice which explicitly transcend national boundaries. Beginning in the United States, especially in the first decades of the twentieth century, manufacturers began to intensify their control over the labor process and to impose upon workers a heightened division between mental and manual labor, planning and execution. Once the resistance of workers was overcome and their consent elicited (the magnitude of this accomplishment should not be underestimated, as we shall see), this facilitated the breaking down of production processes into a series of discrete steps and specialized tasks. These steps might be integrated into a single mass production facility, as in Ford's pioneering River Rouge complex of the 1920s and 30s, where raw materials entered at one end and automobiles emerged at the other; or, as in the decades since World War II, they could be distributed in ways which rationalize the production process on a vast geographic scale. In the context of the postwar global order, the growth of transnational production and intra-firm exchange has to a significant degree displaced international trade. Today multinational firms orchestrate their production and trade on a world scale, and may in that sense partially erode capitalism's structured separation between "division of labor in the workshop" – in which the power of the capitalist enforces rationalization of the labor process at the micro level – and "division of labor in society" – in which the market mediates between independent producers, and no conscious macro-level social coordination prevails. The mystifying effect of the market – which disguises relations of class power as impersonal, naturalized market forces confronting individuals – may then be lessening as huge firms more directly manage production and exchange world-wide and the social power of capital becomes less opaque.[45] Corresponding with this internationalization of production has been an internationalization of Gramsci's extended state and the more explicit development of a global civil society through which the hegemony of international capital has been organized in the postwar world.[46] While these long-term tendencies may have encouraged some fragmentation of the working class (e.g., between workers in globally oriented industries vs. those which are more nationally based), now more than ever it is possible to speak realistically about a global class structure, and the possibility of explicitly political struggles which may challenge it.

In the context of this transnationalization of capitalist production, a transformative critique of IPE makes it possible to envision globally radical political practices emerging even within the industrial workplaces of the North and, in particular, in the USA. In an era when production and jobs are potentially globally mobile, it becomes increasingly difficult for these relatively privileged workers to take for granted the standard of living they have enjoyed. Multinational firms seeking to minimize overall costs may impose draconian wage or benefit cutbacks upon these workers, may try to break their bargaining patterns or their unions, or may simply pack up and move to a more "hospitable business climate," that is, one with a compliant, non-unionized, low-wage workforce. This in turn could lead to the explicit politicization of class conflict and open up new horizons of political action which need not be limited by conventional boundaries of political–economic, state–society, domestic–international. Such a struggle could extend to the construction of transnational coalitions among workers and other subaltern groups to confront their exploiters, exert collective control over their lives, and explore new modes of social life. Of course, such conditions could also foster resurgent xenophobia, racism and jingoism among Northern or American workers. I cannot be confident of the more progressive outcome. Yet, it seems to me that it is precisely this historical openness, this absence of guarantee, which makes it so important for a critical IPE to point toward the *possibilities* for progressive social change which inhere in the social relations we so often take for granted, the historical processes which we tend to accept the same way we resign ourselves to the onset of inclement weather.

3 The quality of global power: a relational view of neoliberal hegemony

State–society relations and the politics of world order

In the remainder of this study, I intend to develop a more concrete historical interpretation of a Gramscian politics of world order in the twentieth century. Drawing heavily on the work of scholars outside the IPE mainstream, I will sketch in this chapter a synthetic account of the historical genesis and relational contours of the neoliberal hegemonic order. This discussion will raise a number of questions which have not been explicitly posed within the mainstream IPE literature, and which subsequent chapters will seek to address more directly. The questions posed in this chapter, then, will frame the historical interpretations to be constructed in the rest of the study.

The general approach adopted here seeks to develop a "relational" understanding of the state radically different from the abstract and ahistorical understanding common to both neorealism and world-system theory. Rather than taking the state to be – by definition – the primary locus of political action, this approach views politics as (explicitly or implicitly) omnipresent in social relations and socially productive practices. Hence the modern "political" form of state appears not as a presupposition of inquiry, but as an historical outcome worthy of explanation. Instead of taking the political state (generally, following Weber, identified with its juridical and organizational characteristics as an instrument of territorial rule) to be an empirical datum (as does neorealism) or a functionally necessary structural artefact (as does world-system theory), the approach adopted here calls for inquiry into the underlying social relations which generate the *possibility* of such specialized organizational forms, and into the specific historical processes which actualize this possibility in one form or another.

From this perspective, one of the most important such conditions in the postfeudal era has entailed the division of social reality into apparently separate spheres of "economic" and "political" activity. This historical condition enables the differentiation of a sphere of private, economic activities from one of public, political action, and hence entails the possibility of the modern form of state as well as the capitalist organization of production. To the extent that this condition – i.e., formal separation of the economic and the political – is reproduced in capitalist states–societies, it distances state managers (i.e., executive officers, bureaucrats and administrators) from the immediate imperatives of market competition which confront individuals (both capitalists and workers) in the capitalist economy. It thus creates the possibility of a state apparatus which acts in ways autonomous from the narrow economic interests of particular members of the dominant class, which represents itself in terms of the universal interests of the political community (for example, as the guarantor of national security), and which attempts to preserve the coherence and stability of the social formation as a whole, thus reproducing (in historically variable ways) the core relations of capitalism. How – indeed whether – any of these possibilities may be realized by particular states depends upon the historically specific constellation of state–society relations, which is itself eminently contestable. In the modern period, the characteristics of particular states are the result of processes of historical construction linking class formation and conflict, capital accumulation, institutional state-building, interstate competition and warfare. In the course of such struggles, the boundary separating and defining the economic and the political spheres of social activity may become an object of contention, potentially altering the character and meaning of the state in a particular social formation. States, state powers, and the social relations in which they are embedded are thus viewed as socially produced, and historically mutable.

On this view, no abstract, ahistorical understanding of the state can be adequate. Rather, the historical construction of particular states, and the social context in which this occurs, becomes the focus of analysis. A similar view of states and state powers as products of historical social relations and political practices – rather than as a structural artefact or simple datum – is a central theme in the political economy of Robert Cox, to whom this study is very deeply indebted.

In his seminal critique of neorealist orthodoxy in IR, Cox suggests that we question the abstract presupposition of states as sovereign actors and wielders of generic power resources, and instead approach them as aspects of larger historical structures. States, for Cox, are historically constructed (and continually reconstructed) in the nexus between global and domestic social relations – integral to each of which are political, economic, and ideological aspects:

> The world can be represented as a pattern of interacting social forces in which states play an intermediate though autonomous role between the global structure of social forces and local configurations of social forces within particular countries. This may be called a political economy perspective of the world: power is seen as *emerging* from social processes rather than taken as given in the form of accumulated material capabilities, that is as the result of these processes. (Paraphrasing Marx, one could describe the latter, neorealist view as the "fetishism of power".)[1]

In accordance with this vision of power as produced through historically specific social relations, Cox has introduced into the IR literature Gramsci's view of hegemony as entailing those aspects of power relations in which domination commands consent and in which, as a consequence, coercive aspects of social power become less obtrusive. Attention is thus directed toward the bases of power in those socially self-constructive practices in which people engage more or less routinely, central to which are their productive activities. Hence, the complex of social relations enabling those practices, necessarily including ideological and political as well as economic aspects, are seen to be central to the analysis of hegemonic power.[2]

In contrast to both the neorealist and Wallersteinian understandings of international hegemony as a preponderance of material resources – an essentially quantitative superiority – which one state may deploy in its attempts to secure the compliance of others, Cox points to the social organization of production as it operates on a global scale, and to the qualitative relations of power, domination or hegemony which may inhere in such an historical structure.[3] Cox's understanding of socially based power and hegemony at the global level guides inquiry toward historical investigations of the processes by which particular complexes of power relations, such as states–societies, are constructed in the nexus between global and local social relations. Rather than theoretically collapsing state and society into a single category, their relation is instead seen to be a matter of historical contingency and political struggle, and the interaction of global and local processes of social structuring therefore becomes a matter of considerable significance.

The politics of productivity and neoliberal world order

In his most comprehensive work, Cox sketches three historical structures of world order – complexes of social power relations – which have arisen in the last two centuries. "Each successive structure of world order was characterized by the emergence of new forms of state, new historic blocs, and new configurations of production relations."[4] The first hegemonic world order, a distinctively liberal system, was constructed in the nineteenth century (c. 1789–1873). With the political, economic and ideological ascendance of Great Britain – driven by the first industrial revolution – a qualitative change was brought about in global social relations as British statesmen and capitalists transported the norms and practices of liberal capitalism into the world in which they operated. The mercantilistic political economy prevalent in the early modern period was supplanted by the characteristic liberal distinction between political and economic practices and their corresponding spheres of social reality.[5]

The hegemony of liberalism gave way to an "era of rival imperialisms" (1873–1945) in which liberal social relations within and among states–societies had been eroded by the spread of industrial capitalism, the rise of militant industrial workers movements, intensified international rivalry, and more explicitly active forms of state power attempting to reconstruct political community in a conflict-ridden historical situation. In contrast to the seemingly apolitical individualism of the liberal world view, the new state forms of this period were characterized by a common emphasis on political community at home, defined in opposition to other states–societies and fortified with limited concessions to elements of society hitherto disenfranchised. By the time of World War I they had begun to bring elements of labor for the first time into a corporatist, "welfare-nationalist" form of state, combining these domestic political innovations with protectionism and more aggressive international competition.[6]

With the conclusion of World War II, a non-hegemonic period of open conflict and crisis in global order was brought to an end. In the wake of the destruction of fascism and the "containment" of Soviet influence, the postwar era witnessed a renewal of hegemonic order centered upon the United States and constructed on the foundation of a new form of state–society complex which Cox terms the "neoliberal state." In the neoliberal state–society, the social innovations of the previous era (e.g., industrial capitalism, welfare policies) were adapted to a period of relative peace and renewed openness in the world economy. Whereas its antecedent, the welfare-nationalist state, had sought national community in international competition and conflict, the neoliberal form of state would seek "its security as member of a stable alliance system and its economic growth as a participant in an open world economy. Its task was to adjust the national economy to the growth of the world economy, to facilitate adaptation rather than to protect existing positions."[7] This transformation of the welfare-nationalist state form into the internationalist, growth-oriented neoliberal state was in large measure made possible by the United States' active reconstruction of the advanced capitalist states along liberal democratic lines. "The Marshall Plan extended beyond influencing state policies right into the conscious shaping of the balance among social forces within states and the emerging configuration of historic blocs."[8] Purposive American intervention solidified the basis of centrist, liberal capitalist regimes in the occupied and liberated countries of the West, excluding both communist and fascist alternatives to the neoliberal state and clearing the way for a "moderate," consensual politics of growth. It was in these terms that the American global hegemony of the postwar era was expressed.

Cox's theoretical framework and the historical interpretation it supports resonate strongly with a line of scholarship linking American social and diplomatic history. In a path-breaking series of works, the historian Charles Maier has suggested that the character of American global power in the postwar world was shaped by the historical manner in which social power had been organized within the United States during the depression and war years. Based on the social vision which emerged from this historical experience, Maier argued, the United States was able to establish a "consensual hegemony" over the Western world in the aftermath of World War II.[9]

This hegemony entailed a great deal more than a convergence of interests and attitudes among international elites. Underlying the perceived legitimacy of explicit American political dominance was a reconstruction of the socio-political bases of the major states devastated by the war; and the principle which formed the foundation for

43

this reconstitution, Maier argues, was a uniquely American vision of the politics of productivity. Maier's summary statement merits full quotation:

> United States objectives are usually described in terms of enlightened idealism or capitalist expansionism. But much of the way policy makers envisaged international economic reconstruction derived from the ambivalent way in which domestic economic conflict had been resolved before and during the New Deal. In the inconclusive struggle between business champions and the spokesmen for reform, Americans achieved consensus by celebrating a supposedly impartial efficiency and productivity and by condemning allegedly wasteful monopoly. Looking outward during and after World War II, United States representatives condemned fascism as a form of monopoly power, then later sought to isolate communist parties and labor unions as adversaries of their priorities of production. American blueprints for international monetary order, policy toward trade unions, and the intervention of occupation authorities in West Germany and Japan sought to transform political issues into problems of output, to adjourn class conflict for a consensus on growth. The American approach was successful because for almost two decades high rates of growth made the politics of productivity apparently pay off.[10]

The American vision of social harmony through productivity, growth and prosperity was the ideological basis for internationalizing the socio-political relations of the USA, reshaping those of its major partners in the postwar world, and the relations of the world economy more generally. Empowered by their predominance in the global division of labor, American state managers, capitalists, and organized labor leaders sought to foster economic recovery and interdependence among the major capitalist powers as part of an explicit strategy of global order. In the decades after the war, American economic powers would be used to construct a stable, multilateral world economy; while the politics of productivity would facilitate the crystallization of a Western European community of liberal capitalist states and thus resolve the central geopolitical problems of this century by harnessing Germany to the West and containing the USSR. From Maier's perspective, then, it was this productivist vision, along with the underlying social relations and corresponding institutional frameworks in which it was embedded, which may be said to constitute the American-centered world order of the twentieth century.

Following Maier's lead, Michael Hogan has built a strong case arguing that a fundamental continuity characterized American foreign policy in the two postwar eras – deriving from socio-political characteristics of the American state–society and transcending differences between governing parties and their favored instruments of policy. In both periods, American policy-makers sought simultaneously to "refashion Europe in the image of American liberal capitalism" and to ameliorate its chronic geopolitical troubles by encouraging economic integration, interdependence and growth. Elaborating upon the ideas of their Hooverite predecessors of the 1920s, American Marshall Planners took the economic integration of Europe to be essential to the long-run peace and prosperity of the Western world. It was thought that integration would create the large, unified market necessary to support mass production and realize economies of scale, foster the most efficient use of resources, and generally contribute to higher living standards in Europe. In an environment of increasing affluence, these Americans believed, cooperation might displace conflict and diminish the threats to liberalism posed by "extremism." Through the coordinated reconstruction of the advanced capitalist economies, catalyzed by massive infusions of Marshall Plan dollars, American policy would lay the basis for a more open, interdependent and prosperous world economy. In pursuit of this vision, various sorts of transnational networks – including governmental, business, and labor organizations – were fostered as part of the Marshall Plan strategy of economic coordination. "By forging such links, American Marshall Planners hoped to build a transnational alliance behind the [Economic Recovery Program], equip participating countries with American production skills, fashion American patterns of labor–management teamwork, and, in these and other ways, maximize the chances for economic integration and social peace on the Continent."[11]

Productivity politics: labor and neoliberal hegemony

The mainstream of American organized labor envisioned its own future in terms of the kind of transnational productivity politics which Maier and Hogan place at the center of their historical interpretations, and participated actively in its internationalization. As early as 1943, officials of the Congress of Industrial Organizations (CIO) had endorsed the strategy of reciprocal trade agreements as a way to construct a liberalized international economic order and thus to realize the neoliberal vision of global peace and prosperity. In 1944, *CIO News* explained in the following direct language the economic consequences of failing to realize this vision: "Without world trade, America's huge production machine will rot, and millions of people will lack jobs and rot with it." In a liberalized world, however, American industrial products could find markets and fears of renewed depression and anti-union political reaction might be displaced by more generalized prosperity, full employment and social reform. Although there was significant opposition within the American Federation of Labor (largely among old-line protectionist and Republican elements), by 1948 the AFL had joined the CIO in endorsing reciprocal trade agreements, which one AFL official described as "part of the American foreign policy counterattack against Soviet Communist imperialism and its menace to peace and freedom."[12]

Both major labor organizations in the USA supported the Marshall Plan, sent their members to participate in its administration, and propagandized in its favor at home and abroad, in large part because unionists believed that the return of economic prosperity in Europe would help to sustain American exports and output, and would support full employment and higher wage levels at home. But reconstruction was much more than a matter of money and markets. Labor unionists collaborated with American officials, intelligence operatives, and businessmen, engaging together in direct interventions which were designed to submerge class conflict in Europe, isolate "extremists," and create the political preconditions for a liberal capitalist core.

According to the logic of their ideological framework, the Americans believed that productivity growth was a necessary condition for snowballing investment, capital accumulation and recovery in Europe, and (eventually) for higher wages, generalized prosperity and long-run social stability. Increasing productivity required, and would (in time) reward, labor peace and the circumscription of class conflict. A central aspect of this political agenda, then, involved fostering brands of unionism which were more oriented toward American-style collective bargaining than class-based political action. This goal was pursued through both overt and covert interventions by the American government and major American labor organizations, a concert made possible by their common ideological vision of political stability, peace and prosperity, and their construal of communist parties and unions as beyond the pale which this ideological vision circumscribed.[13]

The AFL was historically the more conservative of the two great

American labor organizations, traditionally eschewing any radical or even explicitly political program in favor of a vision of "voluntarism," an ideology of self-help emphasizing an economically oriented brand of "pure and simple" trade unionism for skilled workers organized along craft lines.[14] Industrial unionism, which might support more class-based and explicitly political or even radical forms of action, was anathema to AFL leadership, and so *a fortiori* was communism. The AFL strongly supported anticommunist internationalism and, even before World War II had ended, its American Labor Conference on International Affairs was envisioning an active role in postwar European labor movements, supporting "the democratic side" in "the bitter struggle against the communist onslaught."[15]

With the help of Jay Lovestone, the AFL sharpened its anticommunist predispositions into the guiding principle of its international operations. A former Communist Party official who became bitterly hostile toward the CP after the late 1920s, Lovestone had become influential among AFL leaders by the end of World War II, preaching a labor gospel which identified democracy with market-oriented individualism, and denouncing explicit political ideologies and movements as un-American and anti-democratic. According to Anthony Carew, Lovestone

> now described himself as a small "d" democrat, promoting a philosophy for labor that gave pre-eminence to the freedom of the individual over collectivist approaches. There was, he said, no longer room for "isms" in American politics, and he called upon all radical groupings to bury their "European philosophies" and join American trade unions in preparing to defend democracy.[16]

Lovestone was appointed Executive Secretary of the Free Trade Union Committee (FTUC), an organization founded in 1944 by AFL leaders and supported with AFL funds, but allowed substantial autonomy for its international operations. Through its agents in Europe – most notoriously, Lovestone's follower Irving Brown – the FTUC began to create a transnational network of, and provided technical and financial assistance to, anticommunist labor leaders and organizations in such countries as Norway, Greece, Austria, Britain, Germany, France, and Italy. Beginning in 1948, the Central Intelligence Agency was using FTUC as a clandestine conduit for the distribution of US government funds to anticommunist labor groups in Europe, with Irving Brown serving as a primary agent of this program.[17]

In the afterglow of anti-fascist popular front policies, powerful

communist forces coexisted uneasily with more social democratic tendencies within postwar European labor movements, especially in the
CGIL of Italy and the CGT of France. But American reconstruction
loans and then the promulgation of the Marshall Plan drew more
"moderate" political forces toward the West, while the Cominform
encouraged its member parties to denounce the Plan as a vehicle for
American imperialism. This conflict exacerbated the tensions and
stresses within European labor movements. With the material and
moral support of Irving Brown and the AFL's FTUC, as well as the
Marshall Plan labor staff in Paris, non-communist elements within the
French CGT broke away to form the anticommunist labor federation
known as Force Ouvrière (FO) in 1947–48. In Italy, with similar kinds
of official and unofficial American support, a non-communist labor
organization (LCGIL) spilt off from the CGIL in 1948. Brown and the
AFL believed it was essential to split the communist-led labor federations, and to create anticommunist dual unions which might facilitate
the marginalization of the radical unions and the containment of
communism.

In comparison to the AFL, the internationalism of the CIO was
initially less dogmatically anticommunist. Objecting to the participation of Soviet labor organizations, the AFL had stubbornly refused to
join the World Federation of Trade Unions (WFTU). The CIO, on the
other hand, had been represented at the 1945 founding of the WFTU in
Paris. In the context of an intensifying Cold War, however, the political
center of gravity in the CIO shifted rightward: it was on the way to
purging its own ranks of communists and radicals, expelling entire
unions which it characterized as communist-dominated. When the
member unions of the WFTU split over whether to support or oppose
the Marshall Plan, the CIO leadership interpreted this as incorrigible
communist intriguing. By 1949 the WFTU was politically polarized and
the CIO, along with the British TUC and the Dutch NVV, withdrew
from the WFTU. Appealing to the "Free Trade Union Movements of
the world" to abandon their ties to the WFTU, representatives of these
American, British and Dutch union federations characterized the
WFTU as "completely dominated by communist organizations, which
are themselves controlled by the Kremlin and the Cominform." These
unionists charged that instead of seeking to promote reconstruction
and the material betterment of the conditions of European workers,
the communist elements in the WFTU were attempting to frustrate
recovery in order to fulfill the interest of the Soviet Union in a weak

and divided Europe. James B. Carey of the CIO saw the WFTU as a casualty of Soviet Cold War machinations: "When the communists ... sought to pervert this organization to serve their ends they irrevocably split it in two."[18]

The CIO then joined the AFL and other non-communist labor federations in founding the International Confederation of Free Trade Unions (ICFTU). "The true strength of the ICFTU," Victor Reuther of the CIO wrote in his memoirs, "was the fact that this organization was committed to European recovery within a democratic framework that permitted free and democratic trade unions to function."[19] Nor was this vision limited to Europe; rather it represented a vision of global hegemonic aspirations. According to CIO ideology, "free labor means a free world." If they were free to form voluntary associations and to bargain collectively with their employers, workers around the world could simultaneously defend their individual rights and liberties and improve their material well being, and in both ways make their homelands more resistant to communist infection. A contemporary CIO document envisioned organized labor as part of a global struggle to defend liberal capitalism: "Free world labor, organized in the growing ranks of the ICFTU, stands today as the only firm and reliable bulwark against further infiltration of red totalitarianism among the masses of workers both in the industrial nations of western Europe and in the awakening lands of the Middle and Far East ... [the] most crucial sectors of freedom's global front ..."[20] In other words, a new international labor organization had been created, from which communist unions would be excluded, and which would help to secure the mutual – if asymmetrical – accommodation of international organized labor and American Cold War foreign policy. As a consequence of these polarizations of international and European labor organizations, the emergence of a unified class-based political movement was precluded, making possible the eventual consolidation of the political hegemony of the center; and the bargaining power of European labor movements was fractured, holding down real wages and contributing to the rapid accumulation of capital.[21]

Even as European labor movements were being split, the Marshall Plan's effective priority of capital accumulation, productivity growth, and financial stability was becoming a locus of controversy within the Economic Cooperation Agency (ECA), which administered Marshall aid. The labor staff of ECA, especially those drawn from the American CIO industrial unions, became increasingly disillusioned with the primary emphasis which Marshall Plan policies placed upon capital accumulation, and the ECA's reluctance to take measures which would support the immediate growth of real wages and allow labor's standard of living to increase along with productivity. As Carew summarizes it, "The frustration that Labor staff experienced within the ECA stemmed from the gradual realization that the aid program accorded social justice a lower priority than economic revival and that in ECA's internal debates labor counted for less than business."[22] It is revealing to note the terms in which this conflict was expressed and contained. In the summer of 1950 a joint AFL–CIO delegation to Europe issued an influential report in which American unionists framed the shortcomings of ECA policies in terms of the difficulties which they created for non-communist labor organizations, competing with communist-led organizations in an environment of dual unionism.

> Our productivity programme in France carries serious threats to the welfare of the workers and does nothing to protect them – as the communists so accurately charge ... temporary unemployment caused thereby is ignored ... There is no protection against wage cuts ... [resulting from] the adoption of machine methods ... There is nothing to prevent the direct benefits of increased production made possible by Marshall Plan aid from going entirely to the employer.[23]

Despite the rhetoric of productivity politics, organized labor was at best a junior partner in the emerging transnational historic bloc. Still, American organized labor remained within the anticommunist consensus, and did not fundamentally challenge the terms of capitalist reconstruction in the core, as the CIO reaction to this situation demonstrates. In 1950 the CIO began European operations – outside the official framework of Marshall Plan administration – to support non-communist unions, providing advice and funds, helping to train "a new cadre of young trade union leaders" in the ideology and strategy of American-style unionism, and driving home the potentially positive-sum effects of productivity growth if (non-communist) organized labor could bargain for a larger share of the expanding pie. Victor Reuther, the CIO's European Representative, urged "... vigorous leadership in a European-wide campaign to organize the unorganized [in the basic industries of transportation, mining, and metalworking] and to swing back into the Democratic Trade Union camps, those who now follow Commie unions." On at least one occasion in the early 1950s, the CIO's Reuther brothers acted as a conduit for CIA funds "to assist democratic trade unions in France and Italy," as Victor Reuther later explained it.[24]

Meanwhile, at the same time they were acting independently of ECA to promote "free trade unions" in Europe, American unionists were also active in the joint management–labor productivity councils which were funded by Marshall aid. Victor Reuther, who served as co-chair of the Anglo-American Council on Productivity, described it as a "partnership" between management and labor in order "to encourage a more rapid and uniform application ... of [American-style] methods to increase productivity and speed up postwar recovery."[25] From the perspective of Reuther and the CIO, productivity growth would make possible higher wages and more comfortable standards of living, to be secured by "free" European unions through collective bargaining. The councils sponsored study trips by teams of British and European managers, workers and technical specialists who would visit the United States to see what were represented as typically American methods for labor–management cooperation in the interest of maximizing productivity. These teams would generate reports of their findings which they would publicize and circulate upon their return from America. The reports of the productivity teams emphasized such technical features of mass production as mechanization and factory layout, production planning and management control, efficient handling of materials, and so forth; but special emphasis was placed upon the purportedly cooperative attitude of American labor toward these productivity enhancing innovations. The Anglo-American Council on Productivity described its primary finding in the following terms: "The most important results of the Team visits are ... intangible, and are hardly capable of measurement except on a long-term basis. They derive from the co-operation in a common enterprise of Management and Labor ... High productivity results largely from an attitude of mind on the part of both Management and Labor." It is illuminating to compare this language with the following excerpt from a US Information Service pamphlet entitled *Consumer Capitalism*: "the secret of high productivity in the United States is not in the machine ... it lies in the unreserved collaboration of the worker and the boss." This sort of representation formed a consistent theme in Marshall Plan productivity campaigns, and seems to have been directed at securing European labor's consent to the restructuring of capitalist production in the interests of productivity.[26]

In addition to transatlantic visitations, Marshall funds also underwrote the establishment of national productivity centers in Britain, France, Italy, Germany, and elsewhere, to propagandize for productivity and to publicize what was considered to be the best industrial practice. In France, a "pilot plant" program was set up to demonstrate concretely the benefits which could follow from industrial reorganization. While American unionists had hoped that the program would invigorate non-communist European unions by providing them with a taste of the bounty which productivity growth could make it possible to secure via collective bargaining and wage increases, in practice the program provided technical assistance to firms which were under little pressure to share their productivity gains with workers. French unionists quickly became disenchanted and the major non-communist labor organization withdrew from the program in 1952. Unionists in Italy likewise withdrew from the productivity programs in that country, while the German unions declined to participate in the first place. So disappointed was Victor Reuther of the CIO that he dubbed the productivity program in France "a disgrace ... a labour exploitation programme."[27]

However, despite the dissatisfaction of American organized labor with the immediate results of the productivity programs sponsored by Marshall aid, they did not withdraw from the anticommunist consensus nor did they question the capitalist basis of reconstruction in the core. Unification of communist and non-communist labor federations for the purpose of class-based political action, confronting the ECA and compelling basic reforms, appears to have been beyond the horizon of political imagination within which the American unionists operated. Their disagreements with Marshall Plan administration were over matters of relative emphasis and priority, rather than fundamental divergences of political vision. And, although the unionists did not get what they wanted in the short term (effective regimes of collective bargaining, and wage levels increasing along with productivity), by the late 1950s these goals would be within reach.[28] The significance of labor's participation in the Marshall Plan may then have less to do with the immediate material results and more to do with the processes of cultural change which that participation set in train. Carew assesses them as follows:

> In the longer run the cumulative influence of a plethora of Marshall Aid-inspired productivity institutes, business schools, training centers, academic research and the conventional wisdom that they developed was pervasive throughout Europe. Cultural values, norms

and expectations in industry were certainly changing by the end of the 1950s, and in this the Marshall Plan programs must be seen as an important conditioning force.[29]

From productivity politics to economic security

Official American agencies acting in concert with labor organizations such as the AFL and CIO sought to consolidate non-communist trade union movements in Europe, to exclude radicals from postwar governments and generally to reinforce tendencies toward social-democratic centrism. The Marshall Plan fostered the spread of American productivist, managerial culture in Europe, having as one of its most significant effects the intensification of centrifugal forces operating upon leftist labor and political movements to isolate them from the mainstream, ultimately contributing to the consolidation of a centrist politics revolving around an ideology of economic growth and a limited generalization of prosperity.

Not surprisingly, the construction of a politics of liberal capitalist hegemony was most successful in the occupied countries (where American control was most direct and where the power of radical labor organizations had been most completely crushed by fascism), and they led the way to a world more hospitable to American-style capitalism. "The whole thrust of Washington's effort in the emerging Federal Republic [of Germany], the new Japan, and the members of the Organization for European Economic Cooperation (OEEC) ... was to ensure the primacy of economics over politics, to de-ideologize issues of political economy into questions of output and efficiency."[30] By creating an environment favorable to such an outcome, American state managers moved toward the vision of a vigorous, liberal world economy upon which, they believed, US prosperity and social stability ultimately depended.

Although there were manifest economic benefits to be had from generalizing the politics of productivity in this way, for American state managers it served simultaneously as an instrument of national security policy. Through the reconstruction of the advanced capitalist economies, American policy not only laid the basis for a more open, interdependent and prosperous world economy, but it would also serve to integrate Germany into a viable, cooperative and essentially liberal West European community, thus resolving a central geopolitical problem of the twentieth century. As it became apparent to American policy-makers that the Soviet Union pursued a view of its own national security requirements which was inconsistent with the American liberal vision of economic security in Europe, the Soviets became the object of a policy of isolation and containment. In the context of a worsening Cold War, it was hoped that the constellation of liberal capitalist democracies brought together under US auspices would form an economic and moral bulwark against the spread of Soviet sympathies and the extension of their "closed sphere of influence" outward from Eastern Europe.[31]

American foreign policy goals of prosperity and security were thus directly linked in the vision of a neoliberal world order. In summarizing the perception of national security which guided US policy-makers after the war, Robert Pollard uses the term "economic security" to denote their fusion of the distinctive American vision of liberal world order with the geopolitical concerns of classical statecraft. He evaluates as follows their ability to realize this larger vision:

> The United States had achieved its main economic security goals in Europe by 1950: the reconstruction of Western Europe in an American-centered multilateral system, the alignment of Germany with the West, and the containment of Soviet power in Europe. Significantly, the Truman administration realized these objectives chiefly through the use of economic instruments, rather than military power.[32]

The evidence which I have reviewed suggests that American perceptions of national security and expressions of American global power in the twentieth century consistently reflected a distinctive quality which was grounded in the socio-political relations of the United States. In the postwar years, the USA provided the framework of ideological, political and economic stability necessary for growth to resume on a liberal capitalist basis and for existing welfare-nationalist states to be reconstructed in neoliberal form, in the context of an open, interdependent, American-led world order. Further, in attempting to realize this neoliberal vision, American state managers deliberately and systematically sought to foster a "moderate" and growth-oriented politics in the advanced capitalist countries.

These historical interpretations of hegemonic neoliberalism may appear to be consonant with some emergent tendencies in the IPE literature on hegemony and foreign economic policy, and so a brief digression may be in order to evaluate these. In particular, an interpretation of the social forces which guided American foreign economic policy in the construction of the new hegemony are offered by scholars who examine the political interplay of interest groups, industrial sectors, and electoral coalitions. Thomas Ferguson and Jeff Frieden have each argued that changes in industrial structure and in the interests of particular industrial and financial groups contributed to the reorganization of predominant political coalitions and thereby altered the content of public policy. Prior to assuming the mantle of global leadership, they contend, American politics was transformed by the emergence of an internationally oriented cluster of industrialists and financiers. Coalescing behind the second New Deal, this bloc of capital-intensive, globally competitive industries and their internationally active financial allies could simultaneously support liberalized international economic policy and domestic accommodation with organized labor. For Ferguson and Frieden, it is in terms of this ascendant bloc of industrial and financial interests that the rise of neoliberalism in the USA is understood.[33]

Assessing this line of sectoral coalition research from a Marxian–Gramscian perspective, it is important to keep in mind that the politics of industrial change are not limited to the formation of new coalitions of private actors, attempting to realize shared economic interests by gaining influence over state policy. Industrial transformation entails changing relationships of class power, both in the sites of production and in the larger social formation. This potentially problematic aspect of sectoral research comes to the fore in Ferguson's analysis, where Gramsci is explicitly invoked as the source of a central organizing concept – "historical bloc" – but where the underlying concept of politics is essentially a liberal one, and hence is fundamentally inconsistent with the entire (Marxian) conceptual system from which Gramsci's concepts take their meaning. In this theoretical transplantation Gramsci's concept loses much of its meaning and, as a consequence, aspects of socio-political change which Gramsci held to be integral – in particular, the relationship between social self-understandings, political power, and the social organization of production – are systematically excluded or devalued in Ferguson's account. In contrast to his interpretation, which emphasizes the mechanisms by which changing constellations of private interests gain influence over the state apparatus, Gramsci understood the construction of an historic bloc to entail a reconstruction of state–society relations through organically related processes of political, economic and cultural change (see chapter 2). From a Gramscian perspective, then, research focusing on sectoral coalitions provides a relatively limited understanding of socio-political change.

These limitations inhere even in the strongest examples of sectoral coalition analysis, such as Ferguson's. His argument is indeed elegant and he musters a rich panoply of primary evidence to support it. Yet, the historical record is not unambiguous. When viewed from a perspective which takes changing relationships of class power to be an important aspect of socio-political transformation, a very different kind of story emerges. Whereas Ferguson presents labor militancy as an independent constraint on the choices available to given economic "elites," the perspective adopted in this study suggests that the rise of capital-intensive mass production industry, struggles over the social organization of production, and the formation of an industrial labor movement were bound up together as integral aspects of the process of change which *produced* the particular economic interests taken for granted in sectoral coalition analysis. Accordingly, the historical evidence appears in a different light: the incipient social compromise of the New Deal era seems less the result of determinate calculations of interest on the part of influential industrialists and financiers than the outcome of open-ended processes of socio-political change involving (but certainly not limited to) the construction of new kinds of class power in the sites of production, and the active resistance of industrial workers to those powers.

Take as a case in point the 1937 breakthroughs in industrial unionism: the first giant corporations (General Motors and US Steel) to recognize unions of the CIO (then known as the Committee for Industrial Organization) as legitimate collective bargaining agents were not among the group of industries which Ferguson's theory identifies as those most likely to accept accommodation with organized labor.[34] Nor was the federal labor policy of the second New Deal decisive in these crucial industrial struggles. Rather, it was *the workers themselves* who won recognition from these fiercely anti-union firms by confronting them with the threat of effective work stoppage at junctures considered strategically important by the firms involved.[35] The insecure foothold which industrial unionism had attained in mass production industry before World War II cannot be attributed (in any direct sense) to federal labor policy nor, therefore, to the actions of those elite economic interests who may have supported such policies. I would contend, then, that political struggles in the sites of production merit interpretation and analysis as a crucial aspect of the genesis of a neo-liberal historic bloc in the USA. Indeed, this is the task of chapters 4–7.

To return to the major themes of our historical interpretation and weave together these various strands, then, we may say that a powerful bloc of American socio-political forces came to embrace a vision of the national interest which sought to secure the politics of productivity on an international scale – a system of global order consistent with their vision of social harmony through liberal democracy and capitalist economic growth. Since the sharp economic crises of the late nineteenth century, prominent American capitalists and statesmen had argued that domestic prosperity and social stability depended upon access to foreign markets. As a consequence of the importance attributed to the "open door" in defining American national interests, US foreign policy-makers perceived as dangerous and exhibited consistent hostility toward anti-liberal and especially revolutionary socialist political movements around the world. With the advent of hegemonic neoliberalism – entailing among other things the subsumption of organized labor into the dominant bloc – this interest in an open door world was fused with active commitments to multilateral international economic institutions, reciprocity in trade relations, a more activist state, a limited generalization of affluence through such measures as the official sanctioning of industrial unions and mass collective bargaining, and a more explicit and virulent anticommunism. This distinctively neoliberal understanding of the national interest emerged as the basis of state policy during the 1930s and 40s, propagated by a nascent hegemonic bloc comprising (1) Wilsonian liberals, especially in the State Department (2) those fractions of the capitalist class which were internationally oriented, especially major banks and technologically advanced corporations engaged in mass production, *and* (3) the official leadership (and to some extent the mainstream membership) of organized labor in America. In its struggles with traditional protectionists and isolationists, as well as more "radical" New Deal economic planners and labor militants, this neoliberal historic bloc came increasingly to associate security with prosperity, both at home and abroad, and thus to define American national interest in terms of a neoliberal world order – with a stable, productive, prosperous, and non-communist Europe as its *sine qua non.*[36]

Due in no small measure to the prodigious output of American mass-production industry, the United States and its allies had been able to defeat the militaristic capitalisms of Italy, Germany and Japan in World War II. Thereafter, the greatest challenge to the global vision of the neoliberal bloc appeared to be Soviet-style communism, and the danger that the devastation wrought by the war would serve as an incubator for radical European movements which might be less inclined to align Europe with the United States or to participate actively in the new capitalist order. The Marshall Plan not only provided a massive infusion of funds to alleviate a dollar shortage and stimulate European reconstruction, it also acted as a mechanism for transplanting the seeds of neoliberal ideology, institutions and practices from the United States to Europe. Collective European planning for the administration of Marshall aid represented a first step toward the unified European market which could support mass production and generate the levels of prosperity which the American ideology associated with political moderation and stability. Further, through the Marshall Plan and less overt modes of intervention, the growth of non-communist, economically oriented labor movements was aided and abetted in Western Europe, and the worst-case scenario of a radicalized, politically active European working class, which might steer European politics in a neutralist or even pro-Soviet direction, was not realized. Finally, transnational linkages were established among the capitalist classes of Europe and America, which together would administer the new order based on a common commitment to economic growth and increased productivity as the keys to the preservation of capitalism in the core of the world economy. It was in the era after World War II, then, that neoliberal states–societies were constructed across the core, and the products of the American mass production economy – both material and ideological – were deeply involved in this process of reconstruction.

Central to this interpretation is the implication that processes of social change within the United States were a necessary condition for the hegemony of neoliberalism in the postwar world. If we grant that such a suggestion is not entirely implausible, we may entertain a host of potentially very interesting but conventionally unasked questions. What, for instance, were the historical qualities of the American state–society which fostered a world order of neoliberalism? How were the socio-political relations of the USA – central to the neoliberal world order – themselves constructed? In particular, what was the historical relationship between the development of American productive powers, and the neoliberal ethos in terms of which the American neoliberal historic bloc constructed its global hegemony? The remainder of this study is centrally concerned with addressing these questions.

4 The emergence of mass production practices and productivist ideology

Taylor, Ford, and mass production in America

In the era of neoliberal hegemony, the core of the world economy was reconstructed on the basis of a limited generalization of affluence made possible by institutionalizing mass production and mass consumption in the advanced industrial economies. The politics of productivity – a centrist, growth-oriented political consensus – would eventually emerge out of this long-term process of social reconstruction. As pioneers of mass production and producers of the emerging hegemonic culture, Americans were able to a much greater degree than other peoples to shape the global social relations in which they lived. With the creation of the postwar international economic institutions (Bretton Woods, GATT, etc.), and the reconstruction of Europe and Japan under US leadership, this asymmetrical American influence was, for a time, institutionalized in a neoliberal world order. A central contention of this study is that the asymmetrical power of American statesmen, capitalists, and labor leaders within the neoliberal world order was to a great extent based upon the ideological frameworks they developed and the social relations they constructed as they created a mass production, mass consumption society in the USA. This chapter traces the origins of mass production practices and productivist ideology in the United States, the early stages of their dissemination to other industrial countries, and the contradictions which led to the crisis out of which neoliberal hegemony would eventually emerge.

Mass production involves high output of standardized goods over long production runs using specialized machinery and less skilled labor. According to the conventional economic calculus, in return for a huge increase in fixed costs (relative to variable costs), manufacturers were able to take advantage of economies of scale, spread fixed costs over vast production runs, and suppress unit costs to historically unprecedented levels. The products of mass production, then, could potentially be made available to masses of people who for the first time could afford to become "consumers."[1]

Conventional economic rationalizations notwithstanding, there was another set of reasons – reasons grounded in class-based relations of production – which underlay the great attraction which mass production had for manufacturers. In particular, it allowed them to decrease their reliance on skilled and self-directing craftsmen, and to employ greater proportions of more or less homogeneous (and hence substitutable) unskilled labor to perform standardized and minutely specified tasks, using machines and tools specially designed to minimize the skill and judgment involved. The net effect was to intensify factory discipline and the degree of control which capitalists and managers could exercise over the actual performance of work, to enforce a greater and more nearly uniform pace and intensity of work, to increase the productivity of labor, and thus to increase the ability of capital to extract surplus labor. Around the turn of the century, doctrines of "scientific management" emerged to promote and to justify – in terms of an ideology of technical rationality, efficiency, and generalized social progress – the predominance of managers and engineers in this new production process, and the exclusion of organized labor.[2]

Frederick Winslow Taylor, the preeminent ideologue of this movement, represented these changes as involving a reconciliation of employers and workers in a new shop-floor consensus, a transcendence of class struggle on the putatively objective terrain of science, making possible the realization of a common interest shared by employer and individual workers. What Taylor perceived as erroneously narrow, class-based conceptions of self-interest – which led to unionization, restriction of output, and other industrial ills – would be supplanted with a common dedication to increasing productivity and reward, achieved through the deployment of science and under the tutelage of the technical expert, the scientific manager. Among the "friendly," "helpful," and "cooperative" measures by means of which Taylor's scientific management proposed to realize its productivity gains were intensified division of labor and increased routinization of tasks, heightened supervision and control of work in accordance with managerial planning, and incentive wages – all designed to reduce workers' collective and individual control of their labor and to eliminate restriction of output. Not reducible to an increase in the purely coercive powers of management, Taylor's scientific management was to be embedded in a cultural transformation of the workplace:

> The great revolution that takes place in the mental attitude of the two parties under scientific management is that both sides take their eyes off the division of the surplus as the all-important matter, and together turn their attention toward increasing the size of the surplus until this surplus becomes so large that it is unnecessary to quarrel over how it shall be divided ... They both realize that when they substitute friendly cooperation and mutual helpfulness for antagonism and strife they are together able to make this surplus so enormously greater ... that there is ample room for a large increase in wages for the workmen and an equally great increase in profits for the manufacturer.[3]

In American industry a consensus on productivity and growth would indeed eventually emerge, but not quite as Taylor had envisioned. As we shall see in subsequent chapters, industrial workers and their unions would, after decades of sometimes intense struggle, institutionalize their consent to management control of the labor process and would, for a time, be rewarded with a substantially improved and relatively privileged standard of living, achieved through collective bargaining.[4] A hegemonic politics of productivity, with far-reaching implications for world order, was produced along with the system of mass production in the USA.

The development of mass production in America was favored by a unique combination of conditions. The vast and rich expanses of appropriable frontier land meant that natural resources could be had abundantly and cheaply. Through the brutal displacement of native Americans, small scale and ideologically individualistic agricultural capitalism was implanted early on. As big capital increasingly penetrated into the frontier regions and transcontinental systems of communication and transportation were constructed after the mid-nineteenth century, great agricultural surpluses became available in commodity form and could circulate through an increasingly national (indeed, international) market, contributing to capital accumulation. Further, in a land of great agricultural bounty, food was relatively inexpensive and absorbed a smaller proportion of family income than in Europe.

Such conditions implied a potential market for standardized manufactured goods, produced in relatively large quantities at low prices for predominantly rural, "middle-class" households.[5]

Through the middle decades of the century (1840s–1873), manufacturers in the northern USA enjoyed a growing domestic market, and responded by expanding the scale of production, thereby helping to generate a period of "rapid and more or less continuous growth" which was, however, largely based upon various previously existing methods of organizing production (often still predominantly craft-based).[6] This was, then, a period generally characterized by extensive growth, rather than intensive, qualitative and technological change.

By the later decades of the nineteenth century, however, this process of expansion generated increasingly intense competitive pressure in a context of decelerating economic growth and falling prices. The merciless elimination of weaker competitors compelled capitalists to seek ways to intensify labor, reduce unit costs, and market their products as widely as possible. As they attempted to respond to these pressures, they were confronted with significant resistance from workers. The persistent power of skilled workers to control crucial aspects of the labor process, along with organized and increasingly militant opposition to lower wages and long hours, made more strictly controlled, mechanized and intensive modes of exploitation extremely attractive for American capitalists. In the decades before the turn of the century, then, intensified competition and workplace friction together generated the beginnings of a transformation of production. Concomitant with a tremendous concentration of capital, new ways of organizing production which had earlier emerged in some industries began to be more widely adopted and more fully developed.[7]

Beginning from the mid-nineteenth century, when the "American system of manufactures" first emerged in the production of rifles in federal armories, American manufacturers pioneered methods which would eventually develop into the system of mass production. According to David Hounshell, this early "armory practice" was characterized by striving toward standardization and precision in order to achieve interchangeability of parts. Pursuit of these goals involved "a high degree of mechanization, specifically the use of special-purpose or single-purpose machine tools operated sequentially to carry out a series of manufacturing operations."[8] By the later nineteenth century, the American system which originated in federal armories had spread into other industries such as watches and clocks, sewing machines, agricultural equipment, bicycles, and automobiles. It was in this last industry that the crucial breakthroughs to true mass production were to be accomplished in the USA during the first decades of this century.

Perhaps as early as 1903, Henry Ford articulated a vision of the mass production and ownership of automobiles:

> I will build a motor car for the great multitude ... It will be constructed of the best materials, by the best men to be hired, after the simplest designs that modern engineering can devise. But it will be so low in price that no man making a good salary will be unable to own one.[9]

To realize this vision of a "universal car," the Ford Motor Company first brought together in its industrial practices the various elements which would constitute the modern system of mass production. It adapted the precision methods, specialized machine tools and sequential operations of armory practice to the machining of interchangeable automobile parts; incorporated novel production processes such as sheet metal stamping; intensified the detailed division of labor within the shops; and, in 1913–14, introduced the moving assembly line. In the words of Henry Ford's ghostwriter, Samuel Crowther, "The net result of the application of these principles [of moving line assembly] is the reduction of the necessity for thought on the part of the worker and the reduction of his movements to a minimum." Ford and Crowther were explicit about the heightened division of manual and mental labor which this entailed: "we have made it unnecessary for the highest types of mental ability to be engaged in every operation in the factory. The better brains are in the mental power-plant" – that is, in management.[10]

Integrated as a mechanized system the pace and intensity of which management could control (although not without significant resistance), the new organization of production cranked out automobiles at unheard-of rates and made possible the steady reduction of their price. With the advent of moving line assembly, the labor time required to build a Ford motor was reduced from about 10 worker-hours in the fall of 1913 to around 3.75 worker-hours by the following spring; while for an automobile chassis, the assembly time was reduced from around 12.5 to less than 2 worker-hours.[11] As a consequence of such dramatic improvements in productivity, a Ford Model T touring car which cost $850 when the car was introduced in 1908 could be reduced in price to $360 by 1916. As their products became increasingly affordable, Ford's

Table 4.1 *Index of output per worker-hour in the US automobile industry, 1904–27 (1914 = 100)*

Year	Index of productivity	Year	Index of productivity
1904	40	1923	265
1909	35	1924	258
1914	100	1925	280
1919	141	1926	302
1921	190	1927	278

Source: "Productivity of Labor in Eleven Manufacturing Industries" *Monthly Labor Review* 30 (March, 1930), p. 502.

volume and market share grew to new heights: from a total of 6,398 vehicles in fiscal year 1907–08, Ford sales grew to 472,350 in 1915–16. By the outbreak of World War I, Ford's productivity had allowed it to capture nearly half of the market for new cars in the United States. According to Nevins and Hill, "of all automobiles manufactured [in the USA in 1914], the Ford Company with 13,000 employees produced 267,720, and the 299 other [American automobile] companies, with 66,350 employees, produced 286,770." Ultimately, Ford's universal car would sell over 15 million copies by the time production of the Model T was halted in 1927. Ford enthusiastically publicized the methods which made such high-volume production possible.[12] Variations of the basic model of mass production were rapidly spreading through much of the industry, resulting in the magnitude of productivity growth which is illustrated in table 4.1.

By the late 1920s, leadership of the automobile industry was passing from Ford Motor Company to General Motors. Ford's original system of mass production based upon highly specialized machine tools and its marketing strategy based upon the "universal car" were supplanted by a marketing strategy based on a changing array of models and prices ("Sloanism") and a system of flexible mass production based upon semi-specialized machines which could be adapted to accommodate changes in automobile models. The General Motors system soon became the industry standard. Nonetheless, this newer variant of mass production retained the central feature of Ford's system: management control – through a combination of coercion and consent – of the organization, pace and intensity of production.[13]

Like Taylor before him, Ford propagated a vision of the employer–

employee relationship as a partnership for prosperity. In Ford's version of this partnership, both parties as well as the public at large all benefit because productive and well-paid workers make for a prosperous community which will sustain sales of manufactured goods such as automobiles:

> what overshadows all else in importance is that we have discovered a new motive for industry and abolished the meaningless terms "capital," "labor," and "public" ... The owner, the employees and the buying public are all one and the same, and unless an industry can so manage itself as to keep wages high and prices low, it destroys itself, for otherwise it limits the number of its customers ... It is the thought of enlarging buying power by paying high wages and selling at low prices which is behind the prosperity of this country. It is the fundamental motive of our company. We call it the "wage motive."[14]

High wages and widespread prosperity, in turn, were supposed to support social equality and the generalized ownership of property, thereby providing the crucial preconditions for individual autonomy and freedom in America. But Ford's vision of "the American way" was not seen as uniquely relevant to peculiar conditions in America; it was expressed in terms of the universalistic aspirations which typify hegemonic ideological projects. Writing for Henry Ford in 1926, Samuel Crowther declared: "The essential principles of Americanism are the goal toward which all civilization is striving."[15] According to Ford and Crowther, this global vision would be realized through the spread of the Fordist model of a mass production, mass consumption society. The industrial ideology of Fordism presupposed that all of mankind shared an interest in the furthest possible advancement of productivity. As the agent of this world-historical mission, the manufacturer was engaged not in the selfish pursuit of profit, but was rather a servant of the public interest, an executor of the greater good of mankind.

Also like Taylor, Ford emphatically maintained the necessity for strict labor discipline, and the subordination of workers to the system of production created and run by management, if these potential benefits were to be realized. Management, then, had a duty to show workers what was (as Ford saw it) in their own best interest, and to enforce conformity with this interest upon them, using the stick of the labor market as well as the carrot of wages:

> We expect the men to do what they are told. The organization is so highly specialized and one part is so dependent upon another that

we could not for a moment consider allowing the men to have their own way. Without the most rigid discipline we would have the utmost confusion ... The men are there to get the greatest possible amount of work done and to receive the highest possible pay. If each man were permitted to act in his own way, production would suffer and therefore pay would suffer. Anyone who does not like to work in our way may always leave.[16]

While revolutionizing the production and pricing of automobiles, Ford also dramatically increased the wage levels of his workers – to about double the prevailing rate – in order to secure a more loyal workforce, willing and able to submit daily to the discipline, exertion, and monotony of the new production system and, not incidentally, to conform to Ford's standards of "a clean, sober, and industrious life."[17] As a result of the famous five dollar day inaugurated in January, 1914, the most reliable and compliant Ford workers might aspire to purchase a Ford automobile, or any of a number of other consumer products which would soon be produced according to Ford's basic principles (or so, at least, the Ford legend suggests).[18] For Hounshell, these developments – taken together as a new system of production – constitute a decisive breakthrough in the organization of manufacturing industry: "With highly mechanized production, moving line assembly, high wages and low prices on products, 'Fordism' was born."[19]

This process of intensifying, standardizing and mechanizing production could not be accomplished without corresponding changes in the organization of economic activity. Daniel Nelson, a leading historian of this transformation, describes it in the following general terms: "The dominant themes of this process, the substitution of formal, centralized controls for ad hoc, decentralized controls and the increasing influence of the management over the factory and its labor force, were the bases of the 'new factory system,' which in turn became the foundation of modern industrial administration." The direct, personal and idiosyncratic authority of entrepreneurial capitalists – and eventually that of foremen as well – would be superseded by a complex, hierarchic organization of management which coordinated and controlled every aspect of the production process, including the recruitment, deployment, discipline and dismissal of personnel. Corresponding to this long-term bureaucratization of production was a new emphasis on systematic, large-scale marketing. Modern corporate capital – in the form of the multidivisional, soon also multinational, firm – emerged in large measure as a response to these twin organizational imperatives of orchestrating and making more predictable both the production and sale of huge volumes of standardized commodities.[20] The development of the new factory system was thus accompanied by the growth and consolidation of economic enterprise.

Since the 1870s, American manufacturing had exhibited tendencies toward bigger firms with more employees and higher levels of capitalization and output. Around the turn of the century, further industrial concentration occurred through successive waves of mergers and the formation of giant conglomerates. In basic industry, these tendencies consolidated the economic predominance of oligopolistic firms by the early decades of this century. The huge firms which now dominated the industrial heart of the American economy employed large staffs of professional managers, engaged in systematic research and development, and invested heavily in the new mechanized technologies of increasingly intensive mass production.[21]

Beginnings of global restructuring

By the early twentieth century, American manufacturers were reaping the benefits of a process of industrial development that had spanned several decades. The giant US firms which emerged from this process engaged in mass production and marketing activities which crossed national boundaries. Through trade and foreign investment, American firms came to dominate the global division of labor and propagated standards of efficiency and affluence and concepts of social control which were associated with Taylorism and Fordism. In so doing, they influenced the social organization of production, management practices, political ideology and culture far beyond American borders.

As table 4.2 suggests, the United States overtook Great Britain – the home of the first industrial revolution – to assume the mantle of the world's most productive economy sometime during the 1890s, and further widened its advantage in overall productivity through subsequent decades. While not all of this growth in overall US productivity is attributable to the new manufacturing methods, it seems plausible to suggest that they made a substantial contribution indeed. Angus Maddison has estimated that in 1890 British output per worker was about 54 percent of the US figure in industry, 63 percent in agriculture, and 133 percent in the service sector, suggesting that Americas greatest advantage when it first surpassed Britain was its industrial productivity (including manufacturing).[22] Further, produc-

Table 4.2 *Comparative levels of productivity,* * 1870–1979
(percent, USA = 100)

Year	USA	UK	Japan	Germany	France
1870	100	114	24	61	60
1880	100	107	n.a.	57	60
1890	100	100	23	58	55
1900	100	93	n.a.	61	55
1913	100	81	22	57	54
1929	100	69	26	49	53
1938	100	70	33	56	64
1950	100	56	14	33	44
1960	100	55	19	50	53
1973	100	64	46	71	76
1979	100	66	53	84	86

Note: *Gross domestic product per worker-hour.
Source: Angus Maddison, *Phases of Capitalist Development* (Oxford: Oxford University Press, 1982), p. 98.

tivity in American manufacturing grew more rapidly than overall productivity or farm productivity through the early decades of the twentieth century. Between 1890 and 1930, manufacturing output per worker-hour in the USA increased nearly 150 percent, whereas overall US productivity increased on the order of 110 percent, and farm output per worker-hour grew about 42 percent. The most explosive growth in productivity occurred during the 1920s, after mass production methods had been developed and were beginning to become widespread.[23] Evidence such as this suggests that the system of manufacturing pioneered by US capitalists was integral to America's status as the leading producer in the world economy.

Through the late nineteenth and early twentieth centuries, large American manufacturing firms became increasingly active internationally, realizing the potential advantages of their new productive system through higher levels of exports and direct foreign investment in manufacturing and marketing, especially in Europe and Canada.[24] Alfred Chandler, the eminent business historian, explains in the following terms the effects of the new business practices on the relationship of the American manufacturing economy to the global division of labor:

> The organizational innovations stimulated by the American system of manufactures in both factory and corporate management had almost as great, if less direct, an impact on the European economies as they

did on the economy of the United States. By the turn of the century they were enabling Americans to undersell Europeans in their own countries. But the "American invasion" involved more than just the sale of American products abroad. It soon led to a large direct investment in plants and personnel. As they were creating their sales networks at home, the new mass-producing, mass-distributing firms set up branch offices abroad. Soon, to meet the demand generated by these branch offices, they erected overseas factories and organized purchasing units to buy for these works ... By World War I, the American multinational corporation had become a significant institution in the world economy.[25]

World War I served to accelerate and intensify processes of development which were already at work in American industry, and to spread more widely through the US economy the new technologies of production and organizational innovations.[26] The war also had enormously important consequences for America's relative position in the world economy. It transformed the USA from a net debtor into a leading creditor nation, and the world's financial center of gravity began to shift from London to New York. Further, American trade expanded greatly during the war. The proportion of total world exports accounted for by the USA grew from 12.4 percent in 1913 to 16.9 in 1922.[27] Perhaps even more significant than the growing volume of exports was the consolidation of America's role as the world's leading industrial producer. Table 4.3 suggests that the United States had assumed this role by the turn of the century, and during the late 1920s was producing over 40 percent of the world's industrial output.

America's changing role in the global division of labor was reflected in the increasing importance of manufactured goods in the composition of US exports. Finished manufactures were the leading category of American exports for the first time in 1913, and the volume of US finished-manufactures exports increased nearly 350 percent between 1914 and 1920.[28] American export trade continued to grow in the decade after the war, as did the relative importance of finished manufactures – by 1930 they represented half of all American exports (see table 4.4).

In the period between the turn of the century and the Great Depression, American manufactures assumed increasing importance in the world economy. Especially significant in this expansion of manufactured exports were machinery and other mass produced goods, with automobiles growing dramatically in relative importance.

Table 4.3 *Percentage shares of world industrial production, 1870–1984*

Year	USA	UK	France	Germany	Japan
1870	23	32	10	13	n.a.
1896–1900	30	20	7	17	1
1913	36	14	7	14	1
1926–29	42	9	7	12	3
1938	28.1	10.2	7.7	12.3	5.7
1948	44.4	6.7	5.4	4.6	1.6
1966	35.2	4.8	5.3	8.1	5.3
1973	29.5	3.8	5.0	7.4	7.8
1979	28.3	3.4	4.8	6.4	7.4
1984	28.4	3.0	4.4	5.8	8.2

Source: David M. Gordon, "The Global Economy" *New Left Review* 168 (1988), table 1, p. 32.

Table 4.4 *Finished manufactures as a proportion of total US exports, 1870–1960*

Year	% Finished manufactures	Year	% Finished manufactures
1870	15	1920	40
1880	11	1930	50
1890	16	1940	59
1900	24	1950	55
1910	29	1960	54

Source: US Bureau of the Census, *Historical Statistics*, series U-213 and U-218, pp. 889–90.

From a share of 2 percent in 1910, automobiles were accounting for 9 percent of US finished-manufactures exports by 1920, and more than 20 percent by 1928.[29] The growing importance of cars in US exports reflected the newly established global commercial predominance of the American auto industry (see table 4.5).

Before the turn of the century, French firms had pioneered in the early design and manufacture of gasoline automobiles and Paris was, for a time, "the world center of automobile production."[30] But the market for automobiles in European countries was limited, and many producers chose to concentrate on crafting high-priced luxury vehicles for the wealthy. French manufacturers, although world leaders early

Table 4.5 *Percentage shares of world motor vehicle exports, 1907–34*

	1907	1913	1923	1928	1934
France	57	33	11	6	6
UK	13	16	2	5	16
USA	11	25	54	72	61
Canada	n.a.	n.a.	25	11	11
Italy	8	6*	4	4	2
Germany	7	16	2	1	3
Belgium	4	5*	3	n.a.	n.a.

Note: * Figures from 1912.
Source: James Foreman-Peck, "The American Challenge of the Twenties" *Journal of Economic History* 42 (1982), p. 868.

on, did not follow the strategic path of standardized mass production and progressively lower unit costs. In contrast, during the first years of this century American manufacturers were introducing lighter and less expensive vehicles which could be produced for a (yet to be realized) mass market, a market which was (in comparison to other countries then producing automobiles) relatively large, wealthy, and well protected by tariffs on imported motor vehicles.[31] Even before 1910 – when the Ford Motor Company opened the Highland Park, Michigan plant where it would begin to develop the techniques of true mass production – American manufacturers had assumed technological and productive leadership of the world's automobile industry by pursuing this strategy. In the decades to follow this industrial leadership would approach an absolute predominance.

Factories in the United States were producing 80 percent of the world's total output of cars and trucks before the outbreak of World War I, and during the war years produced between 91 and 96 percent. In the decade after the war, the American share of world production declined somewhat from the wartime peak, but did not fall below 81 percent. Furthermore, these figures may understate the degree to which American firms dominated the industry world-wide, since by the late twenties the biggest American automobile manufacturers had established subsidiaries and assembly plants overseas and were building cars in a number of other countries (21 for Ford, and 16 for General Motors). According to economic historian James Foreman-Peck, "By 1928 American multinational production abroad exceeded the total output of both the French and German motor industries."[32]

So, to summarize, while the US had surpassed Great Britain in the overall productivity of its economy as early as the 1890s, and giant US firms specializing in mass production and distribution of machinery, motor vehicles, and other manufactures had established beachheads in European and other markets before the war, World War I intensified the application of the new productive systems in American industry and accelerated the process of expansion into major world markets, and thus set the stage for American domination of the new manufacturing economy in the decade after the war. During the 1920s, however, America's ascendant position in the global division of labor did not induce the abandonment of "isolationism" and protectionism in favor of a consistent and vigorous policy of "internationalism," reciprocal tariff reductions, etc.[33] Nonetheless, I believe it would be a mistake to conclude therefore that the rise of mass production in the USA had as yet little significance for the global political economy or for the emergence of American hegemony. On the contrary, during the interwar years the new American developments influenced the organization of production, as well as political ideologies and discourses, throughout the industrial world. Through the spread of American ideologies such as Taylorism and Fordism, the groundwork would be prepared for the consolidation after World War II of a neoliberal, productivity-oriented consensus in the core of the world economy.

Well before the watershed policy changes which committed the US government to reciprocity and internationalism (beginning with the Reciprocal Trade Agreements Act of 1934), American producers had begun to reshape the manner in which economic activity was organized on an international scale. The American system of manufactures attracted the attention of Europeans as early as the 1850s, when members of a select committee created by the British Parliament to study the feasibility of adapting more machine-oriented methods to small arms production in Britain toured a variety of manufacturing plants in a number of American cities. Hounshell excerpts their report to show that they identified the following as important aspects of American industrial practice: "American manufactures ... were characterized by the 'adaptation of special tools to minute purposes,' 'the ample provision of workshop room,' 'systematic arrangement in the manufacture,' 'the progress of material through the manufactory,' and the 'discipline and sobriety of the employed'". In the conclusion of the committee's report, its leading technical expert made it plain that he believed far more was at stake than the availability of guns for the

British army: "contriving ... and making of machinery has become so common in [the United States] ... that unless the [American] example is followed at home ... it is to be feared that American manufacturers will before long become exporters ... to England."[34] At the peak of British global economic predominance, then, he perceived the American system of manufactures to be an emerging threat to Britain's preeminent status as the workshop of the world, and an industrial model which even Britain might fruitfully emulate.

As American productive practices, technology and ideology were further developed through the late nineteenth century, their diffusion was fostered by various international exhibitions and fairs, spectacular celebrations of technology and "progress." At the Paris Exposition of 1900, the Bethlehem Steel exhibit, featuring the "new high speed" steel cutting tools developed (not coincidentally) by Frederick W. Taylor, created a sensation and generated intense interest in American technology and the organization of production which would most fully exploit its advantages. "Taylorism" was widely discussed among European technical and manufacturing strata, Taylor's writings on the cutting of metals and on scientific management were translated and published in Europe, Europeans came to America to study the new system and Taylor, his followers and imitators, traveled to Europe to spread the gospel. Even before World War I, Taylorist industrial practices were being adopted, albeit unevenly, in European industries.[35]

The unprecedented economic demands of the war served as a stimulus for European adoption of American-style managerial practices and mass production methods.[36] This process of exploration and adaptation accelerated in the twenties. In a contemporary survey of the influence of scientific management in Europe, Paul Devinat found a large number of newly created institutions devoted to research into, education about, or application of scientific management and economic rationalization, spread across fourteen European countries. Further, rapidly mushrooming literatures had appeared – in languages from French to Tartar – which translated, commented upon, or imitated the writings of Taylor, Ford, and other luminaries of American management. According to Devinat, European public opinion recognized the American industrial system as being at once threatening and promising:

> In all European countries may be noted a certain amount of anxiety in regard to the superiority of industrial organization in the United States. Certain authors are struck by the superiority of the technique

73

in the United States, others by the well-being of the working classes and the high wages, others by the greater output of the American worker, others by the decrease in the spirit of antagonism between workers and employers, and others, again, by the success of employers such as Ford, and by the results obtained by means of mass production ... From the economic and social point of view all are agreed that America is undoubtedly superior to Europe and that if the latter does not adopt similar methods of work ... it will become more and more difficult for her to compete with American products. This anxiety is accompanied by keen interest in all the processes and methods that have enabled America to reach her present high level of production.[37]

In addition to the economic threat which it posed to European industry, the American system appeared to promise the possibility of greater productivity and output, generally higher levels of wages and welfare, and a resolution of class antagonisms in the common project of securing this better future. Devinat relates that according to its "foremost exponents,"

Scientific management ... leads in practice to the recognition and the development of the solidarity existing between all the different human elements concerned in production. It causes them to collaborate more and more closely for their mutual advantage, both by eliminating everything calculated to make work materially disagreeable and by exorcising conflicts between individuals or between classes such as are born of speculation or injustice. By necessitating a serious endeavour to secure a more equitable and scientific distribution of profits, it not only strengthens such solidarity but supplies a more legitimate basis for profit itself.[38]

Writing in the preface to Devinat's 1927 study, Albert Thomas, the French socialist who was the Director of the International Labor Office, attributed the growing influence of American-style management doctrines to "the realization by many persons in Europe that the economic progress of the United States threatens disaster to the older continent, and that the only way to salvation lies in the rationalization of production."[39] But Thomas was not simply recognizing the power of American-style techniques of production; he also suggested that the American ideology of scientific management in the public interest "calls for respect":

the doctrine of rationalization [scientific management] ... claims that its purpose is not to increase the employers' profits. In accordance with the American ideal of "service" it aims at serving the interests of consumers as a whole. It holds up the material prosperity of all members of society as one of the goals of civilization. To reduce the cost of production to a minimum, and thus to secure the ample satisfaction of all requirements, to be of service to the consuming masses, these are its aims.[40]

Thomas explicitly acknowledged that scientific management "presupposes" the increasing separation of manual and mental labor, the concentration of the latter in "the 'brain' of the factory – the central offices and the research departments," and an irremediable loss of "intelligence and initiative in the workshops." Yet, he believed that these developments ultimately implied not a heightening of class struggle, but its resolution. Through increases in the efficiency of production, workers could be afforded an improved standard of living and more time off in which to enjoy it, and this in turn would eventually win their consent to the new organization of production. Thomas concludes that the "prophets of scientific management" indeed preach "a noble gospel." That the head of the ILO would speak in these terms about Taylorism and its spawn testifies to the nascent global power of the American productivist ethos and the industrial machine it animated. The writings of Devinat and Thomas suggest that (perhaps with differing emphases) European capitalists and managers as well as social democratic labor intellectuals were increasingly impelled in the direction of American productive practices and ideology by the competitive pressure of American commercial rivals, and also by its promise to lubricate the frictions of class struggle through higher productivity and wages and a culture of scientific cooperation in the workplace.

Doctrines of scientific management and mass production spread from the United States to a great variety of European institutional and industrial settings in the decade after World War I. These tendencies are clearly apparent in the automobile industry. A stream of European auto magnates, managers and engineers traveled to Detroit to study Ford's system in operation. After visiting the Highland Park plant, Louis Renault admitted that he was "very much impressed by the ingenuity displayed in the manufacture of cars." Following his own tour, Karl Neumaier, general manager of Benz, declared that "the Ford plant is the most remarkable in the world; it is the very best in equipment and method." Although Ford's English subsidiary had introduced some Fordist production practices by 1915, the European automobile industry generally began to incorporate important aspects

75

of the American system of production (variously adapted to local conditions) after the war. Specialized machine tools, imported from America, were predominant in many European plants by the 1920s. Citroën adopted the moving assembly line in 1919. Renault followed in 1922, and Peugeot after that. Opel, Germany's largest producer, began to install a moving line in 1924; and the Czech producer, Skoda, in 1925 built along Fordist lines an entirely new auto factory which it called "America." In Italy, Fiat began operating its new Fordist factory at Mirafiori in 1936, increasing Fiat's production by half and generating nearly 85 percent of Italian motor vehicle output in 1937. A number of British manufacturers adopted some of these techniques in the 1920s, but Morris – the largest British producer of the time – waited until 1934 before installing the moving assembly line.[41]

Not all of the American industrial philosophy was embraced with equal enthusiasm. In the twenties, Devinat suggested that despite the growing popularity of American doctrines of scientific management, what he took to be crucial aspects of those doctrines were only slowly, and then "very imperfectly," being understood. In particular, he believed that the "intimate connection" of "the whole structure of American prosperity" with "a systematic policy of high wages and continual reduction in the costs of production" was not widely enough appreciated in Europe.[42] Like many of their American counterparts, European manufacturers who implemented Fordist production methods were attracted by the promise of lower costs to be achieved through increased efficiency in materials handling and assembly, decreasing reliance upon skilled labor, and increasing control over the intensity of work. While they did not generally follow Ford's example so far as to institute dramatically higher wage levels for their workers, European manufacturers were not above invoking the rhetoric of Taylorism and Fordism to promote the new organization of production and justify the subordination of labor to management. For example, as Fridenson relates, "The managers of the Fiat company heralded the emergence of a 'progressive capitalism' which promised abundance and welfare provided 'social pacification' and industrial discipline were achieved."[43]

The significance of the new doctrines of technically rational administration went far beyond the factory floor. Although ultimately conservative in their implications, those aspects of Taylorism and Fordism which promised a suspension of class conflict through economic rationalization and productivity growth held some appeal for political forces of both left and right in the deeply fractured socio-political climate of postwar Europe. In the immediate postwar years, the legitimacy of capitalist control of the workplace (and ultimately, of society as a whole) was challenged by the rise of factory councils as an expression of activist, mass-based working-class politics, aiming to construct the kernel of socialist society through the collective administration of work. After the failure of revolutionary movements across Europe, Taylorism and Fordism provided a justification for the reassertion of managerial authority. According to Maier, "The managerial mystique evoked widespread enthusiasm, assumed a truly cultic importance precisely because it was a modern and supposedly class-neutral alternative to the immediately preceding socialist attack on industrial hierarchies."[44]

Often referred to in Germany as Americanization, "Taylorismus" and "Fordismus" were central inspirations for the German economic rationalization movement of the 1920s, and in the subsequent decade the mass production of a people's car (Volkswagen) was a central aspect of nazi Germany's industrial policy. Italian fascist ideology synthesized Taylorism's emphasis on orderly, managed production with a vision of social unity based upon a virulent and aggressive nationalism. Taylorism had a major impact on the French intellectual climate and, along with the administrative doctrines of Henri Fayol, was especially influential among technical and governmental elites. European art and architecture were influenced as well by the ethos of the new system of production and its mechanized dynamism. And, perhaps ironically, doctrines of scientific management were explicitly embraced by Lenin, Trotsky, and others who held that authoritative and systematic planning and the most efficient use of resources and labor were necessary for the rapid construction of a revolutionary socialist society in backward, impoverished and war-torn Russia.[45] Even as they were emerging in the United States, the new systems of mass production were having significant economic, political and cultural effects across a number of countries.

To bring together and summarize these various threads, then, by the 1920s the new organization of production – based upon intensified exploitation of workers achieved through increasing capitalist control of the labor process, and rationalized through ideologies of management in the public interest – was becoming increasingly predominant in the industrial heart of the American economy. As a result, American manufacturers were the most productive in the world and dominated world commerce in such archetypal products of the mass production system as motor vehicles. Through trade, foreign investment, and various kinds of technical and cultural intercourse, American-style productive practices, technology and ideology had begun the process of dissemination to other industrial countries.

Evidence such as that reviewed above suggests that American manufacturers were redefining the standards of efficiency and affluence by which industrial societies (or their most powerful classes and class fractions) measured themselves, and in terms of which they would (eventually) address and attempt to overcome socio-political conflicts. The groundwork for a transnational neoliberal hegemony was being prepared during these years. The political economy of mass production was as yet, however, deeply problematic, unstable and insecure. In particular, it was plagued by tendencies toward underconsumption and the persistence of various forms of worker resistance. Only after the severe crisis of the 1930s–40s was a hegemonic neoliberalism constructed in ways which would, for a time at least, stabilize and secure the political economy of mass production.

Contradictions, crises and struggles: toward neoliberal hegemony

As their new powers helped American capitalists to drive workers to higher productivity, they were also able to crush organization efforts by industrial labor. As the great war in Europe was brought to an end, employers waged war on unionized employees in a renewed open-shop drive, carried out under the pseudo-patriotic banner of the "American Plan." Further, in the red scare of 1918–20, the power of the state was directed against suspected radicals and aliens; and, in the postwar years, anti-trust laws were turned against labor with great vigor. Aided by a sharp postwar recession, employers were generally successful in reversing the gains which organized labor had made under the special conditions of wartime. Employers had won decisive victories in the strike wave which followed World War I, and drove worker resistance underground, so that it took the form of relatively isolated, uncoordinated and covert opposition and restriction of output by informal work groups. Once the overt militance of organized labor had been coercively put down, many larger corporations attempted to stabilize their workforces and elicit the consent of individualized workers through "welfare capitalism," entailing various combinations of company-sponsored insurance and pension plans, employee stock-purchase plans, company unions in the guise of "industrial democracy," and a variety of organized sporting and social activities for workers. The return to "normalcy," then brought with it the return to a workplace dominated by the power of capital, and the speed-up.[46]

According to figures presented by Gordon, Edwards and Reich, between 1919 and 1929 capital per production worker in the USA grew by 36 percent, horsepower per production worker increased by 47 percent, while value added per worker expanded by 74 percent. They see this kind of disproportionate increase in output as an index of the power of capital to control the intensity of work during the 1920s:

> Value added per worker increased much more rapidly than it had during the previous two decades; this increase cannot be explained by a correspondingly rapid increase in investment or in the value of capital stock ... Thus the available data are consistent with the hypothesis that employers engaged in rapid speedup during the early and mid-1920s, taking advantage of labor's weakness; this speedup explains as much or more of the continuing increase in labor productivity during the 1920s as is explained by continuing mechanization.[47]

The decade of the twenties was thus one in which productivity rose rapidly. Moreover, industrial labor was chronically underemployed, unorganized and relatively cheap. As a consequence, real wages increased slowly and lagged well behind productivity growth. Comparing from the peak of one business cycle to the next, output per worker-hour in manufacturing increased by more than 29 percent in the period 1923–29, whereas real average hourly earnings of production workers in manufacturing increased by roughly 9 percent.[48] Profit margins were correspondingly high, and there was a marked tendency toward an increasing inequality of income. Devine offers the following as a rough indicator of a class-based distribution of income which was moving in favor of capital: the ratio of profits and interest income relative to wages rose from 27.3 percent in 1923 to 32.8 percent in 1929. Viewed in terms of the distribution of individual incomes, the rich were getting richer: between 1923 and 1929 the share of total national income claimed by the top 5 percent of the population increased from 27.1 percent to 33.5 percent, and that of the top 1 percent grew from 13.1 to 18.9 percent.[49]

In contrast to the ease of the affluent, workers' standards of living during the 1920s were, in general, much more grim than is commonly acknowledged. Frank Stricker has estimated that on the order of 35 to 40 percent of non-farm families lived in poverty (by the standards of the day) at the end of this putative era of prosperity. The situation of even the most fortunate workers was tenuous and insecure, as a period of illness or unemployment could bring economic disaster for a wage-earner's family. Preoccupied with securing the most basic elements of material well being, relatively few working-class Americans were able to participate in the nascent consumer culture.[50]

Among the wealthiest Americans, then, there was abundant money for investment, speculation, and luxury consumption; but the class skew of this prosperity meant that consumption was insufficiently widespread and steady to support mass production. By the mid to late 1920s, markets for such mass produced consumer durables as automobiles were becoming saturated, despite the growth of installment credit, and sophisticated advertising and marketing strategies. In short, even before the stock market crash, the new mass production economy was dangerously unstable due largely to the disproportionate power of capital and the unbalanced development of social productive powers and consumption norms.[51] The underlying imbalance of the industrial economy goes a long way toward explaining the basic preconditions for a crisis of the magnitude of the Great Depression.

The crisis, however, cannot be fully understood in terms of economic problems of overproduction and devaluation of capital, for the depression years also witnessed a labor uprising of historic proportions and enormous socio-political consequences. Over the first years of the Depression, the conditions of life for working people deteriorated as workers were subjected to wage and hour reductions, massive layoffs and, for those who managed to keep their jobs, an intensification of industrial discipline and still greater speed-up. Those workers who had placed their confidence in the welfare programs of their employers soon found themselves bitterly disappointed as cost-cutting corporations eliminated these benefits. Together, these factors generated mounting levels of discontent among industrial workers. When section 7(a) of President Roosevelt's National Industrial Recovery Act (NIRA) of 1933 appeared to give federal government sanction to labor organization and collective bargaining, but failed to convince employers that independent unions were mandated, an explosion of labor organizing and militance occurred.[52]

Whereas 1932 witnessed the initiation of 841 work stoppages, 1,695 strikes were begun in 1933. Only 1.8 percent of the total workforce had been involved in stoppages during 1932, some 324,000 workers; but this proportion increased more than three-fold, to 6.3 percent, in 1933 when 1.17 million workers struck. Worker-days lost to strikes increased more than 60 percent, from 10.5 million in 1932 to almost 17 million the following year. In 1932, the proportion of strikers involved in stoppages where union organization was the major issue was about 22 percent; the following year that proportion had increased to around 41 percent, and by 1934 was greater than 51 percent. And this was only the beginning of depression-era unionization and militancy.[53]

Between 1933 and 1937, work stoppages averaged 2,495 per year, an average of 5.8 percent of the workforce – 1.28 million workers – were out on strike, and nearly 19 million worker-days were lost in an average year. In 1937, at the crest of the great strike wave, over 4,700 strikes were initiated, involving 1.86 million workers – more than 7 percent of the nation's entire workforce – of whom almost 60 percent were involved in strikes where unionization was the primary issue. By 1939, over 28 percent of non-agricultural laborers were union members, whereas in 1933 that figure had been only around 11 percent. Born out of the militance of the rank and file, mass industrial unions would eventually come to play a crucial role in mediating between workers and management. But in the great industrial battles which raged through the depression years and World War II, it became clear that the apparently placid 1920s had not signified the permanent subordination of labor to the systems of mass production owned and controlled by capital: capital had not yet secured the consent of industrial labor to the powers of management in the workplace.

If American capitalism was dangerously unstable during these years, then the world political economy was no less so. In the core, the European economies had never really escaped the legacy of economic destruction left by World War I, and were heavily burdened with war debts and reparations. Large inflows of American private investment, and such financial expedients as the Dawes (1924) and Young (1929) plans, were not sufficient to revitalize European capitalism such that it might weather the coming storm. When American private capital ceased to flow into Europe after the great crash, and the Smoot-Hawley Tariff of 1930 precipitated a general increase in international trade barriers, the crisis of mass production in America became a crisis of the global political economy. In the context of a deepening world-wide depression and in the absence of a hegemonic world order in terms of which common responses might be formulated, economic nationalism and militarism threatened to foreclose any possibility of realizing the nascent American vision of a world whose doors were open to American goods and capital. The British and their Commonwealth associates created the Imperial Preference System in 1932. More ominous still, nazi Germany embarked upon an industrial policy of mass motorization and rearmament in the 1930s; while Japan's military-industrial complex prepared to stake out a Greater East Asia Co-Prosperity Sphere from which Western commercial interests might be excluded.[54]

The great political-economic crisis of the 1930s and 40s was then global in its scope, and titanic struggles were waged over the future shape of the capitalist heart of the world economy. Yet, by the late-1940s the global crisis was well on its way to amelioration. The fascist alternative to liberal capitalism had been destroyed and a global war of unprecedented violence and destructiveness had been brought to an end. Under the leadership of the United States, European capitalism was being reconstructed through a process which would pacify or isolate radicals and create a unified European market large enough to support mass production industry. The reconstruction of Japan was designed to provide a moderate, capitalist anchor for the development of Asia. And the institutional framework had been created which would provide the international financial stability and liquidity necessary to support a renewal of world trade, as multilateral negotiations progressively reduced tariff barriers and trade controls. In all of this the United States government, American corporate capitalists, and representatives of the American labor movement played leading roles. But how was it possible for such a bloc of American statesmen, capitalists and labor leaders to come together in order to defeat fascism and reconstruct the core of the capitalist world-economy in ways which would support the internationalization of mass production and mass consumption? How was American liberal capitalism able to overcome its own crisis, ameliorate its own contradictions, and produce the material resources, institutional models and ideological frameworks which contributed decisively to the new world order? The following three chapters attempt to reconstruct the processes through which the consent of industrial labor was secured in the American workplace, and the mass production, mass consumption economy was stabilized in the United States. Then, in the concluding chapter, I will examine the postwar development of this system, and the new forms through which its contradictions are manifested.

5 State–society relations and the politics of industrial transformation in the United States

A central argument of this study is that the neoliberal politics of productivity presupposed the creation of new social powers in the privately controlled sites of production, and hence, the subordination of industrial workers to these new "private" powers – a process entailing decades of struggle in which this subordination was contested. In the remainder of this study, I will further develop the argument that the extraordinary global powers of the United States were made possible by the formation of a neoliberal historic bloc, constructing a new social consensus on the basis of steadily increasing productivity, economic growth and a limited generalization of prosperity. More specifically, in this chapter I will argue that this neoliberal hegemony entailed a reconstruction of state–society relations in the USA, simultaneously creating the social infrastructure of mass production and consumption while maintaining the formal separation between the spheres of politics and economics, public and private, which is characteristic of liberal capitalist social formations. This peculiar politics of production, then, is a central – if conventionally unexamined – aspect of the social power complex of American hegemony, and as such merits historical interpretation and critique.

Liberalism and neoliberalism in America

In a classic study, Louis Hartz suggested that politics in America was different from that of other democratic capitalist countries, for America had no historical experience of feudal social relations. Not having been through the long and arduous process of defining itself through opposition to the rule of aristocratic privilege, American liberalism represented not so much an explicit, deliberate and active ideology of revolution as an underlying and generally unquestioned presupposition of political community. As implicit social convention, liberalism in America could itself become traditional, even conservative. Embodying the values of individual liberty and equality of opportunity, liberalism in America could appeal to a much broader spectrum of the public than in the traditionally stratified societies of Europe, and hence could more credibly present itself as common sense, self-evident, universal. Political contests were waged between groups whose differences were largely defined in terms of the aspects of a common liberal tradition which they chose to emphasize. Under such conditions, liberalism could come to be expressed in terms of "Americanism": a national ethos, the self-identification of a political community. A major consequence of this identification was the stigmatization of leftist movements and ideologies as alien, invasive, "un-American." Hence, even moderate Progressive reformers could find themselves politically isolated unless they explicitly pledged allegiance to liberalism-Americanism and eschewed programmatic restructuring in favor of pragmatic tinkering. In liberal America, then, the constitution of the political community, the privileging of the private individual and especially his right to property, and the scope of the public authority, all represent questions which were answered without really having been asked; rather, Hartz argued, these have been the legacy of tradition.[1]

While affirming the power of liberal thought and practice in American history, Samuel Bowles and Herbert Gintis are critical of Hartz's depiction of the American political experience as if Americans had been born into liberalism as one might be born into inherited wealth, distant from its origins, innocent of its social implications. Rather, they would maintain that Americans have come by their liberalism the old fashioned way: they produced it – through historical struggles in which the possibilities of a contradictory social formation were contested.

> the advanced capitalist social formation may be ... represented as an articulation of the liberal democratic state and capitalist production, in which the dynamics of the whole cannot be reduced to the structure of either. Further, under general historical conditions, this articulation renders the social whole a *contradictory* rather than a functional totality.[2]

It is a contradictory whole because its two aspects – capitalist production and liberal democracy – organize socially self-creative practices according to distinct and potentially conflicting ordering principles and practical logics: "the one is characterized by the preeminence of economic privilege based on property rights, the other insists on the priority of liberty and democratic accountability based on the exercise of personal rights."[3] It is the "transportation of practices" between these two sites which may generate fundamental political struggle and structural transformation in liberal capitalist democracies. The relation of state and society, democracy and capitalism, is then historically problematic: the boundary separating public and private realms has been the object of ongoing political struggle, and periodic realignment. Liberalism, encompassing the dual commitments to democracy and private property, is for Bowles and Gintis a continually open political question – quite literally whether we realize it or not.

On this view, state–society relations in the USA have only relatively recently assumed their characteristic neoliberal form. This distinctive constellation of public and private power – the social relations upon which American global hegemony may be said to have been based – was the historically contingent outcome of the political struggles entailed in the rise of corporate industrial capitalism, mass production, and organized labor within a liberal state–society. The neoliberal political economy of the postwar years was based on a reorganization of power within and between the public and private spheres – a reconstruction of state–society relations with major implications for the character of both state and economy – culminating during the years of the Great Depression, World War II, and the early Cold War.

The overall relation between public and private power in neoliberal America may be described in terms of the more active mediation of class conflict, and the rationalization of production and consumption – in an environment of increasing international openness – by the democratic state. This tacit political settlement largely forestalled explicit class conflict and defined for several decades the conditions under which liberal democracy and capitalist production could coexist. In its economic policies the state provided minimal welfare services and managed aggregate demand, thereby stimulating consumption and making possible the (more or less) consistently high levels of demand required to support the apparatus of mass production and keep industry operating somewhere near capacity. Politically, the state officially sanctioned the right of labor to bargain collectively with capital, but has repressed radical elements and otherwise ensured that the demands of labor did not seriously threaten private (capitalist) control over the production process.[4] Although this socio-political restructuring entailed a much more active role for the state than classical liberalism had conceived, and the essential liberal separation between the spheres of public and private became more indistinct around its margins, the fundamental capitalist reality of private ownership and control was preserved despite the increasing complexity, social interdependence, and hierarchic organization of productive activity.

This neoliberal "accommodation" was made possible by, and in turn shaped, the politics of private power in the sites of capitalist production. Class struggle within the political apparatus of production – what Michael Burawoy calls the "factory regime" – was diffused and institutionalized as an integral part of this reconstruction of the liberal state–society. Through its provision of welfare benefits and the legal sanctioning of collective bargaining, the state lessened the direct dependence of workers upon wages and reduced the extent to which capitalists could confront workers with naked, coercive power at the point of production. For Burawoy, this change marks a fundamental shift in the expression of capitalist power within the production regime:

> Now management can no longer rely entirely on the economic whip of the market. Nor can it impose an arbitrary despotism. Workers must be *persuaded* to cooperate with management. Their interests must be coordinated with those of capital. The *despotic regimes* of early capitalism, in which coercion prevails over consent, must be replaced by *hegemonic regimes* in which consent prevails (although never to the exclusion of coercion). Not only is the application of coercion circumscribed and regularized, but the infliction of discipline and punishment itself becomes the object of consent.[5]

In the United States, hegemonic factory regimes have been premised upon the institutionalization of industrial unions as collective bargaining agents, their legal certification and administrative regulation by the state, and the circumscription of class conflict within a framework of contractual negotiation centering on procedural and distributive issues. Within this framework, unions were able to secure remunerative benefits from corporate industrial giants, contingent upon their acquiescence in capitalist control of the production process and in the governance of that process by the imperative of corporate profit. In the corporate manufacturing sector of the American economy, then, higher general wage levels – linked to growth in aggregate productivity – combined with new benefit packages to purchase a more orderly and predictable system of industrial relations. Formal grievance procedures and the increasing bureaucratization of the workplace served to displace shop-floor discontent on to institutional terrain which the company and the union conjointly controlled, and where the militance of the rank and file might be more effectively contained. Under the hegemony of the contract, workers have been defined as private individuals endowed with certain rights and responsibilities, rather than as members of a subordinate class engaged in ongoing collective struggle against the power of capital in the workplace and against the privileging of private property entailed in liberalism's core conception of social reality. In this politics of productivity, overt coercion by capital and the state has faded into the background as industrial unions have become brokers of consent. These, then, are the general outlines of the institutional changes which accompanied the hegemony of neoliberalism in the United States. It remains to give an historical overview of the construction of neoliberalism in the USA, and of the restructuring of production and politics which this entailed.

From craft control to systematic management

By the end of the nineteenth century, social dynamics were gathering force which would transform the process of production and restructure the classical liberal delineation between politics and economics. Capital concentration had begun to increase the scale of economic operations, to create the corporate form of enterprise and the modern factory. In their efforts to accelerate accumulation and survive in an era of intense competition and attrition, capitalists sought to expand their operations, reduce unit costs, and consolidate markets. Capitalists found themselves on the one hand driven by this competitive imperative of the market, on the other severely hampered by the prevailing organization of production. In the workplace, the centrality of skilled labor in the production process, along with the mutualistic ethical codes and tightly knit work groups of the craftsmen, enabled them to exercise substantial control over the conditions of their work. If labor productivity was to be significantly increased, therefore, the collective power of craftsmen in the social organization of production had to be broken, supplanted by the private power of capital and the prerogatives of management. "Once the managers and foremen had taken control of the work routine from the craftsmen, science and technology could be fully exploited to increase productivity and profitability. Management could eliminate skilled workers ... and replace them with semi-skilled machine tenders, and immigrant laborers who worked under the close supervision of foremen."[6]

Standardization and mechanization of production along with the ideology of scientific management held out for capital the possibility of minimizing the power of skilled labor over the production process, increasing output and lowering costs. This new ideology of efficiency through managerial control supplanted the traditional vision of the craftsman's labor as noble, "manly," and creative, with a conception of labor as simply another input into the production process, no less subject to the logic of economy – and the discretionary powers of management – than any other input.[7] Thus the mutualistic self-direction of skilled laborers was directly assaulted by the new management and the social powers it sought to create. In their efforts to actualize more fully the dominance relations made possible by the privileging of private property in capitalist states–societies, employers provoked challenges – sometimes explicitly political – to their "private" social powers.

In the struggles which this process entailed, the organizational asymmetry between newly consolidated corporations – integrating and coordinating production on a national scale – and an ethnically, racially and sexually fragmented working class – only partially organized along craft lines – allowed corporate capital to contain trade unionism, undercut craft autonomy, and intensify control over production. After the powerful Amalgamated Association of Iron and Steel Workers was decisively defeated by Carnegie Steel in the great Homestead strike of 1892, militant unionism was put on the strategic defensive. In the early years of this century came a resurgence of business hostility toward labor, actively supported by the middle classes and the courts. In the face of this "open shop drive," discretion could appear the better part of valor as national craft unions displayed little enthusiasm for risky battles over issues of shop-floor control. As a consequence, workers' resistance to the transformation of production and the intensification of control for several decades remained local, isolated, and sporadic; but it was by no means eliminated.[8]

Especially significant in these struggles over control of the production process were metalworking and machine-building industries, both because of their centrality in the developing mass production economy and because the indispensable role of skilled labor in machine production made these industries an early battleground over techniques of scientific management designed to maximize the effort and output of workers. Standardization of products and specialization of work tasks, detailed supervision and piecework pay incentives did violence to the culture of craft autonomy from which skilled machinists drew their collective identity. Through the first decades of the twentieth century, machinists and other skilled workers resisted as best they could these attempts to subordinate their craft to the new management systems.[9]

These conflicts festering within American industry for several decades became acute during World War I. Officials of the AFL national trade unions sought to collaborate with the reformist Wilson administration: "to secure the political loyalty of the AFL to the war effort, to place union leaders in administrative agencies, and to write union wage and work standards into government decrees."[10] Meanwhile the smoldering unrest of rank and file workers exploded in confrontations which would set important patterns for the future of industrial conflict in America.

The Great War and its extraordinary economic demands accelerated the rate at which the new management methods were implemented in the shops. As production expanded and management attempted to further intensify its control, labor shortages developed which weakened the coercive power of employers and increased the scope for systematic worker resistance. The wartime combination of deteriorating working conditions, eroding real wages, and the sudden vulnerability of employers traditionally hostile to organized labor but now deprived of the discipline of a tight labor market resulted in shop-floor militance and record levels of strike activity beginning in 1915–16. While some of these strikes were explicitly oriented toward control issues and hence constituted direct challenges to the private power of capitalists, many of them interfered with war production and prompted innovative policy responses from state managers which altered the institutional terrain of class struggle.[11]

In an attempt to obtain labor's cooperation with the war effort, the Wilson administration provided for official labor representation on the numerous boards and agencies created to oversee the wartime economy. The eight hour day, overtime pay, new industrial safety standards and increasingly rule-governed employment practices all represented concrete gains for labor under the federally administered wartime economy. Most significant, however, was the new labor relations policy. The state officially sanctioned organization and collective bargaining by "responsible" and "loyal" elements of labor (but did not support the closed shop or proscribe company unions), and attempted to isolate and eliminate more radical influences. As part of this effort, the tripartite National War Labor Board (NWLB) was created in 1918 to resolve labor disputes and uphold fair labor practices. Membership of AFL unions increased markedly in these more favorable circumstances. In short, for the duration of the war emergency the state used its administrative powers to selectively shield labor from the effects of open shop drive and to strengthen the apparatus of collective bargaining.[12]

Under such conditions, skilled metal trades workers could draw upon their mutualistic craft traditions to begin to develop an alternative vision of democratic self-control in the workplace, and one which was more inclusive and broadly class-based, less narrowly defensive, than had been earlier craft resistance to scientific management. In the years between the open shop drive and the war, skilled machinists had developed novel forms of local organization (e.g., citywide metal trades councils, uniting members of various metalworking crafts) which bypassed inert national trade union bureaucracies and provided craft conservatives and radicals alike with a forum for expressing common grievances arising from the onslaught of the new management. Yet, in the era of the open shop, these local organizations remained isolated from national unions, vulnerable to employer retaliation, and without significant organizational strength within the shops themselves. Without a secure foothold in the workplace, these new local organizations could neither effectively resist the erosion of the crafts nor unite with the unskilled to articulate a class-based alternative to capitalist control. With the coming of the war and the new federal labor relations policy, that condition was, for a time, reversed.[13]

By shielding unionism in the shops precisely when wartime conditions had aggravated grievances shared by workers of all trades and skill levels and had simultaneously lessened the disciplinary power of the labor market, state intervention facilitated the consolidation of local, rank and file organization under radical craft leadership. As a result, a significant aspect of the strike wave of 1917–18 was a broad-based challenge to the authority of capitalists in centers of wartime production such as the metalworking and munitions industries of the Northeast. In Bridgeport, Connecticut, locally organized metalworkers put forth a set of "demands focused ... on workplace control, seeking to limit employers' discretion in classifying workers and to secure for representative shop committees a voice in factory management."[14] In the face of intransigent employers, the Bridgeport metalworkers staged a general strike, defying national trade union officials and the NWLB.

To contain the threat of labor rebellion and end the strike President Wilson intervened, threatening the strikers with loss of their jobs and their draft exemptions. Once the strikers were back at work, the NWLB imposed a shop-floor reorganization: non-union shop committees would bargain for the employees. The organizational basis of the workers' control struggles was undermined by severing the linkage between independent local organizations under radical craft leadership and the workers in the shops. As was common in NWLB cases, the form of labor organization which received federal support was something other than independent rank and file unionism: "the cardinal aim, always, was to secure maximum uninterrupted production."[15]

New adaptations of management practice combined with federal labor policy to contain the potential for radical labor unrest. During the war manufacturers began introducing on a widespread basis systematic personnel policies, job ladders based on individual performance, and welfare benefits; all designed to secure for the firm the loyalty of workers, to encourage competition among individual workers for the most desirable jobs, and to ameliorate a major source of common grievance among workers – the arbitrary rule of the foremen. The power of management was consolidated through the increasing rationalization of work, supplanting the mutualistic ethic of the crafts with company unions and the individualized incentives of the intra-firm labor market. Once this transformation was accomplished, craft culture could no longer serve as a medium for the radicalizing transportation of practices from the democratic polity into the industrial heart of the capitalist economy. With the end of the war, federal sanction for collective bargaining was withdrawn and the open shop drive was renewed with a vengeance. Through the next decade management would proceed to intensify its control of the production process, largely unopposed by organized workers.[16]

Mass production, industrial unions, and neoliberal hegemony

The social powers concentrated under the private authority of management during the early decades of this century were used to construct systems of large-scale, standardized production in which the typical worker was no longer a skilled, self-directing craftsman, but a tender of machines designed and controlled by management. However, this transformation of the social organization of production was hardly automatic; it entailed a transformation of the political terrain upon which the private power of management was contested. With the rise of an industrial union movement during the Great Depression, organized mass resistance to capitalist control in the new workplace became a possibility which, in some circumstances, was actualized. These uprisings of industrial workers prompted active responses from state managers and capitalists, embroiling them in a three-way political struggle.

The outcome of this phase of socio-political struggle was a series of institutional changes which, when finally consolidated during World War II and the early Cold War, served to isolate rank and file militants within individual production sites and marginalize radicals, to depoliticize the workplace, and to integrate mass industrial unions into the fabric of liberal society. Industrial unions were legally recognized as legitimate collective bargaining agents on the condition that they acknowledge in practice the basic norms on which liberal social relations are constructed: most importantly, that they respect the property rights of their employers, uphold the sanctity of contracts into which they enter, and assume the corresponding responsibility for controlling their memberships and enforcing compliance with contractual commitments. By incorporating industrial labor within the hegemonic culture of liberalism, celebrating a putatively apolitical growth-oriented consensus, the separation between economics and politics was reproduced in neoliberal form.

An industrial union movement, potentially capable of systematic resistance to the institutionalization of private power in mass production industry, emerged in the USA during the Depression. Those workers who managed to retain their jobs found themselves subjected to an intensification of shop-floor control by capitalists who were both compelled to cut costs and able to tighten industrial discipline by virtue of the extremely slack markets for goods and labor.[17] When in 1933, after a particularly severe decade of business and government hostility toward organized labor, the Roosevelt administration's National Industrial Recovery Act (NIRA) appeared to give federal sanction to collective bargaining, the result was explosive. Section 7(a) of the NIRA declared:

employees shall have the right to organize and bargain collectively through representatives of their own choosing, and shall be free from the interference, restraint, or coercion of employers of labor, or their agents, in the designation of such representatives or in self-organization or in other concerted activities for the purpose of collective bargaining or other mutual aid or protection.

Further, the law stated that no one "shall be required as a condition of employment to join any company union or to refrain from joining, organizing or assisting a labor organization of his own choosing." Thus seeming to legitimate for the first time truly independent labor unions, but providing no authoritative enforcement apparatus, section 7(a) of the NIRA had the effect of simultaneously rekindling worker militancy and stiffening employer intransigence. It triggered a sustained and increasingly intense wave of mass strikes, especially in the mostly unorganized mass production industries, during 1933–34.[18]

The significance of these early New Deal era strikes goes beyond a simple tally of "wins" and "losses." Their most far-reaching effects were to prompt the formation in 1935 of a national organization of industrial labor independent of the old craft-based AFL – the Committee for Industrial Organization, as the CIO was originally known – and to press reform-minded officials led by Senator Robert Wagner to strengthen legislatively the federal machinery for dealing with conflicts over unionization. The National Labor Relations Act of 1935 reaffirmed that "employees shall have the right of self-organization," and proscribed as "unfair labor practice" activities of an employer which "interfere with, restrain, or coerce employees in the exercise of [this right]." Yet, the peaceful resolution of the uprising of industrial labor for which the sponsors of the Wagner Act had hoped did not materialize. The National Labor Relations Board (NLRB) and its vision of a representative system of collective bargaining faced even stiffer resistance from capitalists, despite (or perhaps because of) its reinforcement by the Wagner Act and the belated support of FDR. Unless forced to do so by the courts, employers felt no compulsion to comply with NLRB rulings; and challenges to the constitutionality of the Wagner Act were certain to delay its full legal impact.[19]

Thus, the newly formed CIO and the traditionally anti-union corporations of mass production industry were on a collision course, and the federal government was unable to restrain either party. In an historic recognition strike which ended in February, 1937, rank and file militants in the automobile industry successfully employed the sit-down

93

tactic to break the open shop at General Motors and secured for their union (United Automobile Workers–CIO) the right to represent them in collective bargaining.[20] Within two months, the UAW had also compelled Chrysler to recognize it as a bargaining agent. As the CIO prepared for a hard struggle in the steel industry, US Steel Corporation – traditional bastion of the open shop in basic industry – saw the writing on the wall and recognized the Steel Workers Organizing Committee (SWOC) of the CIO without a strike. Within a year, the CIO had also achieved major breakthroughs in the rubber and electrical industries. By 1937–38, then, industrial unionism was a reality in some crucial parts of the American economy, and the CIO had established itself as a powerful force to be reckoned with.[21]

However, by the time the legal status of the Wagner Act and the powers of the NLRB had been upheld by the Supreme Court (1937), the momentum of the CIO's industrial organization drive had been dissipated by the dramatic economic downturn of 1937–38, the strengthening of conservative political forces hostile to unionism, and crucial failures in the attempt to consolidate unionism in the steel and automobile industries. The SWOC had been ruthlessly repelled by the corporations when it tried to extend its beachhead from US Steel to the other major firms in the industry. In the infamous "Little Steel" strikes, as well as in the UAW's first unsuccessful attempt to break the open shop at Ford, employers used violence, intimidation and systematic propaganda campaigns to bring the CIO's industrial organization drive to a halt. So, after the drastic economic deterioration and the nation-wide resurgence of conservatism which coincided with it, the newly sanctified legal authority of the NLRB became the primary defense of a tenuous industrial union movement. A rough stalemate between capital and labor in mass production industry prevailed through the remainder of the decade.[22]

This stalemate was broken with the outbreak of World War II and the dramatic economic and political changes this brought about. With the war production boom came the end of slack labor markets and hence a temporary easing of the shop-floor power of management. The industrial union movement soon got its second wind as the unrest of the rank and file could once again find organizational expression. Hence, beginning in 1941, tightening markets facilitated a resurgence of the labor militance which had been stifled by the conservative backlash of the late 1930s. The federal labor policies developed to contain industrial conflict during the wartime emergency created the institutional context in which the American system of industrial relations would emerge.[23]

In a period of global political crisis and imminent involvement in general war, state managers could hardly remain impassive in the face of industrial labor's renewed offensive, especially since many of the industries most affected by the strike wave were engaged in defense-related production. The institutional precedents set during World War I were drawn upon by federal authorities in response to this latest national crisis. As in the first war, moderate labor leaders were co-opted into the nominally tripartite agencies created to administer the wartime economy. Such representation served to strengthen moderate forces within the CIO and to identify their leadership with the legitimacy of the state. Thus it began to isolate left-syndicalist militants from the mainstream of union organization, and to reinforce the dependence of union hierarchies upon the state.

Moreover, FDR also followed the precedent of World War I in creating special administrative organs to minimize the effects of industrial conflict on wartime production. He established the National Defense Mediation Board (NDMB) in 1941, which was succeeded in January 1942 by the National War Labor Board (NWLB). More powerful than any of its predecessors, the NWLB "... had full authority, as a result of executive orders under the war powers of the presidency, to settle any labor dispute by conciliation, mediation, or compulsory arbitration." As Nelson Lichtenstein makes clear, the long-term consequences of interjecting such powerful administrative apparatus into the yet uncertain struggle over industrial unionism at this crucial juncture were momentous:

> The NDMB and its successor, the National War Labor Board, were as important as the Wagner Act in shaping the American system of industrial relations. For the next four years, these boards were instrumental in setting for the first time industry-wide wage patterns, fixing a system of "industrial jurisprudence" on the shop-floor, and influencing the internal structure of the new industrial unions. They were a powerful force in nationalizing a conception of routine and bureaucratic industrial relations that ... the Wagner Act and the NLRB had thus far failed to implement fully.[24]

The NWLB, in short, administratively ended the industrial unionization stalemate produced by a decade of inconclusive class struggle and ambivalent New Deal policies, and, in the process, created the institutional basis for a bureaucratized system of industrial relations centered on collective bargaining. Howell Harris summarizes its impact in the following terms:

> The NWLB made important contributions to several critical developments. It established institutionally secure unions, constrained to behave "responsibly" as the price of acceptance by employers, and tolerance or support from the state. It further defined the scope and area of collective bargaining, confining it to matters of wages, hours and working conditions, for the most part at the level of the plant, firm or community, rather than region or industry. It developed orderly grievance procedures, in which the union's role was strictly reactive, and there was little room for fractional bargaining and "enhancement" of the contract by pressure and "interpretation, "by imposing a legalistic system of arbitration.[25]

This outcome, however, was hardly a simple matter of administrative fiat. Throughout the war, class struggle centering on issues of shop-floor control interacted with state policy to reshape the American system of industrial relations. These home front struggles transformed the character of the industrial union movement by severing the complementary relationship which had existed between rank and file militance and the power of national union leaderships, thus isolating control struggles within particular production sites and institutionalizing unions as pillars of a neoliberal accommodation between the private power of capital and organized industrial labor.

In the spirit of patriotism following the attack on Pearl Harbor, national unions had agreed voluntarily to desist from striking for the duration of the war. This wartime "no-strike pledge" by major union leaders was a crucial aspect of the institutional context for wartime resistance to capitalist control. Having reached an accommodation with the state and adjourned for the indefinite future their campaigns against the open shop, wartime union leaders became justifiably concerned about their ability to hold their memberships when national unions had disavowed the strike weapon and when wages and working conditions were administratively determined by the state. In order to prevent the disintegration of its new framework of industrial relations, the NWLB in June of 1942 announced a "maintenance of membership" program which provided for mandatory membership and dues checkoff to those unions which upheld the no-strike pledge. "By tying union security to the question of strikes," Joshua Freeman argues, "the WLB shrewdly used the unions themselves as the chief instrument of wartime labor discipline." The experience of Frank

Marquart, a UAW activist, supports this conclusion: "During the war," he recalled, "the union was increasingly becoming a disciplinary agency over the workers."[26]

Not surprisingly, the size and financial health of industrial unions immediately began to show marked improvement. Yet, even as the unions grew, bureaucratic tendencies within them became more pronounced, and the distance between union leaderships and the shop-floor grew. With their memberships assured by federal regulation, union officials could become less sensitive to the problems and grievances of the rank and file under the demanding conditions of wartime production. The result was a political crisis within the CIO, the resolution of which would in large measure determine the character of the postwar system of industrial relations, and ultimately reaffirm the separation of work and politics.[27]

The war brought a renewal of the battle between workers and capitalists for control of the shop-floor. At first, the conditions of wartime production favored worker's control. Demand for labor was up dramatically and "cost-plus" contracts for military goods eased downward pressure on wages. Conversion to production of sophisticated weaponry – less amenable to assembly line production than consumer goods – allowed groups of workers to reassert control over their labor process by informally setting production quotas and work norms. Finally, the influx of war workers led to the recruitment of foremen out of the rank and file which, in combination with the increasing influence of personnel and engineering bureaucracies within the firm, eroded the power and prestige of foremen and led to a unionization movement among them. All these factors contributed to an increase in the scope for worker resistance to the private powers of management in the shops. Lichtenstein explains the resulting dynamic in the following terms:

> As long as production remained paramount and labor scarce, there was little factory managers could do about their loss of shop control. Depending on the company, however, the opportunity for tightening up on discipline and abandoning the policy of making concessions to guarantee uninterrupted production came somewhere between mid-1942, when conversion problems were generally resolved, and the end of 1943, when output peaked and layoffs began at certain factories.[28]

It was at this point, then, that management began aggressively to reassert its authority over the production process and to defy the claims of unionized workers.

The result was a great wave of unauthorized and illegal wildcat strikes having mostly to do with control issues (but some racially motivated "hate strikes" as well) beginning in 1943. As a consequence of this renewed militance the CIO faced a critical dilemma. On the one hand it could lose contact with the rank and file and become an empty institutional shell if it failed to respond to this resurgence of the militancy which had been the basic source of its bargaining power in the industrial unionization battles of the thirties. On the other hand, it might earn the active hostility of state managers – and risk all the hard-won gains since the open shop days of the twenties – if it renounced the no-strike pledge and used its wartime strength to try to consolidate its position in basic industry. In response to this predicament, CIO leadership denounced wildcat strikes and "clung tenaciously to the authority of the NWLB." The leadership of the nation's greatest industrial unions (with the significant exception of John L. Lewis of the miners) opted for the security offered by the state.[29]

As national union leadership become more closely identified with federal policy, the organized expression of rank and file unrest and resistance to the intensification of control devolved increasingly upon the secondary and local union leaderships. However, in the face of their institutional isolation, the new militancy remained sporadic, strategically uncoordinated, and largely delimited within the work-place itself. In the end, it served only to prompt the elimination of those organizational elements which, during the peacetime struggles of the 1930s, had mediated between national union leaderships and shop-floor activists and fused them into a more or less coherent movement.[30]

Under the doctrine of "negative leadership," local union leaders were held responsible for work stoppages by their memberships and were disciplined or removed by union hierarchies, in cooperation with the NWLB, if they proved too responsive to rank and file restlessness. Moreover, the tendency of corporations to supplant the powers of the foremen with more systematic and predictable organizations and pro-cedures of management was tremendously accelerated by wartime pressures. The marginalization of foremen indirectly contributed to the decline of union counterparts such as shop stewards who had provided crucial rank and file leadership in their shop-floor dealings with foremen. "Ultimately," Lichtenstein argues, "the routinization imposed on all shop-floor bargaining relationships helped accelerate the demise of a vigorous steward system and transform local union officials into virtual contract policemen."[31]

The effect of these wartime struggles over the politics of production was to disempower the secondary, local and shop-floor leadership of the industrial unions such that resistance to the combination of intensified control and the no-strike pledge remained relatively isolated and incoherent. The militance of the informal work groups which had for decades been the heart of worker resistance to capitalist control was quarantined within individual production sites and subjected to the conjoint repression of capital, the state, and the newly consolidated hierarchies of the industrial unions themselves. Whereas many CIO loyalists saw these measures as wartime expedients and hoped independent unionism would see better days in the postwar world, the long-term consequences of the wartime system could not be wished away: "... the maintenance of labor peace in an era when grievances were rife required the permanent weakening of those elements in the union structure upon which trade union power ultimately rested."[32] By the end of the war, the institutional pattern of bureaucratized, hierarchic, and fundamentally conservative industrial unionism had emerged from the interaction of state policy and political class struggle.

The process of subjecting the rank and file to the control of "responsible" union leaderships continued into the postwar years, when the political climate turned dramatically against the militant unionists and radicals who, although a minority, had played a crucial role in the creation of the industrial union movement. Since 1937–38, a powerful coalition of businessmen, conservative Republicans and Southern Democrats had been attacking New Deal reforms and labor legislation as "un-American" and socialistic. Out of this hostile milieu had come charges that the New Deal administration and the labor movement were infested with communists, depicted as insidious agents of a foreign power engaged in a conspiracy to subvert American democracy. A special committee charged with exposing such nefarious activities was created by the House of Representatives in 1938, and in 1945 was made a permanent committee: The House Un-American Activities Committee (HUAC). Its sensational hearings suggested that under complacent or complicit Democratic administrations, communist fifth-columnists had infiltrated every area of American life.[33]

Under intense partisan political pressure after the Republican electoral victories of 1946, and seeking a way to consolidate popular support for an emerging internationalist foreign policy, President Truman attempted to turn anticommunism to his own advantage. In March of 1947, he announced the Truman Doctrine in a speech which portrayed a global struggle between two "alternative ways of life," one free and democratic, the other terroristic and totalitarian. In this epic contest, he claimed, totalitarianism was already on the march, violating the Yalta Agreement in Eastern Europe and threatening Greece and Turkey. If America failed to respond, the result would be disastrous for the all the "freedom-loving peoples of the world," as one after another fell under the sinister influence of the totalitarian menace. Therefore, Truman announced, it was incumbent upon the United States "to help free peoples to maintain their free institutions and their national integrity against aggressive movements that seek to impose on them totalitarian regimes." Having scared the hell out of the country (as Senator Vandenberg had recommended) with his depiction of the global communist threat, Truman announced measures putatively designed to protect America's internal security. Nine days after the Truman Doctrine speech, he promulgated an executive order mandating investigations into the loyalty of US government employees. The loyalty order was specifically aimed at those who were engaged in espionage or who advocated revolution, treason or sedition, those who acted in "the interests of another government in preference to the interests of the United States," or those who could be shown to have "... membership in, affiliation with or *sympathetic association* with any foreign or *domestic* organization ... designated by the Attorney General as totalitarian, Fascist, Communist, or *subversive*" (emphases in original). By framing it as a nonpartisan issue of national security, in the context of an imminent global crisis, Truman legitimated and lent credibility to the anticommunist bile of the right wing and contributed mightily to the gathering momentum of the postwar red scare.[34]

In such an atmosphere, radical unionists and especially Communist Party (CP) members, fellow travelers, and even those popular front progressives who continued to be willing to work with radicals, were all denied the status of legitimate political actors or trade unionists; they were instead cast as potential, if not actual, traitors and spies. This hostile milieu influenced the content of federal labor law. Passed over Truman's token veto in June, 1947, the Taft-Hartley Act constrained organized labor to act "responsibly" and to eject radical leaders under penalty of law. It enabled employers to sue unions for breach of contract if their members initiated a strike while under a collective bargaining agreement, and made union officers subject to penalties if they failed to oppose such wildcat strikes. To preclude potentially radicalizing transportation of practices, it outlawed such manifestations of class-based solidarity as sympathy strikes and secondary boycotts, and forbade unions to contribute to electoral campaigns for federal office. Perhaps the most pernicious of its provisions was the denial of NLRB protections to any union whose officers did not sign affidavits in which each would swear "that he is not a member of the Communist Party or affiliated with such party, and that he does not believe in ... the overthrow of the United States Government by force or by any illegal or unconstitutional methods."[35]

The corps of dedicated and militant radical unionists who for decades had striven to help create the industrial union movement thus became a political albatross around the neck of union leaderships attempting to portray themselves as responsible and sober bargaining partners in a mildly reformed American capitalism. An industrial labor movement in which communists and fellow travelers held prominent positions, and in which entire unions were permeated by radicalism, began to look increasingly vulnerable to the forces of anticommunist reaction. In anticipation of such attacks, the CIO had begun to take defensive measures. At its 1946 convention, the CIO passed a resolution which declared that the assembled delegates "resent and reject efforts of the Communist Party or other political parties and their adherents to interfere with the affairs of the CIO. This convention serves notice that we will not tolerate such interference." The following year, a speech by Secretary of State George Marshall was warmly greeted at the CIO convention and a resolution favoring "sound programs for postwar rehabilitation" was passed. The CIO was moving to support the Truman administration and its global policy, while it suppressed internal dissent and turned against its own radical members. Mildly social democratic union leaders such as Phillip Murray of the Steelworkers and Walter Reuther of the Auto Workers purged their own union hierarchies of communists and fellow travelers, and shifted the balance of power in the CIO as a whole in the direction of anticommunism. The schism was deepened by Communist Party opposition to the Marshall Plan, which the CIO endorsed, and by CP support for the third party presidential candidacy of Henry Wallace in 1948, when the CIO had cast its lot with Truman and the Democrats. Speaking at the CIO convention of that year, Reuther framed the issue in terms which suggested that no conceivable middle ground existed between mainstream American unionists and CP members: "It is a question of loyalty. Are they going to be loyal to the CIO or loyal to the Communist Party? Are they going to be loyal to this country or loyal to the Soviet Union?"[36]

By 1949, the CIO was ready to liquidate its communist minority. At its annual convention, a Resolutions Committee chaired by Walter Reuther denounced the "blind and slavish willingness" of communist unionists "to act as puppets for the Soviet dictatorship and its foreign policy" of expansionism. The Committee recommended harsh measures and the convention enacted them: the CIO constitution was amended so that communists or fellow travelers could be barred from union office, and member unions which deviated from CIO policy and instead followed what was perceived as the CP party line could be ejected from the CIO. Entire unions such as the United Electrical Workers (UE) and the Farm Equipment Workers (FE) were driven from the federation in 1949, and thereupon were subjected to membership raids by CIO unions. Within two years, eleven left-led unions, representing some 900,000 members, were purged from the CIO. In these purges, the CIO lost more than large numbers of rank and file members; it also discarded a cadre of dedicated, experienced and militant unionists, and silenced internal dissent about the growing symbiosis of industrial unionism and liberal capitalism at home and abroad.[37]

Production politics and neoliberal hegemony

Implicit in the liberal form of state–society is a potential for domination of the social process of production by "private" power. In the late nineteenth and early twentieth centuries, American capitalists began much more effectively to actualize this potential through changes in the social organization of production which reduced drastically the element of skilled, self-directed labor and transformed the typical American worker from a craftsman into a tender of machines, designed and ultimately controlled by the agents of capital. The political apparatus of production was transformed as part of this process. Integral to this transformation was the subordination of workers to the new social powers of management, and this involved extended periods of socio-political struggle. The first phase, climaxing in World War I, witnessed the decomposition of the social organization of production centering upon mutualistic and self-directing crafts. The second phase involved securing the consent of mass production industrial workers to their role in the new, complex and highly interdependent division of labor.

Potentially challenging to liberalism's essential separation of public–political and private–economic spheres, the militance of rank and file workers resisting their subordination to the new powers of management was, by the period immediately following World War II, isolated from the organizational apparatus which might have allowed workers collectively to confront corporate capital. Under these conditions, shop-floor insurrection could challenge only the local and direct manifestation of the social power of capital. Transportation of class practices from the shop-floor to the larger structure of state–society relations which enable capitalist production was precluded as industrial union hierarchies grew more dependent upon the state, suppressed radicals and embraced liberal norms, and became contractual agents, brokers of consent. Instead of explicitly politicizing production and undermining the public–private dichotomy, the liberal practices of the larger social formation were reinforced within the workplace. So, even as production in the United States became increasingly social in its character, it could retain its apolitical, "economic" appearance under the hegemonic factory regimes of neoliberalism. The political apparatus of mass production had been woven into the fabric of socio-political relations in the United States, just as a tamed industrial labor movement had been incorporated into the hegemony of the neoliberal historic bloc.

The neoliberal constellation of public and private powers in the USA was integral to postwar American global power in both an instrumental and a substantive sense. Instrumentally, America's mass-production industries produced vast quantities of goods which helped to defeat fascism, arrest postwar economic crisis in Europe and contribute to a renewal of growth. Substantively, the quality of social organizations reconstructed in the core of the world economy was shaped by the American productivist ethos, its putatively apolitical consensus on economic growth and the limited generalization of affluence associated with it. The framework of ideological, political, and economic stability necessary for the emergence of a vibrant core of liberal capitalist states–societies was made possible by the politics of productivity and the reconstruction of state–society relations in the USA.

6 Fordism vs. unionism: production politics and ideological struggle at Ford Motor Company, 1914–1937

I have been arguing that the American global hegemony of this century was made possible, and its contours were shaped, by the development of mass production practices and productivist ideologies in the United States. In the last chapter I sketched an overview of the institutionalization of mass production in the USA and the changes in state–society relations which were integral to that process. In this chapter and the next, I will focus more closely on the politics of ideological struggle and the construction of a socio-political hegemony which incorporated large segments of the industrial working class, stabilizing (for a time) class relations in the United States and generating the ideological framework which would serve as the centerpiece of American global hegemony. It was this ideological framework which provided the common ground upon which American statesmen, capitalists, and leaders of organized labor could undertake the collective project of remaking the world after World War II.

More specifically, in these two chapters I propose to examine the history of class-based power as it was constructed and contested in the Ford Motor Company between the introduction of the moving assembly line system of mass production in 1913–14 and, by the time of the Korean War, the consolidation of a working-class culture of domestic affluence and anticommunist internationalism – implying a social consensus on the basic legitimacy, universal relevance and progressive character of liberal capitalism. Ford represents an especially illuminating case because its labor relations policies ranged from a smothering paternalism designed to reshape the values and lifestyles of its workers and elicit their shop-floor consent, to a coercive regime of pervasive and naked brutality, and finally a hegemonic regime in which working-class organizations and ideologies of unionized

Americanism were themselves incorporated into a more or less stable and consensual system of industrial relations and global political-economic leadership. At Ford, issues of managerial power and explicitly political aspects of the production process were never far from the surface, and so the question of how these issues were resolved into a hegemonic regime stands out more clearly.

Liberal capitalism, "Americanism," and common sense

Before proceeding to interpret ideological aspects of the struggles between Ford Motor Company and its workers, I shall sketch the general contours of the predominant social relations and ideology which were at once the context and the object of these struggles. As I suggested in the preceding chapter, a basic premise of this study is that the socio-political struggles it seeks to reconstruct were made possible by, and were waged on a terrain defined by, the fundamentally contradictory nature of liberal capitalist social formations. Liberalism and capitalism emerged as part of the same historical process in the West and, from a Marxian point of view, they may be seen as two sides of a single coin; internally related such that liberalism represents the ideological aspect of the capitalist organization of society, the perspective and world view of the capitalist class.

I understand capitalism to entail the private ownership of the social means of production; and the corresponding necessity of those who are excluded from such ownership to sell that one commodity which they do "own," their capacity to work, in order to secure the necessities of life. As part of this bargain, they must submit to capitalist control of the labor process and the expropriation of its product. Capitalism is then a social system which is centrally riven by asymmetries of wealth and power which are based upon class. As I discussed at some length in chapter 2, I take these relations of class to be associated with a plethora of internal conflicts or contradictions, which generate the possibility of historically concrete social struggles.

By liberalism I understand a family of modern Western social philosophies sharing a fundamental commitment to a social ontology of abstract individualism; that is, a world view which presumes that individuals are the most basic elements of which our social universe is constituted, that they are in this sense prior to and more fundamentally real than social relations, which are seen as resulting from the choices and actions of individuals. This individualism is "abstract" because it envisions individuals as existing prior to and apart from any social or historical context which might otherwise be seen to shape their identities, the ends which they pursue, their capacities for action. Abstracting from all of this, individuals are understood in terms of some invariant essence or human nature, for example, that they are self-interested and instrumentally rational in the pursuit of ends which are individually subjective and inscrutable. Valorized, then, are those social relations which reflect or support this image of the naturalized individual. Among the network of values which are associated with such a world view are individual liberty, autonomy and privacy, understood in relation to "external" constraints or intrusions; the protection of the "rights" and property of the individual from transgression by others and especially by government, which is seen as properly being the creature and servant of the aggregate of individuals; the rule of law which binds citizens equally and circumscribes the powers of government, preventing thereby the arbitrary or discriminatory exercise of power over individuals; the consent of the individual to the powers of government and to the laws which govern individual conduct in civil society – a value potentially associated with political democracy; and equality of opportunity such that those individuals with the greatest merit, energy or cleverness shall not be prevented from succeeding to the limits of their abilities by entrenched social hierarchies of aristocratic power and privilege.[1] Because they are associated with an image of human nature, the values of liberalism claim universal applicability.

A fundamental ambiguity within liberal thought and political practice, however, revolves around the issue of just who counts as an "individual" whose liberty and "rights" are to be protected, and upon whose consent the just powers of government must be based. This liberal ambiguity is compounded by its relation to issues of property, inequality, and class, and it has major implications for the question of democracy in liberal capitalist society. Take, for example, Locke's account of origins of property in the state of nature wherein, he is at pains to assert, all men are naturally free and equal. Yet, we find among the property to which Locke's labor-mixing formula allows him to lay claim are "the Turfs my Servant has cut."[2] How there came to be this relation of class (master–servant) in the state of nature is unexplained by Locke: this has the effect of implicitly naturalizing class relations while simultaneously proclaiming their non-existence. At the heart of the liberal world view, then, is a double standard revolving around issues of class.

Liberalism proclaims universal human equality in the endowment of individual rights and liberties; but the historic practices of liberal capitalism represent something altogether different. On the one hand, liberalism sees in private property a great source of individual autonomy, which simultaneously provides the property owner with the wherewithal to make decisions independent of potentially corrupting "outside" influences, and provides him with a stake in the future of the commonwealth and thus encourages "responsible" decision making. On the other hand, in its abstract individualism and its stubborn defense of private property, liberalism sustains and legitimizes the class-based maldistribution of property and power, and the dependence and social alienation which this enforces upon great masses of people in capitalist society. On the one hand, liberalism upholds government by the consent of the governed as a key protection of universal rights and liberties against arbitrary rule and tyranny. On the other hand, liberals have feared the extension of this principle to encompass all citizens, since the active participation of the propertyless – whom the middle class has viewed as irresponsible, ignorant and uncivilized – was equated with mob rule and seen as a real threat to individual liberties and especially rights of property.[3]

Such apparent paradoxes as these suggest that liberalism has historically represented the political perspective of the middle class: it supported limited government as an antidote to absolutist monarchy, and formal equality as a weapon against aristocratic privilege; yet it has feared participatory democracy and the empowerment of subordinate classes, and especially the working class, as a danger to middle-class rights, liberties, and property. In 1843 Marx argued that liberalism's emancipatory commitments were impoverished by its middle-class perspective, its ontology of abstract individualism and instrumental view of community:

> The first point we should note is that the so-called *rights of man*, as distinct from the *rights of the citizen*, are quite simply the rights of the *member of civil society*, i.e., of egoistic man, of man separated from other men and from the community ... the right of man to freedom is not based on the association of man with man but rather on the separation of man from man ... The right to private property is therefore the right to enjoy and dispose of one's resources as one wills, without regard for other men and independently of society: the

> right of self-interest. The individual freedom mentioned above, together with this application of it, forms the foundation of civil society. It leads each man to see in other men not the *realization* but the *limitation* of his own freedom. But above all it proclaims the right of man "to enjoy and dispose at will of his goods, his revenues and the fruit of his work and industry" ... not one of the so-called rights of man goes beyond egoistic man, man as a member of civil society, namely an individual withdrawn into himself, his private interest and his private desires and separated from the community ... it is man as *bourgeois*, i.e., as a member of civil society, and not man as citizen who is taken as the *real* and *authentic* man.[4]

As it declares universal rights and liberties and the equality of all human beings, liberalism presupposes and naturalizes the very social structure which makes possible private property in the means of production, and secures the privileged position and social powers of the class which owns them.

The ambiguity of liberalism has historically been resolved in favor of the capitalist class. But the underlying tension remains at the center of liberal capitalist society. In this historical context, declarations of universal liberty, equality and democracy are potentially subversive insofar as these aspirations represent unfulfilled promises of liberal capitalism, promises which could not be fulfilled without endangering the class relations which are the core of capitalism. This discrepancy, then, opens up a space in which conflicting interpretations of the meaning of liberalism may be constructed, and in which challenges to the predominant understandings of liberalism – and to the prevailing organization of society – might be mounted.

Class struggles at Ford Motor Company may be understood in terms of a dialectic of coercion and consent in which these issues of whose rights, what liberties, and the meaning of democracy, were actively contested by Ford management, Ford workers, and ultimately the United Automobile Workers (UAW). Yet, the participants did not frame these issues directly in terms of liberal philosophy. Instead, in a series of struggles stretching over decades, the meaning of "Americanism" was defined, challenged and redefined.[5] Although Americanism has been associated with a range of meanings not all of which were distinctly liberal – for example, strongly nativist and racist versions of Americanism were directed against unassimilated immigrants, African-Americans, Asians, Jews, and others – I would suggest that core meanings of Americanism had to do with the liberal tradition in America, and how it was to be interpreted, reproduced or transformed.

To use Gramsci's term, Americanism was a central element in the "common sense" of popular culture in the USA.[6] The concept of common sense was important to Gramsci's vision of the dynamics of class struggle; he drew inspiration from Marx's statement that it is in terms of ideological forms "that men become conscious of this conflict and fight it out." Although Gramsci believed that ideology was central to the making and potential remaking of society, he argued directly against individualistic or idealist interpretations: "the thesis which asserts that men become conscious of fundamental conflicts on the level of ideology is not psychological or moralistic in character, but structural and epistemological."[7] In other words, Gramsci is arguing that the world views and self-understandings in terms of which people frame their actions are grounded in the social and historical context in which those people live, and will in some way represent their collective conditions of life. In a society which is fundamentally structured along contradictory lines, the world views of the masses of people – their "folklore" or "common sense" – will also be fragmented and contradictory, will be amenable to conflicting interpretations, and will therefore potentially support different modes of political action which grow out of those interpretations.

Gramsci uses the metaphor of a series of "stratified deposits" to depict the way in which the cultural history of society will be registered in the common sense of the masses. "Every philosophical current leaves behind a sedimentation of 'common sense': this is the document of its historical effectiveness. Common sense is not something rigid and immobile, but is continually transforming itself with scientific ideas and with philosophical opinions which have entered ordinary life."[8] Common sense is a contradictory amalgam of such deposits. While this sedimentation will certainly contain some of the ideological representations of the dominant class or historic bloc, it is not univocal. As a consequence, within the common sense of the masses there may be space for critical analysis of social contradictions and self-understandings, and the potential for a transformative political movement to emerge. Gramsci's point, then, is that common sense can be a crucial terrain of political struggle. My point is that a central aspect of the class struggles at Ford had to do with the common sense of the industrial working class: the meanings which they attached to Americanism could either attenuate or exacerbate the contradictions of liberal capitalism.

Fordism vs. unionism

Mass production entailed the exercise of new forms of social power which are commonly subsumed under the rubric of "management." And – in a capitalist context – these powers of management in turn presupposed the subordination of the industrial working class. But this subordination was hardly automatic; it was not produced simply by starting up machine tools and assembly lines in Ford's Highland Park plant in 1914. It was the product of protracted struggle in which management directed at its workers – in various combinations – measures designed to coerce workers into submitting, or to induce them to consent, to workplace regimes embodying the new managerial powers. The workers, for their part, variously resisted, transformed or adapted the conditions which management sought to create in the workplace. From the early decades of this century, management deployed language and symbols of liberal "Americanism" to sanctify the rights of private property holders and to legitimize or disguise their power over workers and work. Through the creation of industrial unions in the 1930s and 40s, workers articulated a broader vision of "democracy" which forced management to modify their notion of univocal authority in the workplace and to accept unions as a fact of life; while in the postwar years a more generalized affluence and a pervasive political culture of anticommunism constrained the ability and willingness of unions to challenge the social basis of managerial powers. By 1950, industrial unioinists were accepting as part of their understanding of Americanism the general legitimacy of liberal capitalism and their own place within it, and were representing America's relation to the rest of the world in terms of the universalistic claims of liberal capitalism.

Coercion and consent: mass production, prosperity and paternalism

Between 1908 and 1914 the Ford Motor Company synthesized the various elements which together would constitute the modern system of mass production. With these changes, the production process was transformed from one centrally based upon skilled and relatively autonomous craftsmen to one based upon intensive mechanization and the use of less skilled labor. The system of mass production would make possible enormous increases in output per unit of labor in large part because it displaced self-directed craftsman from a central place in the production process, and substituted vast numbers of unskilled or semiskilled machine operators and assemblers, performing rigidly defined and highly repetitive tasks under close supervision. With this development, management could attempt more aggressively to assert control over the pace and intensity of work, using the speed of the line and the coercive industrial discipline of the foreman. In the mid-1920s, a Ford worker described the pace and intensity of effort which his mass production job required, and the consequences of failing to meet that standard on a daily basis: "You've got to work like hell in Ford's. From the time you become a number in the morning until the bell rings for quitting time you have to keep at it. You can't let up. You've got to get out the production ... and if you can't get it out, you get out."[9]

Yet, while the system of mass production generated the potential for management to exert greater control over the performance of work, it did not guarantee the realization of that potential. The basic technology of mass production had been put in place at Ford by 1914, but the struggle for control of the labor process – and the dialectic of coercion and consent which this entailed – was just beginning. Ford management became increasingly aware of a multifaceted "labor problem" which threatened their ability to get the most out of their new productive system.

During the period when Ford was developing its system of mass production, it encountered on a correspondingly massive scale the individualized resistance of workers who refused to consent to permanent subordination under the new system. By the time the first moving assembly lines were being created in the Highland Park plant, labor turnover was becoming an acute problem for Ford management: in 1913 the rate of quits at Ford was about 370 percent of the total workforce. Further, according to company officials, during the same period it was not unusual for 10 percent of those currently holding jobs at Ford to be absent on a given day. The company was becoming aware that problems with its labor force were costing it money: hiring and training of new workers on such a massive scale entailed a significant administrative cost, and massive turnover and absenteeism were also seen as impairing the efficiency of production.[10]

Another aspect of the "labor problem" which Ford management perceived was restriction of output or "soldiering" by workers, a form of covert and informally organized resistance which directly challenged the basic presumption of Taylorism and Fordism: management control of the pace and intensity of work. Flow production and moving line assembly were reducing the scope for soldiering, but would not eliminate it.[11]

Ford management was also concerned about more organized forms of opposition and the potential influence among its workers of unions such as the Carriage, Wagon and Automobile Workers' Union (CWAWU) and radical groups such as the International Workers of the World (IWW). Although Detroit had been justly known as an open shop town since around 1902, and labor unions and radical organizations were not particularly strong in the automobile plants, the IWW had launched a well publicized campaign to organize Detroit auto workers, had agitated at Ford's Highland Park plant, and led a strike – all the more frightening to employers because it was organized along industrial rather than craft lines – at Studebaker in 1913.[12]

Ford's problems of labor control were compounded by the large numbers of immigrants who comprised the new industrial workforce at Ford. In 1914, 71 percent of Ford workers were foreign-born, representing at least 22 different nationalities (some Ford publications claimed fifty or more) among which eastern and southern Europeans predominated.[13] Many of these immigrant workers were from a peasant background, and found entirely alien an industrial work culture such as that at Ford. Although the detailed division of labor and specialized machinery in the Ford shops minimized the requirements of skill and judgment and thereby made it possible for unskilled immigrants to become auto workers with minimal training, Ford managers were concerned about the effects which such a culturally heterogeneous workforce might have upon shop discipline and the steady output of their integrated productive system. Differences in language and culture could disrupt the great productive machine or inhibit its efficiency if workers failed to understand instructions or to communicate problems effectively, if their holidays and traditional orientations toward time did not mesh with the schedule of the factory, if their background left them ill equipped to fathom a culture so thoroughly permeated by individualism, commodification and private property, and to respond to its constraints and incentives in ways which the Ford Motor Company considered constructive.

In all these ways, then, Ford became concerned about the labor problem and "the efficiency of the unit – man," as the in-house magazine, *Ford Times*, put it. Meyer assembles data from company records which show that although Ford was attaining significantly higher levels of productivity as the new system of mass production evolved, the rate of growth in average output per worker was uneven, and declined substantially between 1911 and 1913.[14] On the eve of their installation of moving assembly lines at the Highland Park plant, Ford management may well have been concerned about their ability to get the most out of their new system by getting the most out of their workers.

Ford management responded to its labor problem with a series of reforms culminating in the widely publicized "profit sharing plan" and a comprehensive program of paternalism toward its workers, inaugurated in January, 1914. The new labor policies aimed at addressing specific worker grievances by dramatically raising pay, shortening the working day, and curbing the power of foremen, especially the power to fire workers at will.[15] The company also provided medical services to workers at the factory, and a legal department to advise them about investments, insurance and real estate contracts. It established the Ford English School for its non-English-speaking employees and arranged for successful completion of the course to satisfy initial requirements in the process of attaining US citizenship.[16]

Through these reforms and the attendant publicity, Ford sought to send a message to its workers. The immediate goal was to create a strong perception of common interest between the firm and its employees, to convince workers that Ford Motor Company was committed to their well being and expected them to respond in kind. In a 1915 pamphlet with the lengthy but significant title *Helpful Hints and Advice to Employes* [sic] *to Help Them Grasp the Opportunities which are Presented to them by the Ford Profit Sharing Plan*, the company appealed to its workers on the grounds that "Those who benefit by the profit-sharing plan should realize that it is in their best interest to help in insuring its continued success, and it is therefore hoped that each employe will show a reciprocal interest, and give his best efforts toward that end. Each employe should feel that he is one of a big organization, and take a personal interest in its welfare."[17]

In order to underscore this sense of a common enterprise, and to blur the class-based distinction between workers' wages and capitalists' profits, Ford quite deliberately represented the then-astonishing increase in pay to a $5.00 daily minimum, not as a simple increase in the wage, but as a share of the company's profits paid in addition to regularly earned wages. The profit share Ford claimed to bestow upon its workers as a matter of justice and concern rather than contractual obligation.[18] At the announcement of the Ford profit sharing plan in

January, 1914, company treasurer James Couzens encapsulated this central aspect of the plan in the following terms: "We want those who have helped us to produce this great institution [Ford Motor Company] and are helping to maintain it to share our prosperity. We want them to have present profits and future prospects." Roughly a year after the plan was introduced, testifying before a Federal Commission on Industrial Relations, Henry Ford cast in the following terms the motive behind the profit sharing plan: "Our first purpose was substantial justice to our co-workers without whom we could have accomplished nothing." When the plan was two years old someone identified only in class-neutral terms as "a member of the [Ford] organization" told the *Detroit News*, "Each profit-sharer considers himself a partner in the Company and the Company considers him a partner."[19]

While workers were to think of themselves as partners in a collective enterprise, they were quite clearly assigned a subordinate role in the Ford ideology of profit sharing; for the partnership between management and workers at Ford was to be a distinctly asymmetrical one. Management might allow workers to share in the "profits" of the enterprise, but they would not be empowered to participate in decisions about the future of their collective enterprise. According to Henry Ford, "The average employee in the average industry is not ready for participation in the management. An industry, at this stage of our development, must be more or less of a friendly autocracy." Control over the labor process, as well as pricing and investment decisions, and the future of profit sharing itself, all were retained by Ford management.[20] The price which Ford hoped tacitly to extract from workers for their inclusion in its version of the American dream was the recognition of management's right and its superior ability to run the business in the interest of all concerned. Ford's paternalistic labor policies of 1914–21 thus reflected the double standard of liberal capitalism: at the ideological level, the central theme was formal equality premised upon abstract individualism; while the effective result was to protect and extend inequality of wealth and social power based upon concrete relations of class.

For Ford management, the primary connotation of Americanism was security of private property and the right of the owner to dispose of his property in whichever fashion he desired, free of the interference of government or of such dubious collective agencies as labor unions. That this property might be a large-scale industrial enterprise in which many thousands of people were engaged in socially cooperative production was not held to contradict the "private" character of the property or of the rights to its control. On the contrary, the legitimacy of private ownership and control was bolstered by a doctrine which held that property owners had secured their property through their own hard work and special merits, and thus had distinguished themselves from those more ordinary men who constituted the great bulk of their employees. To allow the employees a significant voice in management of the enterprise, then, would be both unjust and unwise: it would deprive the owner of the just reward for his own efforts; and it would place the most important decisions in the hands of the least capable, and would thus endanger the survival of the enterprise. Therefore, the reasoning went, it was actually in the interests of the employees to submit to the leadership of the employer, since he was obviously best able to guide the enterprise to success and thereby better the condition of everyone associated with it. In the words of Arnold and Faurote, two technical journalists writing about Fordism for a professional audience of businessmen, managers and engineers: "All economists are agreed that the only reason why any one man works for another man is because the hired man does not know enough to be the director of his own labor. And, incontrovertibly, the employer being wiser than the employed, the wisdom of the employer should be applied to the benefit of the employed, to some extent at least."[21] The intellectual superiority of management was unequivocally invoked as a justification of their power over the enterprise and (with somewhat more equivocation) for paternalism toward employees. Thus Henry Ford's unorthodox labor policies were explained to other businessmen in terms of their own class-based common sense, the principle which justified their control over the workplace. In their profit sharing plan, however, this basic presupposition of capitalist power was submerged beneath representations of Ford employees as co-workers, partners and profit sharers. In this way, Ford attempted to secure the consent of its workers to management control.

A second major purpose in representing the pay increase as "profit sharing," rather than as wages to which workers were legally entitled by virtue of their labor contract with the company, was that this created for the company a discretionary power to grant rewards (and, by working-class standards, very substantial ones since $5.00 a day was more than double the basic wage rate) to those workers whom it deemed worthy, and to deny those rewards to others.[22] Under the plan, the company explained, "A man's pay consists of two parts . . . his wage and his profits. The wage is conditioned on skill and length of service. The profits are shared on condition that a man measures up to a given moral and economic standard." In other words, "You have to live right to get it and continue to live right to continue to get it." The company believed that a worker's family life was directly related to his reliability and productivity on the job, and it used the profit sharing plan as a lever to enforce upon its workers, not just industrial discipline at work, but also what it considered to be "improv[ed] living conditions, better morals, and . . . habits of thrift and saving."[23]

To insure that its profit sharers were "living right" the company created a surveillance arm which it called the Ford Sociological Department. This department had a staff of full-time "sociological investigators" who maintained records on each employee, visited his or her home, observed family life and living conditions, checked marriage documents, bank books, insurance policies, leases, real estate deeds or contracts, and inquired among neighbors as to the employee's leisure activities and "habits."[24] Investigators gave "advice" to workers about the kinds of neighborhoods and houses in which Ford workers were expected to live, about "home comforts and sanitation" and the superiority of single family dwellings, about what constituted appropriate supervision and education of children, about budgeting and thrift. Despite – or because of – the intrusive nature of these investigations, the company made it clear to workers that "It is the duty of every employe to aid the investigators in every way possible in their work." It further signaled its seriousness about this surveillance by warning workers that even in the new, kinder, gentler Ford Motor Company – where according to Henry Ford, "No man will be discharged if we can help it, except for unfaithfulness or inefficiency" – failure to inform the company of a change of address was grounds for dismissal.[25] Moreover, anyone who, upon investigation, consistently failed to satisfy the company's criteria for becoming a profit sharer would be given six months to ponder the inducement of withheld profit shares and the threat of dismissal if the employee failed to change his ways; after six months, the threat was made good. There was, then, a coercive side to Ford's paternalistic labor policies.[26]

As Stephen Meyer argues, these policies created mechanisms through which Ford could reward certain kinds of home and work practices, and punish others, in order to address the turnover problem and stabilize its workforce; to increase shop-floor control and efficiency; and to realize more fully the potential productivity gains from the new system of production by stabilizing relations between employees and employer. But there was more to this policy than the simple application of carrots and sticks. Ford Motor Company was attempting to reconstruct the "common sense" of its employees so that they would recognize the inducement of the carrot and the threat of the stick. Ford attempted to secure workers' consent to management control by shaping a collective vision in which its predominantly unskilled and immigrant workers could find a new identity, a vision of Americanism in which workers and management were represented as a collection of self-interested individuals, voluntarily cooperating in a common enterprise, a partnership for prosperity. As a result of this partnership, individual workers could succeed to the limits of their abilities and become property holders and even investors. Thus, the Ford policies implied, workers too would benefit from the American system of liberal capitalism and its protection of individual rights and private property. A central underlying theme in Ford's policies toward its workers, then, was the establishment of a common American identity through integration into a culture of abstract individualism.

The ideological core of the profit sharing plan was the explicit extension of liberal rights and liberties – as Ford construed them – to industrial workers. In Ford's America of equal opportunity, one's position in the industrial proletariat was not a barrier to individual realization of the American dream: as *Ford Times* put it, "a worker had a right to advance."[27] The individualized incentives of liberal capitalism could be used to manage Ford's heterogeneous labor force if its members could be brought to see themselves as unbound by multi-faceted identities of class, ethnic group, and so forth, so that their self-interest might be more effectively harnessed to the company's purposes. In discussing the basic philosophy of the plan, John R. Lee explained that it was strikingly simple: "We have learned to appreciate men as men, and to forget the discrimination of color, race, country, religion, fraternal orders and everything else outside of human qualities and energy."[28] The message was clear: anyone could succeed at Ford Motor Company (with the implicit proviso that they played the game by Ford's rules). This message was reinforced by Ford's policy of providing jobs for African-Americans in numbers much greater than other employers.[29] Further, Ford proclaimed that a man's past mistakes or misfortunes should not prevent him from earning a living, that is, from becoming a self-supporting and autonomous individual. The transcript of Ford's 1915 testimony before the Federal Industrial Relations Commission records applause when Ford declared:

> My idea is, aid men to help themselves. Nearly all are willing to work for adequate reward. We have all kinds of cripples in our employ, and they are making good. We have a great many who have been in prison and are outcasts from Society. Everyone of them is making a good showing and is gaining in self-respect and strength of character. We will guarantee to take every man out of Sing Sing and make a man of him.[30]

So central was the reconstruction of abstract individualism to Ford labor policies that Samuel Marquis, who administered Ford's Sociological Department from 1916 to 1921, could claim that automobiles "are but the by-products of [Ford's] real business, which is the making of men."[31]

Ford management perceived in this individualistic Americanism a powerful solvent which could break down class-based self-understandings and contribute to the establishment of a more productive and profitable industrial harmony. After his departure from the company, Samuel Marquis told the following story which shows how class conflicts ceased to exist in the company's official ontology of individualism:

> When I went with the Ford Motor Company, Mr. Ford said to me, "I do not want you to come here with the idea that the problems which you will be called upon to meet arise out of the relation of capital and labor. The only problems here, or in any other industry, are those arising between man and man. Forget labor and capital and think of your problem as between man and man, and your problem is half solved before you begin." My experience proved that to be a fundamental truth.[32]

The company wanted its employees to think in these terms as well. Ford's company magazine, *Ford Times*, represented as an exemplary credo an item allegedly written by a Ford worker (himself represented as an abstract individual identified as "Employe No. B 8074, Ford Factory") and entitled "My Future":

> I know that my future depends upon myself, as the manner in which I perform the duties assigned me shall determine my value.
> I shall always give a heaping measure that my pay may be in proportion to my service.

It shall be my aim to work for, talk for and boost my employer, because I am one of the organization.

Under no circumstances shall I listen to, or take part in, discussions affecting the welfare of my employer or others employed ...

I know that excellence is never granted but as reward for labor, therefore it is necessary to excel, that promotion be assured.

The ideal Ford employee, then, saw his interests as coincident with those of his employer, worked as hard as possible for the betterment of both, avoided any illegitimate intrusions upon the rights of his employer and his fellow employees (presumably, by such sinister collective agencies as labor unions), and was confident that all of this would bring individual advancement. Indeed, *Ford Times* assuredly declared, "With his evident knowledge of self, and an inspired determination to scale the pinnacle of success, B 8074 will succeed."[33] The condition of such "success" was an individualized self-understanding in which categories of class had no place.

Ford also tried to dissolve the ethnic and national identities of its largely immigrant workforce through "virtually compulsory" attendance at the Americanization classes conducted by the Ford English School, which was created in 1914. According to the company, "... our one great aim is to impress those men that they are, or should be, Americans, and that former racial, national and linguistic differences are to be forgotten."[34] Ford imputed to immigrants a view of America as the "land of liberty and generous chances for success," and the company undertook to show them how – through employment at Ford – they might realize these cardinal values of Americanism.[35] In the words of Samuel Marquis: "The object of this English School is not only to make the men more efficient in our work in the shop, but also to prepare them for citizenship. The first thing we teach them to say is, 'I am a good American,' and then we try to get them to live up to the statement."[36] And the single most important aspect of constructing for these workers new identities as "Americans" was to get them to see themselves as autonomous individuals who could find liberty and success in their new land by severing ties of dependence with ethnic communities and institutions, and casting their lot with Ford Motor Company. Discussing the dependence of immigrants upon ethnic communities and the bilingual agents and brokers who mediated between immigrants and their English-speaking milieu, John R. Lee declared: "We have actually found in Detroit petty empires existing."[37] Through the Americanization of its immigrant workers, Ford

Motor Company represented itself as the agent of their liberation from such Old World relations of dependence.

Integrating immigrant workers into the culture of liberal capitalism required more than just "liberating" them from their ethnic/national communities, however; they also needed to develop the ability to recognize and respond to the constraints and incentives of an individualized, commodified culture, and this is what the Ford English School sought to instill in its students: "By treating employees as Men and making it possible for themselves and their families to live respectably, it has become possible – yes, easy – for these thousands of foreign-born workmen to be refashioned and woven into the warp and woof of a greater Americanism. And with education will come the fruits of a broadened intelligence – and greater opportunity."[38]

The instructional program which the Ford English School adopted had been designed by Peter Roberts and the YMCA, and emphasized the practical use of language in everyday contexts. These contexts were defined in terms of three spheres of life, with corresponding sets of lessons for each: workers were taught a language of the home; a language of production; and of the market, the commodity economy. Workers were taught to envision and describe – in terms of an individual's daily experiences – objects and actions in each of these spheres. Embedded in these language lessons were cultural orientations and normative predispositions which would integrate the worker into an individualized, commodified industrial culture, in which he would be expected to sell his labor time in order to survive. For example, one lesson in the domestic series implicitly emphasized the importance of the clock in governing the rhythms of daily life:

> I awake from sleep.
> I open my eyes.
> I look for my watch.
> I find my watch.
> I see what time it is.
> It is six o'clock.
> I must get up.

Among the relational terms which Roberts' course manual suggests that instructors work into their lessons are several which would be near to the heart of an industrial employer such as Ford: fast/slow, busy/idle, hard/leisurely.[39] By teaching immigrants the practical language of workers in a capitalist society, Ford helped them to situate

120

Figure 6.1 Ford's "melting pot"

The Ford English School graduation ceremony (c. 1916) symbolized the transformation of immigrant workers – bearing various ethnic–national traditions and cultures – into "Americans" – understood as abstract individuals. Photograph from the collections of Henry Ford Museum and Greenfield Village.

themselves in such an order, and to accept its presuppositions as the given parameters of daily life.

In its elaborate and theatrical graduation ritual (depicted in figure 6.1), the Ford English School symbolized the transformation of immigrants – bearing various ethnic/national traditions and cultures – into Americans – understood as abstract individuals. On a stage was represented the side of a steamship, from which a gangplank descended into a large cauldron labeled "Ford English School Melting Pot." A stream of immigrant workers came down the gangplank variously dressed "in the poor garments of their native lands." As they poured into the melting pot, the mixture was stirred by Ford English School instructors. Through this process, their concrete distinctions were dissolved and thereupon "they emerged dressed in American clothes [suits and ties], faces eager with the stimulus of the new opportunities and responsibilities opening out before them. Every man carried a small American flag in his hand."[40]

The company was quite explicit about its belief that this kind of socialization enabled immigrant workers to grasp the constraints and incentives in terms of which Ford had structured its industrial regime: "With the acquirement of the English Tongue, the language of his foreman, his superintendent, the workman's ambition is aroused and he is started on the road toward advancement in his work."[41] Further, Ford claimed that this translated into increased control on the shopfloor: "So thoroughly has the spirit of the school permeated the factory at large, that a foreman holding a prominent position in the plant recently remarked that it was now easier for him to handle 300 men than 25 before the school was started."[42]

Ford wanted its workers to come to know "the meaning of the phrase, American standard of living," and to appreciate the role which employment at Ford played in making such a life possible. As the company saw it, this standard of living entailed the ownership of one's home, and was associated with responsible citizenship: "We encourage these men to buy homes, knowing that the ownership of property will lead to interest in civic matters."[43] Workers were urged to purchase single-family houses in what Ford sociological investigators considered "good neighborhoods." The houses were expected to be clean, well lit and ventilated, and roomy. Practices such as taking in boarders or keeping farm animals such as chickens, thought to be common among immigrant workers, were vigorously discouraged as detrimental to proper American family life: wives and mothers were expected to look after the needs of husband and children, not take care of animals or boarders to earn extra money.[44] In addition to its ideological significance – casting industrial workers as property owners and patriarchs and fragmenting their class identities – all of this had the effect of reinforcing the worker's dependence upon his labor contract with Ford Motor Company to provide for his family and pay the mortgage.

An investigator with the Ford Sociological Department assessed in the following terms the "progress among foreigners" which had been made possible by the company's programs: "The people are now able to think independently and appreciate the value of money." Observing that foreign employees contemplating the purchase of a home were making decisions based upon a balancing of cost against need, and taking into account criteria of future financial security, the investigator concluded "All this, indicates that the employees have become capable of reasoning for themselves."[45] In other words, the common sense of these workers was being reconstructed to incorporate a particular kind of reasoning – the instrumental calculation which is so central to the individualized, commodified culture of liberal capitalism – and this was seen as a clear indication of success for Ford's labor policies.

The company claimed success for its policies on the basis of a number of other indicators as well. Between 1914 and 1919, its sociological investigations documented the steadily increasing value of savings accounts, insurance policies, real estate contracts and homes owned by workers. In the years immediately after the introduction of the profit sharing plan, Ford workers apparently were enjoying something like the "American standard of living" of popular imagination. Labor turnover had been dramatically reduced from a high of around 370 percent in 1913 to around 54 percent in 1914 and 16 percent the year after that. Absenteeism had also been reduced to manageable proportions. Further, the enforcement of factory discipline seemed to depend much less upon actually exercising the power to discharge workers: whereas there had been 1,276 discharges in March 1913, the company claimed that only 166 men were fired in March 1914. Best of all from Ford's perspective, the company reported an immediate increase in overall productivity of some 15 to 20 percent.[46] Although the company's public statements claimed that this increase was the "voluntary" and spontaneous product of workers' gratitude, William Klann, a senior foreman at Ford's Highland Park plant, explained in rather more straightforward terms how this was accomplished: "When we gave the $5 day ... [top management] called us in and said that since they [the workers] were getting twice the wages, they [management] wanted twice as much work ... On the assembly line, we simply turned up the speed of the lines."[47] For the time being, Americanized, individualized and unorganized Ford workers appeared to be willing to submit to management power, intrusive paternalism, and speed-up on the line, in order to earn the relatively high pay made possible by their own subordination to Ford's system of mass production.

Coercive regime: speed-up and secret police

Ford's educational work and profit sharing plan had not created the basis of a stable industrial regime and, in the years following World War I, the balance between coercion and consent in the Ford shops shifted steadily toward coercion. By the 1930s, work at Ford took place under a regime of such overt and ubiquitous duress that the National Labor Relations Board could liken it to martial law.[48] It was in opposition to this harsh open shop regime that industrial unionists of the United Automobile Workers (UAW) would articulate a vision of Americanism in which the rights of labor were to be legally safeguarded alongside those of capital. Industrial hegemony at Ford, and a variant of the politics of productivity formula, would ultimately arise out of this conflict between coercive Fordism and unionized Americanism. The origins of coercive Fordism are thus an important part of the process I am outlining.

World War I signaled the end of the liberal world order which had been based upon the industrial revolution in Britain, and the beginning of a period of global struggle and transition.[49] Eventually, a new world order would be constructed and at its center would be a neoliberal politics of centrist prosperity made possible by mass production; but the regime of mass production was not yet stabilized even in its country of origin. Perhaps ironically, among the far-reaching effects of this opening round in the great global struggle of the twentieth century was to bring to the surface the latent tensions within Ford's paternalistic industrial regime. In so doing, the war set in motion processes which would develop the darker side of Ford's Americanism: from an industrial culture of individualism and shared prosperity, to a repressive conformity in which difference or dissent was equated with disloyalty, and in which covert operatives of an industrial secret police supplanted the intrusive but open advisors of the Ford Sociological Department as a primary instrument of labor control. Whereas under the former regime, Ford had tried to induce workers to consent to speed-up by offering them a greater share of its product, under the new regime they would be frightened into compliance through intimidation and physical violence.

Underlying the Ford profit sharing regime were the tensions and contradictions of liberal capitalism; almost as soon as the plan went into effect, these tensions began to emerge. Workers resented the sociological investigations and the heavy-handed meddling of their employer in their "private" lives. In framing their objections, they demonstrated that the classical liberal values of privacy and autonomy of the individual had been internalized within their own common sense and that such values could be marshaled for criticism of Ford's paternalistic Americanism. In an oral history interview, William Pioch framed his recollection in terms which suggest an awareness of the contradiction between such republican principles as formal equality and rights of the individual, and the ability of the employer to extend his effective power into the "private" sphere of the home:

> I remember when they first started the Sociological Department. They had a group of men on their staff that went out and checked all the employees ... They picked on your life history, how you lived and where you went to church and everything. They went to my home. My wife told them everything. There was nothing to keep from them. Of course, there was a lot of criticism on that. It was kind of a funny idea, in a free state.[50]

Ford Motor Company was aware of these objections, and seemed to recognize their potential power as a rallying point for opposition. In order to downplay the intrusive surveillance which underlay its labor policy, and to contravene the implication that it treated its workers as objects of study and manipulation, it changed the name of the Sociological Department to the Department of Education, and began calling its investigators "advisors."[51] Through its employee newspaper – *The Ford Man*, initiated in September, 1917 – the company represented itself as simply taking "a personal interest" in the workers welfare, making helpful suggestions, not "dictat[ing] to him how to spend his money or run his home."[52] The company's public statements were almost invariably defensive on this count, asserting that their policies were not paternalistic but rather "friendly, fraternal," suggesting a concern for one's equal rather than an exercise of power over subordinates. However, as the following recollection of Samuel Marquis demonstrates, their implicit presumption of social superiority allowed company officials simultaneously to recognize and to minimize the significance of workers' objections to profit sharing paternalism:

> There were employees who objected to it as subjecting them to humiliating experiences. They said that it interfered with their personal liberty and independence. So far as my experience went I found such complaints came from men whose individual liberties had been interfered with, but they were such liberties as getting drunk and beating up one's wife, abusing one's family, and wasting one's money.[53]

In any case, the reasoning went, since the employment relation was a purely voluntary contractual arrangement between two equals, any employee offended by Ford's labor policies was always free to decline the offer of employment. In Marquis' words: "... there is no law in Michigan compelling any man to work for the Ford Company who does not care to do so."[54] Acting as an autonomous individual, the employee chose to submit himself to the conditions of his employer; therefore the employer's power was legitimate, Marquis implied.

The double standard of liberal capitalism was at work here, and both sides knew it. Employment at Ford was represented as a contract between free and equal parties, yet management believed that its implicitly class-based superiority entitled it to dictate and enforce conditions of employment which extended beyond the factory and into the homes and private lives of its workers. This contradiction offended the intuitive liberalism of workers' common sense, and they called upon this cultural legacy to assert their rights to privacy and to question the legitimacy of Ford's intrusions into this private sphere. Their consent to Ford's paternalistic industrial regime, then, was not unequivocal.

As World War I changed the context of industrial relations at Ford, the paternalistic regime began to unravel, and the coercive aspects of the capital–labor relation began to predominate. Wartime inflation seriously eroded the material incentive for submission to Ford paternalism. According to the US Bureau of Labor Statistics, the cost of living in Detroit increased 78 percent between December, 1914 and the same month in 1918. As Nevins and Hill point out, this meant that the purchasing power of the five dollar day had been reduced to about $2.80, not much more than the basic wage rate in effect before the profit sharing plan. Further, other manufacturers had increased their wages since the announcement of the five dollar day in 1914, so that the enormous gap between Ford's pay and the industry average no longer existed. As the relative magnitude of Ford profit sharing declined, so too did the incentive for Ford workers to tolerate the Ford regime. The wartime boom had created a greater variety of job opportunities, and once again increasing numbers of Ford workers were voting with their feet: from 16 percent in 1915, the turnover rate rose steadily during the war years, reaching close to 51 percent in 1918. In the face of worker discontent and high costs, Sociological Department investigations were being scaled back, and the differentiation between wages and a conditional profit share soon would be dropped altogether. Management attempted to reestablish some of the incentive power of Ford pay by raising the minimum wage to six dollars per day in 1919 – a 20 percent increase over the original profit sharing minimum wage – but by the end of that year the cost of living in Detroit had climbed to almost 108 percent above what it had been in 1914. In a further effort to recapture some of the aura of profit sharing, Ford announced an end-of-year bonus plan in December, 1919, but it too was devoured by price increases and added the equivalent of only one or two cents per hour to the real wages of Ford workers.[55]

Along with the bonus plan the company announced an employee investment plan through which, workers were told, they might become owners of the company and share still more in its prosperity; and Ford opened company stores to sell food and clothing to employees at reduced prices in order to help offset the rapidly rising cost of living and the relatively meager wage increases. The company's employee newspaper modestly suggested: "No other business organization in the whole world since time began has done so much for its employes [sic] as has this grand Company with whom we co-operate, the Ford Motor Company."[56] Ford continued to bombard workers with the claim, central to its original profit sharing plan, that Ford Motor Company was a cooperative venture in which employees "are working with Mr. Ford, and not working for him"; and that this partnership for prosperity had resolved "the problem between Capital and Labor that has existed since the days when men first began to work as servants and masters." As a consequence, "The opportunity to 'move up higher' is wide open to every Ford worker," whose success was said to depend entirely upon his own "individual effort."[57] *The Ford Man* called upon workers to show their appreciation and to realize their interest in the company by working more diligently, staying with Ford instead of looking for more attractive work elsewhere, and paying no heed to "disloyal" malcontents, labor agitators, and "Bolsheviks" in their ranks (between whom the company did not clearly distinguish).[58] The company paper represented Henry Ford as "a pioneer in recognizing the rights of Americans and of laborers" and suggested that an enlightened employer such as he could do more than un-American radicals or unionists to advance the interests of workers.[59] In these ways, Ford sought to contain growing worker discontent and retain some vestiges of the profit sharing regime even after its foundation had eroded away. Just as wartime conditions strained the bonds which Ford had sought to create between the company and its workers, the war also introduced the atmosphere of repressive conformity, intimidation and the large-scale covert surveillance which was to become a central part of the coercive regime of the interwar years.

Upon formally entering into hostilities in April, 1917, the American government was acutely aware that the public was not altogether unified in support of the war; yet, a massive social mobilization was required if the USA were to participate decisively in this great and terrible struggle. Almost immediately upon entry, then, President Wilson created the Committee on Public Information and launched a systematic propaganda campaign of unprecedented proportions in order to forge a popular consensus behind the war policy. The public was barraged with representations of the enemy as militaristic, brutal and inhuman, and the war was depicted as a holy crusade for freedom and democracy. Whole-hearted ("100 percent") support for the war effort became the *sine qua non* of patriotism; anything less came to be viewed as treasonous. Tendencies toward the enforcement of consensus through the suppression of dissent were intensified by the passage of legislation – at the federal level, the Espionage, Trading with the Enemy, and Sedition Acts – which effectively criminalized opposition to the war or public criticism of the government, the constitution, the prevailing social order. To protect the arsenal of democracy, the Sedition and Espionage Acts specifically proscribed speaking or writing in ways which might be construed as interfering with production for the war effort. In the context of this belligerent Americanism, Socialists and Wobblies, radicals and militant unionists (together with pacifists, German-Americans and others) were presumed to be suspect, disloyal almost by definition, and became the objects of official, semi-official, and outright vigilante-style oppression.[60]

This wartime oppression extended into the Ford works through the offices of the American Protective League (APL). The APL was created in 1917 as a citizens auxiliary to the US Department of Justice; organized nation-wide, its 250,000 hyper-patriotic volunteers collaborated with the Justice Department's Bureau of Investigation, military intelligence and local authorities to sniff out putatively disloyal or subversive persons or activities. Surrounding themselves with the aura of official sanction and authority, "Its 'agents' bugged, burglarized, slandered, and illegally arrested other Americans."[61] To prevent the much-feared disruption of war production, the APL extended its spying into workplaces and factories. Employers, who might be the beneficiaries of government war contracts and who were in no case friends of Wobblies or militant unionists, were generally inclined to do their patriotic duty by cooperating. Ford's surveillance arm, the Sociological Department, furnished officers for the Detroit APL and coordinated their activities in the Ford shops.[62]

According to Stephen Meyer, the APL organization at Ford's Highland Park plant consisted of around a hundred secret agents scattered through forty-five different departments and shops. When a worker somehow aroused the suspicions of an agent, the worker's Sociological Department files provided a head start on an investigation of the worker's background and loyalties. Supplemented by the agent's account of the "suspicious" actions or statements, the worker's file could then be forwarded to the Bureau of Investigation, military intelligence, or local authorities for further action. The Ford organization also imposed its own sanctions to enforce loyalty upon its workers. Supervisors harassed and pressured employees to contribute to the Red Cross and to buy Liberty Bonds. For the foreign-born, Ford's Americanization classes became one litmus test for loyalty. Those who resisted these pressures, those who did not seem to work with sufficient enthusiasm, or who made remarks construed as anti-war, anti-government, or anti-Ford, were deemed disloyal and transferred to the most difficult and least desirable jobs in the plant, or were simply discharged.

The new, militant Americanism of wartime found its way into Ford's employee newspaper, which helped to foster the general atmosphere of intimidation by publishing on its front page an explanation of the Espionage Act, emphasizing for the benefit of Ford workers the Act's provisions against "inciting or advocating the curtailment of production ... of anything essential to the prosecution of the war ..."[63] Articles, editorials and letters to the editor called upon workers to denounce as disloyal Hun-sympathizers, if not traitors or spies, anyone who was not obviously giving his all to the war effort (and, by happy coincidence, to Ford Motor Company). In one example of this genre, J. D. Young cautioned his fellow employees thus:

> . . . a man not fulfilling his daily duty, no matter in what capacity he is serving, opens the way for just suspicion of [being] a co-worker to the enemy.
>
> We cannot accuse any man of being a party to any form of espionage without due evidence, but we can place a man under secret suspicion until he has proven beyond question his loyalty.
>
> Be on the alert for the man that questions our principles in this, the greatest struggle of history, for the man that doubts the outcome, for the man that stands by and allows another to let a questionable statement go unchallenged.[64]

Since the company was engaged in war work, Americanism could in this way be explicitly linked to performance on the job and, by extension, loyalty to Ford. While this could be used to create a chilling atmosphere of fear and conformity, it also had its ridiculous side. For example, *The Ford Man* of October 3, 1918, depicted labor turnover as a sinister conspiracy to disrupt war production – this "well organized campaign" presumably orchestrated by the devious Hun – and suggested that workers who looked for better jobs elsewhere were dupes of the enemy or worse. In general, Ford's wartime propaganda urged workers to redouble their efforts in order to win the war and demonstrate their gratitude to Ford, their great benefactor and symbol of the American way.[65]

The conclusion of the war in November, 1918 did not bring to an end the covert surveillance and malignant Americanism in the Ford plant. After the war there was an intense bout of labor unrest which gripped the country, touched the automobile industry, and approached the outer edges of the Ford empire. Organized labor had gained strength during the war, when the federal government extended some protections to "responsible" and "loyal" unions which were seen as contributing to industrial peace during the wartime emergency. Afterward, as the war economy shifted back toward civilian production and consumption, there was a brief boom in the auto industry which increased the demand for labor and potentially, therefore, its bargaining power. As a result of these apparently favorable conditions, and the desire of industrial workers to recover some of the real wages lost to wartime inflation, the Carriage, Wagon and Automobile Workers

Union (or AWU) experienced a surge in membership in the immediate postwar years. Employers, for their part, were seeking to reassert control over their businesses as government wartime regulation abated. As these social forces collided, a huge strike wave occurred and a number of auto plants in several cities were struck. Among these was the Wadsworth Manufacturing Company, a major supplier of auto bodies to Ford. Not only did this strike constrain Ford's output during a period of potentially booming sales, but the AWU seemed to be gaining influence and membership among Ford workers themselves.[66] In response, Ford sent strike-breakers to Wadsworth and in its own plant began to institutionalize its espionage network under the leadership of an APL veteran, charged with the destruction of nascent labor organizations.

Ford's labor spies were placed in the shops alongside other employees, and reported to management about the activities and statements of their co-workers. They were especially concerned with rooting out radicals and unionists, but they also reported soldiering, inefficient use of company time (for example, workers spending "excessive" time in the toilet), violations of various Ford shop rules, and comments disparaging of Henry Ford or the company. Further, Ford's labor spies followed workers outside of the factory and infiltrated radical and labor organizations in order to report on their membership and activities. Ford management took action to transfer, isolate or discharge those whom its spies designated as disloyal or undesirable.[67]

Meanwhile, in the pages of *The Ford Man*, the company continued to identify itself and Henry Ford as friends of the worker and avatars of the American Way; and to equate labor organizers of any sort with radicals, who in turn were represented as dangerous, alien and uncivilized. Thus the company played upon the major themes of the postwar red scare to sow suspicion and fear among its workers. One letter to *The Ford Man* suggested to fellow workers that

> [W]e must help this government to fight Bolshevism in its infancy ... Who would think that employes [sic] of such a democratic organization as the Ford Motor Company would work in the interest of such a party. Still it is a fact ... [B]eing in America and being blessed with abundance of everything I cannot see how they will help to advance the cause of revolution ... and by doing so destroy life, property and their own homes and happiness ... [A]nyone spreading such [Bolshevik] propaganda [should] be reported to the Service department [Ford's factory security arm] ...

Others demanded that foreign workers take Americanization classes and speak English, and urged workers to report non-English speakers to the company. Another declared: "If we had more Henry Ford's, we wouldn't need labor unions to protect our interest."[68]

By 1920–21, the brief postwar upsurge of unionism had been crushed by a concatenation of powerful counter-tendencies. Employers had defeated strikes and broken unions around the country under the banner of the militantly open shop "American Plan." In the rhetoric of the American Plan, unions were depicted as illegitimate combinations which constrained the freedom of individuals to enter into contracts for their mutual benefit: they were, then, "contrary to the fundamental principles of the American economic system and a hindrance to the nation's progress." As the open shop drive attacked the labor movement, the postwar red scare and Palmer raids created an environment of suspicion, fear and hostility toward radicals and labor activists who were represented as quintessentially un-American. And finally, the economy entered a sharp recessionary period in which jobs of any kind suddenly became more scarce.[69] This period witnessed the ultimate demise of Ford paternalism, and a hardening of Ford labor policies which would endure until the UAW insurgency of the early 1940s.

As sales and revenues dropped off during the recession, Ford Motor Company faced a severe financial crisis: at a time when he was investing heavily in the development of the giant new River Rouge facility, and purchasing coal and iron mines to supply it, Ford had to pay off large debts incurred in order to buy out major stockholders and assert exclusive control over what was now effectively his company. To meet this crisis, Ford slashed Model T prices in an effort to boost sales of his car, and forced Ford dealers to buy more cars than they could sell. According to "the rule that everything and everybody must produce or get out," he made massive cuts in office and administrative staff.[70] During the winter of 1920–21, Ford shut down the factory and laid off his workers for a period of weeks, effectively casting them adrift in the stormy recessionary sea. Having thus accentuated the fragility of his workers' economic security and their sense of dependence upon the company, Ford rehired fewer of them upon reopening the plant and – to get the maximum possible production at minimum cost – enforced a brutal speed-up upon those who were rehired. Ford and Crowther boasted about this increased efficiency: "Before we had employed fifteen men per car per day. Afterward we employed nine per car per day." Ford foreman William Klann, whose job it was to effect the speed-up on the shop-floor, recalled: "We were driving them in those days ... Ford was one of the worst shops for driving the men."[71]

The paternalism of the old Sociological Department seemed out of place in the new regime with its hard-edged emphasis on production, and was viewed by Ford's production executives as frivolous, an unnecessary impediment. As their influence increased and his own declined, Marquis perceived the sea change in the following terms:

> The humane treatment of employees, according to these men, would lead to the weakening of the authority of the "boss," and to the breaking down of discipline in the shop. To them the sole end of industry was production and profits, and the one sure way of getting these things out of labor was to curse it, threaten it, drive it, insult it, humiliate it, and discharge it on the slightest provocation; in short – to use a phrase much on the lips of such men – "put the fear of God into labor."[72]

After a series of conflicts with Ford's production executives (especially Charles Sorenson), Samuel Marquis resigned from Ford Motor Company in January, 1921 and the Sociological Department which Marquis had headed was subsumed within the Factory Service Department.[73]

At that time, the Factory Service Department was responsible for plant security and the detection of theft, for fire fighting, delivery of communications within the plant, escorting of visitors and employees, and enforcement of company rules and regulations.[74] By 1927 – when Ford finally supplanted the Model T with the Model A and moved its primary manufacturing facilities from Highland Park to the River Rouge plant – Harry Bennett had become the Service Department chief at "the Rouge" and was building it into a formidable secret police, enforcing a severe shop discipline, sniffing out and extinguishing dissent among those connected to the Ford empire. Under the personal sponsorship of Henry Ford, Bennett's influence within the company grew until, in 1937 as the UAW began to challenge Ford's open shop, the old man made it clear to both his son, Edsel, and his production chief, Charles Sorenson, that neither was to interfere with Bennett's handling of labor relations: Bennett had become the labor czar of the Ford Motor Company.[75]

Ford's labor policy in the interwar years was simple and direct. Ford himself was unequivocal in denouncing unions on individualist grounds. "Labor union organizations are the worst thing that ever struck the earth," he said, "because they take away a mans independence." Sorenson was more specific about whose independence was being protected, and its real basis: "Mr. Ford doesn't need any outside advice on how to run his business." Sorenson disparaged unionists' claims to be able to increase productivity above the level which management could attain by its own methods. Reflecting the class-based common sense of managerial superiority, he implied that management had nothing to learn from unionists, and that any compromise over managerial control of the plant would undermine the system of production. "Everything Henry Ford and I had done to build up that plant and its organization would be jeopardized if we allowed the unions to have a voice in management." The company's statement of its labor policy embodied the ideological presuppositions of its masters: "The industrial relationship between the Ford Motor Company and its employees is purely individual and every policy is designed with the intention of keeping it so." During the early depression years, Ford defied Roosevelt and the National Industrial Recovery Act (NIRA), refusing to sign the automobile industry code because he saw in it a dual threat to managerial prerogative – it was seen to orchestrate governmental regulation of industry, and section 7(a) of the NIRA explicitly recognized workers' right to organize for purposes of collective bargaining.[76] Bennett's mandate was clear: no union activity was to be tolerated among Ford workers, federal policy and popular opinion notwithstanding.

As the balance between coercion and consent at Ford shifted toward the former after World War I, employee newspapers became less important as a means of attempting to mobilize consensus and build a sense of community among Ford workers. Accordingly, the *Ford News* (successor to *The Ford Man*) metamorphosed by the late 1920s from a shop paper aimed at Ford's production workers into a slick glossy magazine for dealers and customers. Gone were regular features about thrift, shop safety, productivity, and workers' suggestions; as Ford lost interest in even the appearance of dialogue with its workers, its publication was reoriented toward a very different audience and these sorts of features were supplanted by upbeat articles on travel, fashion, driving, and sports, as well as advertisements for Ford cars and accessories.[77]

In the interwar years, Ford's primary instruments in the execution of its open shop labor policy were covert surveillance and overt coercion:

dismissal without appeal, or actual physical violence, could be visited upon any worker at any time. Bennett's enforcers were a specially recruited cadre of former policemen, college athletes, professional boxers and wrestlers, mobsters and ex-convicts – tough guys and thugs of every description. Service men guarded the plant gates and checked employee identification badges as workers entered. They patrolled the factory floor watching for signs of union activity or soldiering, and they enforced shop regulations such as the proscriptions against talking or sitting during working hours. Ford worker John Fitzpatrick suggested how the Service Department was able to create a pervasive atmosphere of intimidation within the plant through the exercise of arbitrary power:

> Once you got by the gate the tension began, because in there, no matter how good a man you were ... a service man would come up to you, tap you on the shoulder, and tell you to pack your tool box and go off to ... the Employment Office [to be discharged]. There, in the service man, was the supreme authority so far as your job was concerned – right there at the gate when you walked in.[78]

Nor was Service Department discipline limited to summary discharge; they had a well-deserved reputation for brutality and violence. A manager of Ford's Lincoln plant, J. M. Wagoner, explained how the Service Department punished insufficiently docile Lincoln workers by transferring them to the River Rouge assembly line for "toughening up": "I don't know what happened to them over there, but when they came back you wouldn't even know they were the same men. They had black eyes and pushed in noses ... They really dressed them down." So severe was the regime in the Ford plant by 1940 that laughing and smiling was taken as a sign of insubordination and a provocation which could not be allowed to stand.[79]

The labor espionage upon which Ford began to rely after World War I found an institutional home in the Service Department, and contributed to the chilling atmosphere of intimidation. One of a group of Yale students who worked summers in the Ford plants indicated that as early as 1926 workers were aware of the existence and purpose of Ford's secret police: "It is a current rumor that the Company has a very efficient secret service system with detectives scattered all over the factory to watch for any symptom of labor disturbances. Action is taken before any attempt on the part of workmen to organize could come to fruition."[80] By the late 1930s, when the UAW began its campaign to organize Ford workers, Bennett's in-plant spy network included roughly 10 percent of the 90,000 employees of the River Rouge plant. As they worked, these men would take note of the actions and statements of their fellow workers and report un-Fordly behavior to the disciplinarians of the Service Department. Outside the plant, Bennett's henchmen would follow suspected unionists, infiltrate union meetings, observe union-related sporting events and social occasions in order to identify Ford employees with union sympathies. Sheldon Tappes, a union activist who worked in the River Rouge foundry, recalled how Ford's secret police singled him out: "In 1939 when I was marching in the Labor Day parade, I had my Ford [employee identification] badge pinned to my lapel. And as I got to the Fox Theater, a man stepped out from the curb and took a good look at my badge ... The next day I found myself fired."[81]

In the infamous "Ford Hunger March" of 1932, the Dearborn police and Ford's Service men showed themselves willing to use deadly force to protect Ford's private property rights against the claims of unemployed workers and radical activists. Detroit and the auto industry had been especially hard hit by the Depression, and the city's Welfare Department was simply overwhelmed by the magnitude of the destitution which resulted. Since Ford's major plants were in adjacent Dearborn and Highland Park, the company contributed no taxes to ease Detroit's fiscal crisis, even though some 15 or 20 percent of the families on the city's welfare rolls were thought to be unemployed Ford workers. Further, Henry Ford's individualist ideology was both unsympathetic toward the unemployed and opposed to charity, and accordingly the company announced that it would make no contributions to private relief organizations. On March 7, 1932, the Detroit area Unemployed Councils – organized largely by Communist Party (CP) activists – led a protest march of some three thousand to the gates of Ford's River Rouge plant, where they planned to deliver a list of demands aimed at improving conditions for both the unemployed and those still working in the Ford shops. After Dearborn Police attempted to disperse the crowd with tear gas and fire hoses, and were answered with stones from the protesters (one of which struck Harry Bennett), police and Service men guarding the gate fired into the crowd, killing four and wounding at least fifty. What radicals called the "Ford Massacre," Detroit Prosecutor Harry S. Troy labeled a red riot, seeking to blame the violence on un-American elements. A number of demonstrators (including injured) were detained by the police, leading communists were sought, and the police raided offices of the CP and various ethnic associations seeking radicals and deportable aliens who could be accused of "criminal syndicalism."[82]

Five years later, another violent episode drew public attention to the coercive underpinnings of the Ford empire. After UAW organizers were severely and quite publicly beaten while preparing to pass out union leaflets at the gates of the River Rouge plant on May 26, 1937, the National Labor Relations Board (NLRB) launched an inquiry to determine whether Ford's labor policies were in violation of the National Labor Relations Act of 1935 (the Wagner Act).[83] In a report dated December 22, 1937, the Board found that Ford's Service Department had planned and executed the "almost unbelievably brutal" beatings as part of a systematic policy – "a relentless campaign of intimidation and coercion" – to suppress unionization among Ford employees. In addition to the violence against unionists, the NLRB report cited Ford's distribution of anti-union propaganda among its workers, discussed its attempt to impose a company-dominated pseudo-union called the Ford Brotherhood of America, and described the cases of twenty-nine workers discharged for pro-union activities or sympathies. Based upon its review of this evidence, the Board concluded:

> The record leaves no doubt that the Service Department has been vested with responsibility of maintaining surveillance over Ford employees, not only during their work but even when they are outside the plant, and of crushing at its inception, by force if necessary, any sign of union activity. Thus within [Ford Motor Company's] vast River Rouge plant at Dearborn the freedom of self-organization guaranteed by the [Wagner] Act has been replaced by a rule of terror and repression.[84]

The NLRB found Ford to be in violation of federal labor law at its River Rouge plant. Between 1937 and 1941, eight subsequent NLRB investigations revealed a larger pattern of illegal intimidation against Ford employees at other plants in various cities. Notable among these cases was the record achieved by the Service Department at the Dallas branch plant, who in just six months of 1937 carried out as many as thirty beatings, floggings, and at least one public tarring and feathering. Following (with greater vigor) the same basic strategy that it had in the early 1920s, during the depression era Ford was using violence and intimidation to enforce an intensified speed-up upon its workers and to preclude any organized attempts at resistance.[85]

Although an industrial pioneer in this regard as well, during the New Deal era at least Ford was not exceptional in its systematic intimidation of employees and violation of federal labor law. Chaired by Robert M. LaFollette, Jr., the Senate Committee on Education and Labor began hearings in 1936 in which it documented that American corporations were engaged in illegal anti-union activities on a truly massive scale. Typically justifying their actions on grounds that labor organizations were somehow linked to communism, and that they undermined the idyllic harmony between management and workers, American capitalists were hiring detective agencies to carry out labor espionage, obtaining weapons and munitions for use against crowds of people, hiring strikebreakers and using private police in order to sustain their control of the workplace. Subsequently, the committee investigated campaigns through which corporations involved in labor disputes sought systematically to organize "community sentiment" and arouse the middle class against labor unions by depicting them as dangerous, communistic and un-American.[86] Ford was perhaps outstanding in the degree to which these various functions had been institutionalized within the company itself and by 1937 constituted something of a tradition, but it was not alone in using such means to resist the upsurge of labor organization of the 1930s. In the interwar years the Ford Motor Company was an exemplar of the coercive ways in which the social powers of capital may be exercised.

Unionism is Americanism: production politics and ideological struggle at Ford Motor Company, 1937–1952

Americanism vs. Fordism

By the spring of 1937, through effective work stoppages, the United Automobile Workers (UAW) had compelled both General Motors and Chrysler to recognize the union for purposes of collective bargaining. Of the "big three" auto makers, Ford was the only remaining hold-out, stubbornly refusing to recognize the UAW and thereby threatening to undercut the union's ability to bargain effectively with the other auto makers.[1] From the outset of the campaign to unionize the Ford plants, launched that spring, the unionists appropriated and reinterpreted the language of Americanism which had for so long been used to bolster and legitimate the powers of capital. The UAW articulated to workers its opposition to Ford's authoritarian industrial regime, which the union represented as "un-American," fascistic. In its place, the union envisioned an "industrial democracy" which would safeguard the individual rights of workers and enable them to exercise a significant measure of self-determination in their working lives; the UAW cast itself as the vehicle of this democratization. The union organizers who were attacked outside the River Rouge plant on May 26 were distributing leaflets which counterposed "unionism" to "Fordism": in addition to demanding higher wages and shorter hours, better working conditions and job security through a seniority system, the union also promised Ford workers that "union supervision" of the production process would put an end to the regime of the speed-up and the Service Department. Ford's violence only underscored the poignancy of this aspiration. As Victor Reuther put it, after his brother Walter recovered from the beating he received at the River Rouge plant, "he was more determined than ever to bring the Ford plants within the laws of the United States and to free the workers from what amounted to serfdom."[2]

When the National Labor Relations Board (NLRB) issued its report on Ford's labor policy and the River Rouge beatings, the union's newspaper took the opportunity to counter explicitly the folk wisdom manufactured by Ford spokesman W. J. Cameron. In his nationally popular weekly radio broadcasts, Cameron presented the perspective of the Ford Motor Company in the guise of "a few plain, unpartisan American impressions," often highlighting such putatively patriotic values as free enterprise and democracy. In response, the *United Automobile Worker* reprinted graphic excerpts from the NLRB report, and implied that this kind of blatantly illegal violence against unionists showed what "Ford's idea of democracy" really meant: it entailed the brutal degradation of working people and contempt for their legal rights. The union's paper took note of the NLRB finding that Dearborn police had watched the beatings without intervening. The corrupting influence of the Ford Motor Company over municipal affairs in Dearborn was seen as suggesting that "Democracy in politics cannot prevail without democracy in industry." The union also sought to convey to its readers a sense of their collective responsibility to actively oppose this undemocratic regime: "We, the UAW, are charged with the most active part in the destruction of Fordism and all its brutalities ... The government can bring its legal power to bear; the general public can show its opposition to Fordism; but the only body that can actually end the evil ruthlessness of Fordism is the UAW ..."[3] Industrial democracy was presented as the antidote to industrial autocracy, and the necessary complement of political democracy.

The opposition of unionism and Fordism – and the equation of the latter with a private tyranny in which the property rights of an employer allowed him to run roughshod over the rights of workers and citizens, and to place himself above the law – was a central ideological theme of the unionization struggle at Ford. In counterposing citizen rights vested in all equally, to property rights which legitimized implicitly class-based relations of power, the unionists aimed their ideological campaign squarely at a central contradiction of liberal capitalism. Thus reinterpreting the language and symbols of Americanism, they began to carve out a space for unionism in the common sense of Ford workers.

The unionization campaign at Ford soon stalled, however. The company's intimidation tactics and the climate of fear prevailing among Ford workers kept union activity underground and prevented the union from signing up masses of new members. Moreover, the steep recession of 1937–38 deepened unemployment and, along with the conservative reaction which set in during those years, created an atmosphere which was hardly conducive to militant unionism. And the UAW itself was disabled by bitter factional in-fighting in the wake of its first great successes against GM and Chrysler. Together, these conditions drew the vitality out of the Ford campaign until it was reinvigorated in mid-1940. By that time, the first great bout of UAW factional fighting had been resolved (in part through CIO intervention). Output and employment were on the upswing, increasing the union's potential leverage and attenuating one major source of fear among industrial workers. Further, the UAW by then had won a string of NLRB cases against Ford alleging unfair labor practices in violation of the Wagner Act, more cases were pending, and the original River Rouge case had been largely sustained by a federal appeals court: the sense that Ford was beyond the law, that Ford's Service men could get away with anything, was beginning to dissipate. In response to these more favorable conditions, the CIO and UAW provided a large infusion of cash and a cadre of experienced organizers to jump start the Ford Organizing Committee.[4]

The organizers immediately challenged a Dearborn ordinance, enacted after the River Rouge beatings, which prohibited the distribution of literature in "congested areas" such as the gates of the Ford plant at shift change – precisely the time and place where the union could get direct access to the largest numbers of Ford workers. The union newspaper, *Ford Facts*, exposed the anti-union purpose of the "traffic" ordinance by pointing out that it did not cover other areas of Dearborn as congested as the vicinity of the Ford plant, and that the ordinance was not enforced when organizations such as the American Legion distributed their material outside the plant. Commenting upon Ford's pervasive influence in his home town, the newspaper situated Dearborn within "the Ford empire," which it likened to "a totalitarian state." In opposing this sinister force, the union cast itself as the defender of free speech and the bill of rights, the agent which would "Americanize Ford" and return Dearborn to the United States. The basic issue was framed in the following terms: "Shall the Ford Motor Company be permitted to murder the constitution, and to steal a fundamental American right from its citizens?" When the UAW challenge successfully overturned the ordinance, Michael F. Widman, director of the Ford organizing drive, said "Ford workers find in this decision another stimulus to assert their American rights and to improve their working conditions." Union president R. J. Thomas suggested that the implications extended beyond the workplace and into the sphere of citizenship, upholding the principle of equality before the law as opposed to the prerogatives of property: "Step by step, the UAW–CIO is establishing law and order in Dearborn in place of Ford rule. Not only Ford workers, but all citizens of Dearborn are the beneficiaries of this decision."[5]

Following this legal victory in the fall of 1940, the union stepped up its campaign to persuade Ford workers to join the UAW. Union leaflets and newspapers such as *Ford Facts* were distributed in tens of thousands of copies at the plant gates. In them, the union claimed that Ford's longstanding reputation as a high wage employer had become an anachronistic myth and that the union would secure better wages and working conditions, "winning an American deal" for Ford workers. But the UAW appeal to Ford workers went beyond straightforward bread and butter unionism, and spoke of "matters which American workers, free men, born with the guarantees of life, liberty and the pursuit of happiness, value as highly as they do wage rates." Drawing upon the egalitarian and participatory strains in liberal common sense, the union emphasized the antagonism between industrial democracy and respect for the legal rights of all citizens on the one hand, and Ford's industrial tyranny and lawlessness on the other: "there is no American freedom in a Ford plant." This anti-democratic menace was not limited to the shops; it was depicted as spilling over and corrupting the political community as well. By supporting the union, workers were told, they could see to it "that the Ford workers may enjoy the right of workingmen and citizens of a free republic."[6]

A major recurrent theme in union mass communications was the contempt for the law and for the rights of workers which was manifested in Henry Ford's labor policies. In its attempts to maintain the subordination of its workers, the Ford Motor Company placed itself above the law which, according to the liberal common sense which the union was seeking to reconstruct, should be binding upon all citizens equally. Typical of these representations was a *Ford Facts* cartoon in which a uniformed policeman labeled "NLRB" had pulled over a car driven by Henry Ford and a Service Department thug (figure 7.1). As the policeman looked in the trunk of the car and discovered a cache of tear gas, blackjacks and guns, the Service man demanded privileged treatment: "Say, do you know who we are?!!" Upholding the principle of equality before the law, the policeman responded, "I don't care who

Figure 7.1 "Caught with the goods"
A cartoon published in the UAW's newspaper, *Ford Facts* (October, 1940),
portrayed the National Labor Relations Board upholding the principle of
equality before the law as Henry Ford and a Service Department thug
demand privileged treatment in conducting anti-union violence. From the
Archives of Labor and Urban Affairs, Wayne State University.

you are! You can't get away with this rough stuff!" At this, the
discomfited Henry Ford was depicted blowing his top. One purpose of
such representations was to reassure long-terrorized Ford workers
"that they can join the UAW–CIO with full security and the protection
of the Federal government."[7] But these representations also sought to
legitimate the union by casting it as the defender of the law and of the

rights of citizens against the depredations of industrial pirates such as Ford.

In seeking such legitimation, the unionists felt obliged to defend themselves against the longstanding association, deliberately fostered by employers, of industrial unionism with alien ideologies and dangerous radicals. The national conventions of both the CIO and the UAW passed resolutions in which they explicitly condemned totalitarian dictatorships and ideologies such as "Nazism, Communism and Fascism," which were denounced as "inimical to the welfare of labor, and destructive of our form of government." The CIO resolution warned that in carrying out the unions' primary task of organizing the unorganized, "we must not be diverted by strange, foreign doctrines opposed to our concept of industrial and political democracy." Reporting these resolutions, *Ford Facts* declared (in bold type): "When you join the UAW–CIO, you join a hundred per cent American organization!"[8] Another attempt to situate industrial unionism within a reconstructed American mainstream was an article by CIO President John L. Lewis – illustrated with a flag and an assertive caption reading THE CIO IS AMERICAN – in which he reassured his readers that union members were loyal Americans and would not place their own interests ahead of those of the American people as a whole. Lewis expressed his confidence that unions would "at all times exercise reasonable restraint in the adoption of their policies," and that the CIO would defend American institutions against the domination of selfish interests. He closed with a ringing declaration: ". . . the CIO is a mighty power for democracy, peace and prosperity. The millions of organized workers banded together in the CIO are the backbone of resistance to all the forces that threaten our democratic institutions and the liberty and security that Americans hold dear."[9]

In a global context where conflict between liberal and anti-liberal forces was building toward world war, fascism appeared as a formidable and sinister threat to liberal democracy. The union strove to associate its own struggle against Ford's industrial regime with this global conflict. In the newspapers, handbills and placards with which the UAW represented the terms of its struggle, Henry Ford and his company were frequently identified with fascism. In its efforts to establish this association, the union was aided by the fact that Ford's industrial empire, his vision of mass motorization, and his anti-Semitic writings were much admired in the Third Reich, and in 1938 Ford had accepted from diplomatic representatives of the Reich the highest

Help Americanize *Ford*

Why did Ford receive the highest Nazi decoration?

Why did Ford employ Fritz Kuhn, <u>Convicted</u>
Bund Leader?

Why did Ford refuse to build plane motors
for England?

Why has Ford refused to abide by the laws
of the U. S. A.?

BE AMERICAN: BUY UNION-MADE CARS

Ford, Only Non-union Car Made in America

 FORD COMMITTEE
UNITED AUTOMOBILE WORKERS

Figure 7.2 "Help Americanize Ford"
A UAW organizing handbill (c. 1940) impugned Henry Ford's Americanism
and showed him being decorated by diplomatic representatives of Hitler's
Third Reich. The handbill urged readers to "help Americanize Ford" by
supporting the union. From the Archives of Labor and Urban Affairs, Wayne
State University.

decoration which it could award to foreigners (only three others had received this award, among whom was Mussolini). In a UAW flyer bearing the bold caption "Help Americanize Ford," the union reprinted a photograph of Ford being formally decorated by the German consul (figure 7.2). The flyer cast aspersions on Ford's Americanism by asking its readers to ponder Ford's esteem by the nazis and his refusal "to abide by the laws of the USA." After the River Rouge beatings, union flyers urged workers to band together to protest "Ford Brutality" and "Ford Fascism," and to "Save American Democracy." The original issue of *Ford Facts* asked whether Dearborn was a part of the USA or if it was "a province of Fuehrer Henry Ford's totalitarian empire." Photographs of UAW protests in this period show unionists displaying banners and signs which declare "Fordism is Fascism! Unionism is Americanism," and "Make Dearborn a Part of the United States." Another such slogan defied Ford's authoritarianism by counterposing the unionists' citizen rights to Ford's property rights: "Ford Owns Millions But He Doesnt Own Us" (figure 7.3).[10]

In UAW communications with Ford workers, a vision of industrial democracy was counterposed to the "autocratic bossism" in the Ford shops. In 1940–41, *Ford Facts* was replete with articles and letters from Ford workers discussing grueling working conditions, abusive foremen and the terrorism of the Service Department. The newspaper continually asserted that the collective strength of the union would put an end to the manifold abuses which Ford workers had daily to endure. "You take the work thrown at you, you accept the low pay, you break your back to meet the speed-up, you hide your true thoughts from stool-pigeons and service men – you submit to all that and worse – *because you are alone*."[11] Industrial democracy – understood in terms of collective bargaining over wages and working conditions, and a shop steward system to guard against abuses on the shop-floor – would abolish the tyrannical regime of the speed-up and the Service Department. As one article loudly declared, "the union GUARANTEES TO YOU YOUR DEMOCRATIC RIGHT TO HAVE SOMETHING TO SAY ABOUT YOUR CONDITIONS OF WORK."[12] In appealing to the egalitarian, inclusive and participatory aspects of liberal common sense, the UAW also reached out to African-Americans. Racism, and Ford's patronizing policies toward black workers, were cast as evil not only because they divided industrial workers and undermined the foundation of union strength, but also because they constituted an offense to the kind of Americanism which the union was attempting to reconstruct.[13]

Figure 7.3 "Fordism is fascism; unionism is Americanism"

UAW members at a rally in Monroe, Michigan, June, 1937. In keeping with the general ideological orientation of the union's Ford campaign, their banners associated Fordism with fascism, and unionism with Americanism. They also highlighted the tension between Ford's property rights and the workers' rights as citizens. From the Archives of Labor and Urban Affairs, Wayne State University.

Just before the climactic showdown between the union and the company, *Ford Facts* encapsulated the UAWs vision of Americanism in the form of an invitation for workers to reflect upon their own political identities: HOW GOOD AN AMERICAN ARE YOU? The union provided a convenient checklist to help workers in this self-assessment, among which were the following questions:

> Are you, as a real American, concerned with the glory and future of your nation?
> Do you believe that democracy is the keystone of American Life?
> Do you believe that all men and women who work have a right not only to a decent standard of living, but also to a measure of democracy on their jobs?
> Do you agree that if our democracy is to be real, it must rest on the economic and social well-being of all the people?

Workers who found some resonance in this vision were called upon to help realize it by joining "that happy American army," the United Automobile Workers.[14]

The company made a number of relatively feeble attempts to counter the influence of UAW rhetoric and to reclaim as Ford property the terrain of Americanism. When the union first began its campaign to "Americanize Ford," a series of company-dominated pseudo-unions emerged, one of which called itself "The Liberty Legion of America, Inc." On letterhead graced with an image of the statue of liberty, the Legion explained to Ford workers that in addition to negotiating with Ford Motor Company on behalf of its workers, the Liberty Legion had been "organized for the purpose of combatting radicalism, communism and all other subversive activities toward our government." In a direct appeal to visions of political community based upon abstract individualism and a social contract, Legion leaflets represented excerpts from the organization's "Constitution," complete with a high-sounding preamble declaring dedication to "God and Country," "personal liberty," "security of property," etc. The UAW newspaper quickly unmasked the Legion as a Ford company union. As the UAW challenge intensified, an anti-union newspaper calling itself the *Independent Ford Worker* was distributed at the River Rouge plant. The paper asserted that by threatening industrial peace in America, the UAW–CIO was acting in the interests of communists and nazis. Responding explicitly to R. J. Thomas' allegation that there was "no American Freedom" in a Ford plant, the paper characterized Ford Motor Company as a bastion of "American freedom ... the kind of freedom this nation was built upon. It is the freedom which permitted Henry Ford to rise from utter obscurity to the highest industrial position in the world. It is the kind of freedom offered any Ford worker to go and do likewise." Henry Ford's Americanism was beyond challenge, the paper declared, and he would never "submit to any union." As part of an eleventh hour nation-wide propaganda offensive, Ford bought full-page advertisements in major newspapers defending the companys labor policy and denying that any labor problems existed at Ford.[15]

While Ford and Bennett remained intransigent, in late 1940 and early 1941 the union began to gain strength and to set up its shop steward system within the various buildings and departments of the vast River Rouge complex. When the Supreme Court refused to hear Ford's appeal of its original NLRB case in February 1941, Ford was legally compelled to rehire discharged unionists and to post notices of compliance with the NLRB ruling. A snowball effect began to gather momentum: in the shops union buttons appeared in greater numbers as the workers' confidence in the union and the law began to grow; and, as the union proclaimed its presence more openly, confidence grew. It was further bolstered by a series of localized stoppages and confrontations with management in which the union began to demonstrate its growing strength.[16]

On April 1, when Ford fired several union committeemen, work stoppages occurred all over the plant, and the UAW quickly moved to coordinate and support the strike: the giant River Rouge plant was shut down. Bennett attempted unsuccessfully to prompt government intervention to end the strike by branding the strikers as communists bent on red revolution and disrupting war production. More ominously, he employed black workers to remain at the Rouge as strikebreakers and to attack UAW pickets, hoping thereby to incite race-based violence, polarize the union and provoke government intervention. Fearing a race riot, and securing promises from the union that it would actively pursue anti-discrimination causes in the workplace, some leaders of the African-American community positively endorsed the UAW while many more urged blacks not to be used as strikebreakers. In one instance, pro-union state Senator Charles Diggs spoke at a rally to thousands of African-American constituents, and appealed for unity in terms which resonated with the themes of Americanism and the equality of citizens understood as abstract individuals: "We shall prove that there are no Negro workers or white

workers. We are just American workers willing to live or die together."
With the black community divided so that Ford's clients were no
longer the predominant voice, and with significant segments actively
supporting the CIO, it became clear that Bennett and Ford could not
count on exploiting racial divisions to break the strike.[17]

After eleven days, Ford gave in. The UAW–CIO decisively won the
ensuing NLRB elections, held in May, and entered into negotiations
with Ford Motor Company. In a stunning reversal of longstanding
company policy, Ford agreed to all the major UAW demands and then
some: wage increases and seniority, grievance machinery based on the
UAW shop steward system, transformation of the Ford secret police
into a uniformed plant protection department, as well as a union shop
and dues checkoff. Although standard explanations of this extraordinary settlement refer to the humane influence upon Henry Ford of
his son Edsel and wife Clara, Ford management may well have
decided that the UAW could be useful as a way to impose discipline
upon rank and file workers and to oppose unauthorized "wildcat"
strikes, as the union had done in the North American Aviation strike
which occurred during the Ford contract negotiations.[18]

Unionized Americanism and neoliberal hegemony

The struggles against Ford Motor Company's tyrannical factory
regime had produced a huge, militant and rambunctiously democratic
union: UAW Local 600, representing over 60,000 workers at the River
Rouge complex. Through the war years, any expectations the
company may have had about a workforce pacified and disciplined
through unionization were sorely disappointed. The union's shop
steward system confronted foremen and supervisors with union committeemen who were not reluctant to challenge managerial authority.
As managerial control lost its iron grip in the Ford factory, shop rules
and production standards were increasingly contested. In these contests, the militance of rank and file workers was expressed in frequent,
if not generally large or long, wildcat strikes (some 733 from 1941 to
1945), most over issues of shop-floor control (working conditions and
production standards, supervision, discipline, etc.). Nelson Lichtenstein notes that Local 600 leadership often "adopted" and supported
job actions initiated by the rank and file, and interprets these strikes
accordingly as "an extracontractual dimension" of the union's

grassroots-based power. The militant and participatory culture of Local 600 incorporated a small but active cadre of communists and fellow travelers who had contributed disproportionately to the building of the union and were respected and influential in the local, serving as stewards and playing an important part in the left-center coalition which governed the union on and off through the 1940s (alternating with an anticommunist coalition of social democrats, Catholic corporatists, and others). The obstreperous Local 600 was a thorn in the side of both the Ford Motor Company and the "responsible" national leadership of the UAW, and in the postwar years each took action to subdue it.[19]

At Ford, Harry Bennett's brutal methods had been supplanted by the more sophisticated management style of Henry Ford II, who succeeded his grandfather as company president in September, 1945 and promptly fired Bennett. The younger Ford quickly acquired a national reputation as the prototype of a new generation of enlightened "industrial statesmen" who pointed toward a future of cooperative effort and mutual prosperity for business and labor. Speaking to an audience of leading automotive managers and engineers in 1946, Ford sketched his vision of liberal capitalism in America: "In a free, competitive Democracy, mass-production is a tool for raising the standard of living by *reducing costs* and thereby bringing more and better products within the budgets of more and more people." However, he warned his audience, "We have not yet solved the problems of mass-production, for our failure in human engineering is creating waste and inefficiency which handicaps the very purpose of mass-production – lower costs." The generalized prosperity which mass production seemed to make possible would remain out of reach unless the labor problem could be resolved through "human engineering." As Ford saw it, organized labor was a necessary part of any cooperative solution. He suggested to his audience that labor unions had become a fact of life, that his company was willing and able to deal with unions provided that the they in turn took steps to insure that their contractual obligations – which Ford interpreted in terms of his broader social vision – were fulfilled:

> I assume ... that all of us agree that Labor Unions are here to stay. Certainly, we of the Ford Motor Company have no desire to "break the unions" ... We want to strengthen their leadership by urging and helping them to assume the responsibilities they must assume if the public interest [in improved productivity and greater social pros-

perity] is to be served. . . . If they are going to be real leaders they must accept the social obligations that go with leadership.

Ford's vision of labor leadership was, however, a limited one: he was not overturning the common sense of his class by suggesting that labor assume a broader role in the leadership of society as a whole. Rather, labor should lead itself into a cooperative industrial relationship by submitting to the authority of management in the workplace. "Labor has a great opportunity to achieve stature through greater responsibility. But I consider that management is in charge, that management must manage . . ." he said, suggesting that it was the responsibility of management to take the initiative in constructing stable and peaceful industrial relations.[20]

Ford Motor Company took the initiative going into its 1945–46 contract negotiation with the UAW, confronting the union with a list of thirty-one demands which were aimed at increasing managerial control on the shop-floor and containing the militance of the rank and file. A central theme in the negotiations was Ford's claim that it had agreed to the union shop and dues checkoff in 1941 in exchange for union assurances of stable labor relations, secured by collective bargaining agreements. Yet, the company charged, the union had been unable or unwilling to discipline its membership and suppress wildcat strikes and other outbreaks of shop-floor militance which impaired productivity and eroded the security of the business. Ford reassured the UAW that it "accepted the principle of union membership for its employees and collective bargaining with union representatives," but the company demanded that the new agreement include provisions ". . . which will assure company security through exercise of union responsibility, which the union shop and check-off have not provided," and that it should "provide effective guarantees against work stoppages and for increased productivity on the part of [union] members." After months of negotiation, UAW leadership placed on the defensive by the deepening anti-labor climate in America agreed to a contract including "company security" provisions which authorized the punishment or discharge of individuals responsible for unauthorized work stoppages, as well as workers who failed to meet production standards or deliberately attempted to restrict production. Further, the contract codified managerial powers to determine and enforce work standards, and it contributed to the bureaucratization of the union's grievance machinery and its distancing from the rank and file by providing for a small cadre of full-time union committeemen. In the two years after the contract settlement, the number of wildcat stoppages at Ford declined dramatically, and grievances also declined while productivity increased. For a time, it may have seemed that labor peace had finally been attained at Ford, and that the authority of management had been secured.[21]

But Ford Motor Company was not alone in its worry over the militance of Local 600, for it was the largest local union in the world and represented a strategic objective in the internecine power struggles then unfolding within the UAW. In 1946 Walter Reuther had been elected to the presidency of a deeply divided UAW, and the following year the Reuther faction secured control of the union's International Executive Board. Reuther had been associated with the Socialist Party until 1939, and until the late 1940s energetically advocated a reformed American capitalism in which a tripartite relationship between labor, business and government would facilitate full employment and increasing levels of productivity, wages and mass consumption. When American politics took its rightward turn into the Cold War, Reuther backed away from social democratic macro-reforms, and began to emphasize a strategy of national-level collective bargaining as a way for industrial labor to attain what Nelson Lichtenstein refers to as a "privatized welfare state" of pension plans, insurance, and unemployment benefits. Further, Reuther became more accepting of company security provisions and the linkage of wage increases to productivity growth, especially after he defeated his factional opposition on the left.[22]

In the factional struggles for predominance in the UAW, the Reuther group had found anticommunism to be an increasingly powerful weapon against the union's left-center coalition, which included a cadre of communists and fellow travelers and which was critical of the international and domestic anticommunism then gaining mass and momentum in America. Opposition to Truman's Cold War foreign policy and the Marshall Plan, and support for the kind of popular front, third party politics represented by Henry Wallace, were socially construed as indicators of dubious loyalty and rendered opponents vulnerable to Reuther's attacks. Reuther represented his own model of labor-liberalism as a "third force," capable of defending political and industrial democracy against enemies of both the left and the right. He argued that a centrist union movement could help to dispel the threat of communism by securing a more generalized prosperity and thereby resolving the double standards and unfulfilled promises of liberal capitalism:

> Communism is in perpetual war with what democracy preaches, for it cannot abide the sanctity of the individual or the interplay of honest differences. But Communism breeds on what democracy too often practices; it exploits the lapses of the democratic conscience and thrives on the shortcomings of democratic action. It is the task of democrats to bridge the gap between preachment and practice; we must wipe out the double standard in America, and in the world, which divides the masses of people from the minority that controls the preponderance of economic power. It is this double standard which embitters our society.[23]

Reuther's vision of the role of industrial unions in American liberal capitalism called for "Teamwork in the Leadership, Solidarity in the Ranks": that is, it called for the elimination of communist influence in the union in order to destroy his factional rivals and protect the union movement against the very real threat of political reaction in the era of Taft-Hartley, and the effective discipline of rank and file labor so that Reutherite union leadership could bargain credibly with corporate America and secure for workers a greater share of postwar prosperity.[24] Upon gaining more complete control of the UAW in 1947, the Reuther group purged communists and fellow travelers from positions of influence in the union bureaucracy and then set about attempting to tame centers of political dissent and uncontrolled militance within the union locals.

With its tradition of activism and its strong left-wing faction, Local 600 was a hotbed of anti-Reuther opposition forces and a site of resilient rank and file militance. In general, during the postwar years auto workers had begun to win improved wage and benefit packages, but management prerogative clauses in union contracts reinforced managerial control of the production process, and so working conditions did not improve along with remuneration. In an effort to recapture their status as second only to General Motors among American automakers, Ford management was instituting a speed-up in late 1948 in order to hurry their first really new car (the 1949 model B-A) into the postwar automobile market. While rank and file discontent simmered on the floors of the Rouge plant, Reuther and the UAW leadership were focused on their attempt to set a national pattern for the automobile industry by negotiating a pension plan with Ford.

The militant and anti-Reuther communist faction in Local 600 initiated a campaign urging rank and file job actions to combat the

154

speed-up. Although at first the local's leadership as well as the international union opposed the communists, the appeal for action resonated strongly with the rank and file. The local leadership responded to the militant spirit and the growing influence of the leftists by adopting the speed-up issue, the local voted overwhelmingly to strike, and the international UAW then sanctioned the strike. In May of 1949, the great River Rouge plant was shut down for twenty-four days. While appearing to support the rank and file, Reuther needed to bring the strike to a conclusion in order to pursue his national collective bargaining agenda because the strike raised especially thorny issues of shop-floor control (the very heart of capitalist common sense) which could derail negotiations over more readily attainable benefit packages, and because Ford was refusing to negotiate a new contract with the UAW while strikers had made idle the company's main plant.

Reuther agreed to a strike settlement which would not fundamentally challenge the company's unilateral setting of work standards, and then proceeded to negotiate a new longer-term contract with Ford which included the much-desired pension plan as well as improved medical insurance, but in which "[t]he Company retained its right to discipline for wildcat strikes and unauthorized work stoppages." John Bugas, Ford's Director of Industrial Relations, represented the agreement as the start of a new era: "... we believe that it opens the door on a long period of sustained labor peace and productivity." Reuther lauded the contract as "a historical step forward in labor's drive to destroy the double economic and moral standards in American industry."[25] Interpreting the contradictions of liberal capitalism largely in terms of economic inequality and related problems of underconsumption and unemployment, Reuther was able to envision their resolution through national-level collective bargaining, supported by "solidarity in the ranks." According to Reuther, "the basic problem of our free society consisted in finding a democratic means of ensuring an equilibrium between the faculty of creating new riches and the possibility of consuming them."[26] By constructing convergent visions of liberal capitalism characterized by labor–management cooperation (under the contractually sanctioned direction of management), growing productivity, and mass consumption based on high wages and generous benefits achieved through collective bargaining, Reuther's UAW and the Ford Motor Company had found common ground.

This vision was not universally accepted among the rank and file, and Local 600 in particular remained a site of contestation between Reutherism and more militant and radical unionist tendencies. Many militants and leftists were dissatisfied with Reuther's handling of the speed-up strike and the contract negotiations, and the left-center coalition within the local gained strength even as Carl Stellato – a pro-Reuther and anticommunist candidate who articulated a militant platform in order to win rank and file support – was elected to the local presidency in 1950. Within weeks of Stellato's election, the USA had entered the Korean War, and he sought to use an antcommunist brand of Americanism to destroy his factional opponents in Local 600.

Stellato initiated a vociferous anticommunist campaign within the local, including a policy endorsing US involvement in the Korean War and requiring loyalty oaths from all representatives of the local. He charged five local union officials with being communists and initiated quasi-legal proceedings to purge them. The local's newspaper, *Ford Facts*, was filled with violent and vitriolic denunciations of "Red Fascism," "Communist aggression," and communists in the union movement. *Ford Facts* printed the names of local military men "murdered by Stalin's Korean Storm-troopers," while Stellato himself accused union communists of complicity in the deaths of American troops in Korea: "Members of the Communist Party are nothing more or less than unpaid agents of a foreign power which at this very minute is destroying the lives of American boys." A series of "educational" articles in the local's newspaper told workers of the dictatorial nature of Soviet communism, depicted communists in the local as a disciplined and devious minority "interested not in the workers' problems but solely in the cause of international Stalinism," and related the anticommunist struggle in the local union to that in the industrial union movement, and the world as a whole. The paper approvingly reprinted a statement by the International Confederation of Free Trade Unions (ICFTU, on which see chapter 3) condemning the Korean invasion as "the latest move in a systematic plan for enlarging – by armed force if necessary – the totalitarian sphere of influence."[27]

Stellato and his supporters portrayed the fate of workers under communism as "slavery of a kind even more horrible than that which existed under Fordism," for communism was Fordism enforced by the power of a totalitarian state. During the unionization struggles of 1937–41, the unionists had consistently and successfully sought to identify Fordism with fascism, now communism was being equated with Fordism. The antidote to communism, they asserted, was the same as the antidote to Fordism – "free trade unions," which were said to be possible only under conditions of liberal capitalism:

> [U]nionism, as we experience it, can only exist in countries where all individuals have political liberty ... The Russian worker actually is a slave of the state through his controlled unions, with no voice whatsoever in the determination of his wages or working conditions ... The abuses of American capitalism are many and of long standing. But the mere fact that the citizens of the United States, a capitalist democracy, have freedom of speech and the freedom of assembly, as outlined in the constitution of the United States, enables us to organize unions and attempt to correct the abuses of the American capitalists.[28]

Liberal capitalism was preferable to communism insofar as it allowed "free trade unions" to petition capitalists for redress of grievances, and thus to control abuses. These abuses were not then construed as intrinsic to liberal capitalism, but were implied to be the product of idiosyncratic conditions and authoritarian employers, such as the elder Henry Ford. Communism, on the other hand, was inherently flawed and irredeemably opposed to the interests of Americans and workers.

In accordance with the emerging Cold War consensus, "Red Fascism" was used as a rhetorical device to equate Soviet communism with the fascist dictatorships against which the American public had so successfully been mobilized during World War II. This usage implied that fascism and communism were essentially alike in that both were premised upon the expansion of state power at the expense of individual rights and liberties, and that this was inimical to the interests of every American, regardless of social class. Further, both fascism and communism were represented as inherently underhanded, subversive, aggressive and expansionist, so that neither could safely be appeased and any attempt to compromise was a dangerous delusion. This imagery suggested that the necessary counterpart of a strong and vigilant foreign policy was a domestic politics in which anyone not vigorously hostile to totalitarianism was suspect. Any group advocating an expansion of the scope of state activity (even – or perhaps especially – measures as seemingly innocuous as the extension of New Deal reforms) could be portrayed as placing the country on a slippery slope at the base of which opened up the totalitarian abyss. At a national level, by reinforcing the individualist core of common sense Americanism and turning this powerful cultural force against dissidents, Cold War liberalism and the popular myth of "Red Fascism" served to isolate radicals, leftists and those moderate liberals who refused to denounce the former, to contain the movement to reform American capitalism, and to mobilize support for a globally active and militant foreign policy.[29] In 1950, Carl Stellato and his supporters attempted to use the same rhetorical strategy to impose a Reutherite conformity upon Local 600.

While this strategy had helped the Reuther forces to achieve predominance in the international union and to contain or undermine local centers of radical and militant unionism (as in the struggles between UAW Local 248 and Allis Chalmers in Milwaukee), Local 600 proved more resistant to this strain of anticommunist Americanism. Stellato encountered rank and file resistance to his attempted purges in 1950–51: elections for local union office increased the strength of his factional opponents and, in an apparent repudiation of his witch trials, the five accused "communists" were reelected to their union offices. Stellato himself was barely retained as local president. Having failed to consolidate the power of his Reutherite faction by appealing to the rank and file on anticommunist grounds, Stellato changed horses and became a vocal critic of Reuther and his leadership of the international UAW. Stellato reversed his earlier support for the 1950 UAW contract with Ford, which reflected the pattern established in the union's GM contract and included a cost of living escalator and an "annual improvement factor" (a pay raise linked to productivity increases). Representing himself as a champion of rank and file militance against both Ford and the UAW bureaucracy, Stellato criticized this latter provision as a union-sanctioned device to speed-up workers. Following hearings by the House Un-American Activities Committee (HUAC) charging communist infiltration of Local 600, and using the local's failure to convict the five alleged CP members as a pretext, the UAW placed the local under a temporary board of administration in 1952. Even so, Stellato was reelected when the administratorship ended and retained his post for many years.

Local 600 did not cannibalize its own left wing as so many other local unions did, and through the 1950s it was to be a continuing source of criticism of Reuther's leadership of the UAW. The union's leftist group had a strong local base among African-Americans and workers of Eastern European descent, but there may be other reasons why the local did not embrace an exclusionary Americanism centered on anti-communism. The local's culture of militant, democratic, and participatory unionism – developed through the hard-fought struggles in which a unionized Americanism was constructed in opposition to authoritarian Fordism – seems to have been able to tolerate radicals who proved themselves as dedicated grassroots unionists. And, within this militant and activist culture, it may be that the communists of Local 600 had been able to integrate their unionism and their radicalism in such a way that they were not generally perceived by the rank and file to be acting as agents of an alien ideology or functionaries of a foreign government, and were therefore less vulnerable to the strategies of isolation which were so central to Cold War liberalism. Indeed, in 1949 (the year of the speed-up strike) the Michigan CP hierarchy bemoaned the extent to which Party members and fellow travelers in Local 600 had become preoccupied with "trade union issues" at the expense of those ideological and organizational activities which the Party considered to be important for its own future.[30] The unionized Americanism of Local 600 was sufficiently inclusive to prevent the destruction of the local's left wing, and it seems to have incorporated communists and fellow travelers in ways which reinforced its identity as a militant, democratic union; but its formative concept of individual rights and liberties as the foundation of industrial democracy may well have precluded the embrace of a Marxian revolutionary vision as the core of a counter-hegemonic culture in the local. The struggle against Fordism had produced a democratic culture of unionism, but it remained a *liberal* democratic vision, and therefore did not pose an explicit and coherent challenge to the basic structures of capitalism.

Even if it did not develop a revolutionary program, the culture of unionized Americanism prevalent within the local retained its militant, democratic edge through the darkest years of the Cold War red scare, and might then have implicitly challenged the right of capital to control the production process. Yet, the potential militance of the local was largely contained by the national structure of collective bargaining in the USA and the corresponding disempowerment of such rank and file representatives as shop stewards and committeemen; and the local's political culture was reduced to an island of heterogeneity in the midst of the rising Cold War consensus during the Korean War. Despite the failure of anticommunism to homogenize and pacify it, Local 600 ultimately was unable to challenge Reutherism for control of the UAW, to challenge Ford Motor Company for control of the factory floor, or to create an alternative social vision which might challenge the hegemony of liberal capitalism in the core of the world economy.[31]

A hegemonic vision of liberal capitalism: prosperity and anticommunism at home and abroad

With the destruction or containment of the radical left wing of the union movement, Reuther's vision of liberal capitalism became the predominant framework within the UAW and defined the horizons of the "legitimate" left in the postwar American political economy. Reuther's world view envisioned liberal capitalism as a bastion of individual liberty and an engine of economic growth which, when corporate power was properly counterbalanced by unionism and collective bargaining, could raise the standard of living of the great majority of people in America and, indeed, the world. Reuther believed that liberal capitalism was doubly challenged in the Cold War era, from both the right and the left. At home, right-wing reaction and economic inequality threatened to contain unionism and perpetuate disastrous tendencies toward underconsumption, unemployment and economic insecurity. In the world at large, widespread poverty and hopelessness created an environment in which the "propaganda promises and systematic confusion" spread about by deceptive communists could win for them massive popular support which they could not otherwise attain. Here Reuther seems to have presumed that liberal capitalism, with its central provision for individual rights and liberties, was better suited to an essential human nature and would exert greater natural appeal for the peoples of the world than communism, if only it could demonstrate that "bread and freedom can live together in the same house."[32]

In an ambitious 100–year plan which he presented to President Truman and which was represented to workers in union newspapers such as *Ford Facts*, Reuther laid out his vision of how Americans should respond to these challenges at home and abroad. Explicitly accepting as his own starting point the premise of a global contest between "democracy" and an aggressive, oppressive "Communism," he declared: "We must meet the challenge of Communism, not by pious slogans about democracy's virtues, but by a positive program of social action that can and does win a fuller measure of economic and social justice for people everywhere." "Democratic unionism" was to be a central weapon with which to win the Cold War for liberal capitalism. To realize his vision of global peace and prosperity, Reuther proposed the creation of an internationally administered development fund through which large amounts of US aid – made available by a high-output, full-employment economy at home – might be channeled into the creation of positive examples of the material advantages of liberal capitalism, contrasting starkly with the negative example of Soviet militarism. "Instead of driving their bodies in speeded up production for the Soviet war machine, we propose to assist them [those peoples under, or putatively threatened by, communist domination] in achieving decent wages, hours, working conditions and the right to collective bargaining ..." Reuther believed his liberal capitalist vision held a universal appeal: "This is an offer understandable in any language because it talks in terms of tools, food, housing, health, education, security and freedom." He depicted a future in which the cooperative task of building a productive, prosperous, and "free" world would supplant international conflict, and eliminate the need for military machines and production for war. In producing and distributing the products of this global economic machine – generalizing the fruits of prosperity and securing the political stability of liberal capitalism – unions would play a central part both at home and abroad.[33]

Reuther's image of American liberal capitalism as a model for the world is remarkably similar to the ideological representations of Ford Motor Company during the Korean War, when it began once again to convey explicitly political messages to its workers through shop papers like *Ford Rouge News*. Ford too began from the premise of a global competition between two antithetical ways of life, one of which held the promise of unlimited prosperity and individual freedom:

> Right now the peoples of many nations are faced with a choice between Communism and Democracy – a choice between life and death. And they are looking to us for help and leadership.
>
> They are looking at the promise of individual reward that has stimulated American invention and business enterprise; at American technical progress which has performed miracles of mass production; at *American workers free to organize, to bargain collectively with their employers*, to choose their jobs and to change them at will, with no ceiling on advancement, and constantly increasing real wages for shorter working hours.[34]

And, like Reuther, Ford asserted that although American liberal capitalism might require minor adjustments here and there, it was the system of social organization best able to preserve individual freedoms and advance individual welfare. "Sure, our system has its faults," Ford admitted. "... But the truth is that the average American makes more, has more, and enjoys more than any other citizen under any other system in the world. And above all this he has a freedom of choice throughout his life that is possible only under our American system."[35] Presuming that liberal values were (or ought to be) universal, Ford concluded that American liberal capitalism was the one best system upon which other peoples should model their own societies.

By the time of the Korean War, what had been one of the most authoritarian and violently anti-labor corporations in America, and one of the most militant industrial unions, had constructed convergent visions of a neoliberal world order. Reuther's UAW and Ford Motor Company had come together on an ideological common ground which accepted unionism as a potentially stabilizing aspect of liberal capitalism, which proclaimed the goal of liberal capitalism to be social peace and a more generalized prosperity, and which envisioned the ends and means of American liberal capitalism to be universally relevant and desirable. Through four decades of struggle, the common sense of industrial capitalists at Ford had been reconstructed in such a way that institutionalized labor unions and collective bargaining were no longer unthinkable. Instead, unions were to be faced as a fact of life and forward-thinking employers like Henry Ford II believed that they could be useful in securing the consent of most workers to shop-floor relations of authority, and containing any residual militance and dissent.

For their part, the common sense of mainstream unionists was reconstructed such that the central ambiguities of liberal capitalism were apparently resolved in its favor. The potential challenge to capitalism posed by ideologies of industrial democracy – which addressed an unfulfilled promise of liberal capitalism, and demanded that employees should enjoy in some measure the participatory rights of the citizen rather than being reduced to the status of an appendage to private property – was contained within a vision of that democracy as formal representation by union officers, rather than as the collective practice of rank and file activism. This vision was encapsulated in a 1950 *Ford Facts* cartoon: the caption reads "Quiet Please ... UNION-ISM at work"; beneath is an image of a unionist alone in a voting booth (figure 7.4). His hat off, he is carefully, respectfully, registering his individual preferences on a sheet of paper labeled "your ballot." Thus

Figure 7.4 "Quiet please, unionism at work"
A cartoon published in the UAW's newspaper, *Ford Facts* (April, 1950),
represented unionism in terms of liberal democracy and its individual,
electoral mode of participation. From the Archives of Labor and Urban
Affairs, Wayne State University.

the *Ford Facts* reader was invited to identify with this lone unionist and his electoral mode of participation.[36] Liberal democracy, a political expression of capitalism (see chapter 2), was represented as the model for industrial democracy. Individual rights were to be formally safe-guarded through representative democracy in the union and through institutionalized collective bargaining which would establish a frame-work of rules and regulations to govern work life. This "workplace rule of law," in David Brody's apt phrase, would constrain the arbi-trary (that is, in this context, extra-contractual or individually inequita-ble) exercise of power by the employer; it would in principle apply equally to each worker; and each might be said to have consented by virtue of his or her participation in union elections. This regime would also sanction more coercive measures by the union, the company or the state, against those who acted outside of the established frame-work of industrial law and order.

Through comparison with fascism and Stalinism, liberal capitalism was represented to industrial unionists as the best possible social system. Its abuses were attributed to idiosyncratic conditions or authoritarian employers such as the first Henry Ford. Once these abuses had been corrected by protective legislation and "industrial democracy," liberal capitalism appeared to recognize and safeguard the rights of workers, and seemed to promise freedom, peace and prosperity for the masses of Americans, and the world as a whole.

Since the introduction of moving line assembly and true mass production in 1913–14, the common sense of industrial workers at Ford had been a terrain of struggle, first between the company and unor-ganized workers, and later involving the United Automobile Workers. Before World War I, Ford had begun attempting to "Americanize" its largely immigrant workforce as part of a systematic campaign to foster an industrial culture based upon abstract individualism. At the heart of Ford's Americanism was a vision of the wage relation as a contractual arrangement between an individual worker and his employer, volun-tarily entered into for mutual benefit. This, in turn, implied that workers should accept a responsibility to managerial authority, and a work ethic, in the interest of their own economic self-betterment. Ford's ideological campaign was a two-edged sword: Ford workers appear to have internalized the cultural norms of abstract individual-ism to the extent that they became increasingly effective practitioners of market rationality and accumulators of property, but also drew upon the political language of individual rights and liberties to frame protests against Ford's labor policies of intrusive paternalism. In further attempts to secure the consent of its workforce, Ford used a liberal vocabulary during World War I and the ensuing red scare to identify as loyal Americans those workers most closely identifying their own interests with those of the company, and to stigmatize as "enemies" those who resisted the authority of Ford and the power of capital. Owing to inflation, intensified competitive pressures, and renewed restiveness among auto workers after the war, Ford began to rely more heavily upon a coercive workplace regime and explicit ideological appeals to workers largely fell by the wayside until the rise of the UAW–CIO.

In the late 1930s, as the United Automobile Workers struggled to unionize Ford, the ideological theme of "Americanism vs. Fordism" was central to the union's appeal to Ford workers. Highlighting a central contradiction of liberal capitalism, Fordism was portrayed as a tyrannical regime in which the power and privilege of one wealthy man enabled him to violate the rights of his workers. Unionism – explicitly counterposed to Fordism as an alternative organizing principle – implied the construction of "industrial democracy" in which the rights of workers would be protected and they would be afforded some measure of participation in their working lives. Constructing their self-understanding in terms of unionized Americanism, the unionists simultaneously facilitated and constrained the collective project of organized labor.

By speaking to workers in terms of their own liberal common sense, the UAW was able to counter employers' anti-union propaganda and to identify itself with the aspirations of broad segments of the industrial working class. The unionists equated Ford's harsh open shop regime with "un-American" values, and articulated their own vision of an "American way of life" in which values such as self-determination and equality were extended into the workplace, and in which workers were enabled to secure an "American standard of living" for themselves and their families. The unresolved ambiguities of "Americanism" and "industrial democracy" allowed the union to embrace workers at every position along an ideological spectrum ranging from communists and Trotskyites to Catholic corporatists, and to confront their employer with a unified movement effectively demanding industrial reforms. Subsequently, as the Cold War unfolded, the scope of these ambiguities was narrowed such that radical leftists and their liberal sympathizers were excluded from the ambit of legitimate

Americanism, and alternative visions of industrial democracy which entailed potentially explicit challenges to the social power of capital were marginalized. Promising mass prosperity and a "democratic" alternative to totalitarianism, liberal capitalism – modified to accommodate collective bargaining and a more activist state – constituted the consensual basis of the mass industrial society of the postwar era. It was on the basis of such an ideological framework – with an ontology of abstract individualism residing at its center – that industrial labor could reach an accommodation with corporate capital in America, and both could work together to reconstruct the core of the world economy along liberal capitalist lines.

8   Fordism and neoliberal hegemony: tensions and possibilities

Labor as a junior partner: Fordism and neoliberal hegemony

Between the era of the Great Depression and the early years of the Cold War, a great insurgency had broken out in the manufacturing heart of the American economy. Demands that liberal capitalism fulfill its promises of equality and democracy fueled unrest which was eventually ameliorated in large part through the institutionalization of "industrial democracy," administered by hierarchic, bureaucratic and contractually oriented industrial unions. The mutual accommodation of Ford Motor Company and the UAW resembled similar processes across the industrial core of the American economy.

Rank and file union memberships were disempowered by union bureaucracies and the "workplace rule of law," a union-endorsed regime of procedural rules which legitimated and enforced control of the production process by corporate capitalists even as it defined the "rights" of workers. This formal, legalistic regime – premised upon an ontology of abstract individualism – served to reproduce workers' identities as private individuals endowed with certain rights and responsibilities, rather than as members of a subordinate class engaged in ongoing collective struggle against the power of capital in the workplace and against the privileging of private property entailed in liberalism's core conception of social reality. Under the hegemony of the contract, potential militancy of the rank and file was contained and channeled, subordinated to a collective bargaining process in which the primary stakes were economic: how much more would corporations deign to share with their workers? Radical unions and unionists – who might have been able to articulate alternatives to the emerging

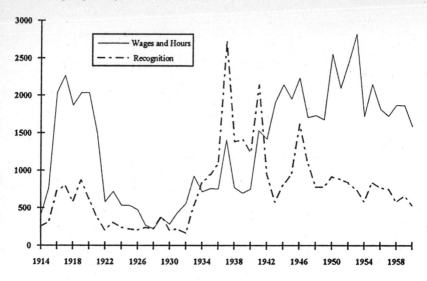

Figure 8.1   Strike frequency by major issue, 1914–60: wages and hours vs. union recognition

Source: US Bureau of the Census, *Historical Statistics of the United States*, series D-978 and D-979, p. 179.

system of industrial relations – were isolated, silenced or destroyed as the Americanism of "free trade unions" triumphed over putative totalitarianisms of left and right.

Class struggle did not cease, but as unions became institutionalized as collective bargaining agents, the character and meaning of industrial conflict changed. In order to secure recognition from corporate capitalists and to make possible any kind of industrial democracy at all, industrial unions had been forced during the 1930s to exercise their mass-based power in potentially violent and politically charged confrontations which to one degree or another, explicitly or implicitly, called into question capitalist control of the production process. Figure 8.1 suggests that by the late 1940s strikes were themselves becoming institutionalized as a more or less routine part of the bargaining process over "bread and butter" issues. After the great industrial uprising which gave birth to the CIO and compelled its recognition by major corporate employers, a declining number of strikes centered on issues of union recognition and an increasing number involved more narrowly economic bargaining over wages and hours.

168

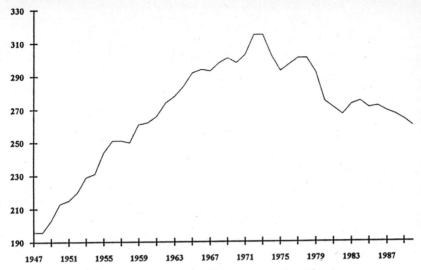

Figure 8.2   Real average weekly earnings of production or
nonsupervisory workers, 1947–90 (in 1982 dollars)
Source: Council of Economic advisers, *Economic Report of the President, 1991,*
tabled B-44, p. 336.

During the period when industrial unions were being institutionalized, workers in the industrial core of the US economy were able to
attain substantially improved standards of living: by one measure (real
average weekly earnings, approximating gross take-home pay more
closely than hourly wages), real wages in manufacturing rose about 60
percent between 1929 and 1951. During the fifteen years after that –
often identified as the postwar golden era – they continued to rise so
that real average weekly earnings in manufacturing had increased 125
percent between 1929 and 1966.[1] Overall in the non-farm US economy,
as figure 8.2 illustrates, real average weekly earnings of production or
nonsupervisory workers climbed steadily through the postwar years
and into the early 1970s (when this long-run tendency was reversed).
This long-term increase in real wages provided the necessary (if not
sufficient) material basis for a recasting of the industrial worker's social
identity from insurgent employee engaged in collective action with
fellow workers, to newly affluent consumer expressing individual
tastes and preferences in the market. The fabulous "American standard
of living" which had eluded industrial workers in the 1920s was at last
becoming a reality for some – if by no means all – working-class families.[2]

169

Such tendencies are evident in the case of Ford workers. During the early postwar years when the UAW was agreeing to "company security" provisions in its contract with Ford Motor Company, and was recognizing the company's authority to set and enforce work rules and production standards, a funny thing was happening in the back pages of *Ford Facts*, the union newspaper which Local 600 distributed to its 60,000 members at the great River Rouge plant. Expensive items like televisions, ranges and home appliances, furniture, jewelry, often available on "easy" credit terms; services like automotive repair, even florists and catering: advertisements for products and services such as these signaled that by 1949 local businesses were envisioning Ford workers as consumers, and that the union was prepared to represent this vision to the workers themselves. The official organ of one of the most militant and politically heterogeneous union locals in the UAW was serving as a vehicle for the culture of mass consumerism.[3]

At the national level, a rising real wage attained through productivity bargaining was being established as the norm in the corporate industrial sector of the economy. In 1950, *Fortune* heralded the "Treaty of Detroit," the unprecedented five-year contract between General Motors and the UAW which set the pattern for the automobile industry and indeed the industrial core in the USA. Ratifying and extending postwar collective bargaining innovations, the landmark long-term agreement provided the union with a cost of living escalator and an "annual improvement factor" – a pay raise linked to aggregate productivity growth – which together almost guaranteed progressively higher real wages for GM workers. For its part, General Motors "regained control over one of the crucial management functions in any line of manufacturing – long-range scheduling of production, model changes, and tool and plant investment." Further, by linking wage increases to productivity gains, the contract represented the union's consent to what *Fortune* called an "all important axiom of American progress": that prosperity depends upon productivity, and that this in turn depends upon capital accumulation and "a cooperative attitude" on the factory floor and across the bargaining table. So significant did *Fortune* deem this establishment of explicit common ground between a major corporate employer and a great industrial union, that they quoted directly the relevant text of the contract:

> The annual improvement factor provided herein ... recognizes that a continuing improvement in the standard of living of employees depends upon technological progress, better tools, methods, pro-

cesses, and equipment, and a cooperative attitude on the part of all parties in such progress. It further recognizes the principle that to produce more with the same amount of human effort is a sound economic and social objective.

Fortune concluded that although the contract buying five years of labor peace might cost GM as much as a billion dollars, "It got a bargain."[4]

While neither man understood the potential of unionism for securing the consent of industrial workers, both Frederick Winslow Taylor and Henry Ford would have recognized and approved of the "all important axiom of American progress." With the significant exception of having been compelled to recognize and bargain with industrial unions, industrial peace had been achieved largely on the terms initially set out by capital. Capital accumulation, management control of the production process, and increasing productivity and profits, were consensually established as preconditions for the granting of rising real wages. It was on these terms that industrial labor and its unions were (grudgingly) accepted into the neoliberal historic bloc as junior partners. Reflecting the terms of this accommodation, real wages did indeed increase during the height of the postwar golden era, but not as rapidly as did productivity: between 1951 and 1966, real average hourly earnings in manufacturing increased about 39 percent, while output per worker-hour grew by 65 percent and real value-added per worker-hour grew by nearly 52 percent.[5]

In his seminal work on "Fordism" as a structural form of capitalism, Michel Aglietta constructed an index of "real social wage cost" – the ratio of real hourly wages to value added per worker-hour. He argued that, in general, this measure varies inversely with the rate of surplus value, a Marxian category indexing the socially prevailing degree of labor exploitation. He then demonstrated that as productivity (in value-added terms) outpaced rising real wages in the USA between 1947 and 1966, this index fell steadily – suggesting a corresponding increase in the rate of surplus value. Aglietta interpreted this as central to the golden era of what he called the "regime of intensive accumulation." The increasing rate of exploitation countered (for a time) the tendency for the rate of profit to fall as capital accumulation revolutionized the social "forces of production" and progressively reduced the proportion of exploitable living labor involved in the production process. Further offsetting this basic crisis tendency of capitalism was the cheapening of both wage goods and means of production which resulted from increasing productivity. At the same time, growing

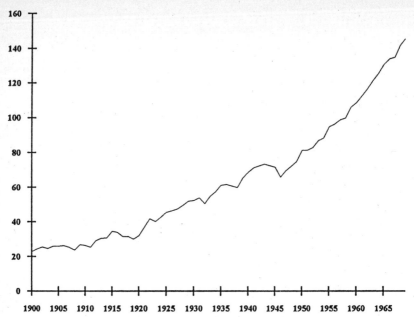

Figure 8.3   Index of output per worker-hour in manufacturing, 1900–69 (in 1958 dollars)

Source: US Bureau of the Census, *Historical Statistics of the United States*, series D-685, p. 162.

productivity and the cheapening of wage goods meant that the real standard of living of the industrial working class could improve markedly even as exploitation intensified. Increasing levels of social consumption in turn promoted a rough balance between the producer goods and consumer goods sectors, thereby avoiding crises of disproportionality such as those which – before to the full development of the regime of intensive accumulation – would violently arrest the accumulation process: in Aglietta's view, it was just such a crisis which generated the basic preconditions of the Great Depression. The golden age of Fordism was supported by an industrial regime which entailed what Mike Davis calls the "socialization of the wage relation": in core sectors of the economy, highly variable individual wage contracts were supplanted by systematized collective bargaining; real wages were stabilized by limiting the extent of mutually undercutting wage competition and by contractually linking wage gains to the rate of increase in social productivity; and a (bare bones) safety net of welfare and social security was instituted.[6]

172

Fordism and the neoliberal world order were integrally related. Under the regime of intensive accumulation in the USA, unionized industrial workers in the postwar era enjoyed unprecedented prosperity (see figure 8.2) and contributed to rapidly increasing productivity (figure 8.3), providing a model for the emulation of other core capitalisms; while internationally the leaderships of mainstream unions participated in the historic bloc which would reconstruct liberal capitalism in the core of the world economy, and seek to fortify the periphery against radical insurgencies. In the postwar decade, through official and unofficial channels, both AFL and CIO had been active in the construction of non-communist, productivity-oriented labor movements in Europe (see chapter 3). American imperial foreign policy at first seemed directly to benefit organized labor: in addition to creating the non-communist world of peace and prosperity in which "free trade unions" were thought to flourish, the great infusions of military spending which supported the global strategy of militarized containment – especially in the Korean War period – accelerated the postwar economic boom and boosted industrial employment and union membership at home. The relationship between neoliberal world order and American unionism appeared, then, to be a symbiotic one. Formally unified in 1955, the AFL–CIO undertook a global mission as part of its founding statement of purpose. The union federation's constitution included a commitment "to give constructive aid in promoting peace and freedom in the world and to aid, assist and cooperate with free and democratic labor movements throughout the world." Further, it explicitly framed this commitment in a Cold War context of global struggle, in which free labor movements at home and abroad faced "the undermining efforts of Communist agencies ... opposed to the basic principles of our democracy and free and democratic unionism." In the official foreign policy ideology of the AFL–CIO, "free" trade unions have been understood as those "independent of state control," that is, labor organizations consisting of autonomous individuals exercising their right to voluntary association in civil society – a fundamentally liberal vision. In addition to serving as a bulwark against communist totalitarianism, the AFL–CIO has envisioned such "free" trade unions as crucial to a global neoliberal order of more widely generalized prosperity and economic growth. In the words of a more recent expression of this ideology: "In the developing world, free unions provide the underpinning for economic growth *and* democracy by contributing to the emergence of a

173

stable, fairly paid, working middle-class." In keeping with these ideological commitments, and in close cooperation with various agencies of the US goverment, the AFL–CIO and its Department of International Affairs (DIA) launched major international programs to support "free" trade unions around the world.[7]

In 1962 the AFL–CIO created the American Institute for Free Labor Development (AIFLD) to sponsor training and support programs for anticommunist unionists throughout Latin America. AIFLD was heavily subsidized by US government funds (from the Agency for International Development) and major American corporations operating in Latin America, the latter actually being represented on its board of directors until 1981. Peter Grace, corporate capitalist and AIFLD board member, represented in the following familiar terms his vision of the organization's purpose: "AIFLD urges cooperation between labor and management and an end to class struggle. It teaches workers to help increase their company's business and to improve productivity so that they gain more from expanding business." As it propagated American-style productivist ideology, AIFLD established a sordid record of support for forces of reaction in a number of Latin American countries, and has been linked to the CIA by former agent Philip Agee, among others. The AFL–CIO formally condemned colonialism of the traditional variety, but in his memoir Victor Reuther of the CIO characterized AIFLD as "an exercise in trade union colonialism, paradoxical as those words may seem." The AFL–CIO was actively propagating paradox in other regions of the world through its African-American Labor Center (AALC, founded in 1964), and the Asian-American Free Labor Institute (AAFLI, 1968) operating in Vietnam, the Philippines, and elsewhere. Victor Reuther's apparent paradox resulted from the construction of the neoliberal historic bloc: the union movement, putatively a countervailing force against the abuse of corporate social power, had been incorporated into the very social formation which sustained and expressed that power on a global scale.[8]

The violent demise of neoliberalism and possibilities for radical renewal

Erected upon a social foundation of manifold contradictions (see chapter 2), the neoliberal world order was subject to stresses and strains at every level, and began to unravel after only two decades. In the late 1960s and early 1970s, as Fordism's remarkable productivity growth began to stall, stagflation set in and conditions of profitability deteriorated across the core of the world economy, tensions within the capitalist class and between capital and labor began to reassert themselves. By the 1980s, major fractures in the neoliberal consensus turned into a largely one-sided renewal of class warfare. Under cover of jingoistic and militantly liberal ideology, right-wing governments in Britain and America dismantled or disabled major parts of the state regulatory and welfare apparatus, imposed higher levels of unemployment in order to control inflation and discipline the working class, and redistributed income upward. The decline of neoliberalism in America has involved the besieging of labor unions by the state and capital, and the virtual expulsion from the predominant historic bloc of that segment of the American working class which had been economically privileged under the neoliberal regime. As the formerly privileged stratum of the working class begins to experience directly the powerlessness, fear and misery which have long afflicted those subaltern groups – in both core and periphery – who were marginalized in the neoliberal order, some kind of collective counter-hegemonic project may become conceivable. Whether this potential is realized will depend in part upon the inclusiveness of the self-understandings which these groups construct. Reflecting the historical ambiguities of their common sense, the "Americanism" of the US working class could either facilitate or hinder such a transnational political project.

Degeneration of Fordism and the neoliberal world order

By the late 1960s and early 1970s, the signs of degeneration were everywhere. At the same time as the USA was losing the war in Vietnam and undergoing upheaval and reform at home, the postwar global economic order was under great stress. The neoliberal order had an inbuilt tendency toward inflation. In large part because the Fordist aspect of the neoliberal regime served to cushion core labor from the full effects of economic downturns and thus helped sustain wage levels during the postwar boom period, and also encouraged oligopolistic corporate capital to grant wage–benefit increases which could be passed on to consumers in the form of price hikes, inflationary pressures were building in the capitalist world. Further, America was effectively exempted from immediate imperatives of balancing international accounts owing to the role of the dollar as world currency under the Bretton Woods regime, and America's war in Vietnam contributed mightily to a rising flood of dollars in the world economy. The increasingly overvalued US dollar undermined confidence in the dollar-centered Bretton Woods regime, led to a drawing down of American gold reserves and contributed to a deteriorating US trade balance. By unilaterally ending the gold-convertibility of the dollar which had been at the heart of the Bretton Woods regime, and imposing an import surcharge, Richard Nixon signaled in 1971 that the positive-sum era of international cooperation and generalized prosperity in the core was coming to a close. Mutual alienation among political communities began to reassert itself as mercantilistic policies of national capitalism challenged the hegemony of an internationally oriented neoliberalism in the core.[9]

The ability of American corporate capital to earn surplus profits in the world economy has been increasingly eroded by resurgent inter-capitalist competition at the global level. Since the late nineteenth century, American manufacturing industry had led the world in productivity, output and exports, especially of those products (such as automobiles) associated with the new mass production economy (see chapter 4). Alone at the apex of the global division of labor, for half a century American manufacturing industry defined standards of efficiency to which other industrial states–societies could aspire. In the decades after World War II, the consolidation of neoliberal hegemony in the core of the world economy, along with Marshall aid and massive flows of direct foreign investment from the USA, led to the generalization of Fordist production methods and consumption norms throughout the core. The upper tiers of the global division of labor became significantly less hierarchic, occupied now by several industrial states–societies producing relatively similar mixes of products, and exporting them to one another. Whereas in 1935, before to the establishment of the neoliberal world order, less than 30 percent of world exports of manufactures took place among the developed market economies themselves, by 1970 that figure had risen to more than 74 percent.[10] The result of these tendencies was a growing excess capacity in industries such as automobiles, steel, textiles and others, and an intensification of global competition among producing firms.

For US-based producers, this global surplus capacity was experienced as a loss of foreign markets and an increasing penetration of the US market by imported products. Between 1957 and 1977, the USA (as a territorial entity excluding foreign operations of US-based MNCs) lost more than one-third of its share of world manufactured exports, which declined from around 21 percent to about 13 percent of the world total. Import competition in the US home market also began to intensify during the 1960s when "imports rose from 4 percent to 17 percent of the US market in autos, from 4 percent to 31 percent in consumer electronics, from 5 percent to 36 percent in calculating and adding machines, and from less than 1 percent to 5 percent in electrical components." This tendency became especially acute during the 1970s and 1980s, with imports beginning to approach half the value of American manufacturing output by 1986.[11]

Among the implications of these changes, US-based corporate capitalists would have perceived a threat to the security of their oligopolistic home markets. Viewed in terms of the conventional economic calculus with which corporate capitalists apprehend their world, it would seem that operating Fordist manufacturing plants at levels well below capacity could only reduce productivity and increase unit costs. "And to make matters worse," Harrison and Bluestone suggest, "while foreign competition raised unit costs, it simultaneously made it more difficult for firms in any one country to pass these higher costs on to their own citizens in the form of inflated prices."[12] On top of all that, the success of the Organization of Petroleum Exporting Countries (OPEC) in regulating the supply and price of oil on world markets in the mid-to-late 1970s led to a dramatic rise in the costs of a crucial economic input. As a result of a flattening of the global division of labor and the appearance of excess capacity in the industrial core of the world economy, combined with resistance in the periphery and increasing costs of imported raw materials such as oil, the global environment faced by American-based corporations was considerably more challenging than the immediate postwar environment had been, and this challenge increasingly menaced the formerly secure home-market position of these firms.

In the USA, the unionized industrial regime of the neoliberal order was also showing strains during this period. By the late 1960s a long period of economic expansion had reduced disciplinary effects of the threat of unemployment just as management was pushing hard to meet growing output goals, working conditions were deteriorating and accident rates were rising. At the same time, the industrial work-force was infused with a younger cohort of workers whose work culture was not shaped by the mythology – more prevalent among older workers – of the Depression and the struggles of the industrial union movement. There was a dramatic increase in strike activity during these years, especially officially unauthorized "wildcat" strikes involving militant movements of rank and file workers rebelling against Fordist industrial discipline and the extreme routinization of work, and willing to challenge business-oriented union leaderships as well as their employers. While the outbreak of rank and file rebellion largely abated after the sharp recession of 1974–75, it signaled that the neoliberal order had not permanently overcome class struggle, that the consent of the working class could not be guaranteed by industrial unions, and that conditions which underlay the golden era might not last for ever.[13]

By the late 1960s, Michel Aglietta argues, the engine of intensive accumulation was stalling. The growth of social productivity decelerated markedly after 1966: the Fordist labor process, based upon the extraction of ever greater quantities of surplus value through the intensification of labor, was reaching its limits. The approach of these limits was signaled by the wave of wildcat strikes and shop-floor rebellions of the late 1960s. Further indicative of a turning point in the Fordist regime, Aglietta's index of "real social wage costs" ceased its steady postwar decline, which he interprets as suggesting that the intensity of labor exploitation (the rate of surplus value) had ceased to grow. Barring the continued growth of relative surplus value – which had allowed workers' standards of living to increase even as exploitation intensified – real wages could not continue to grow at their former pace and began also to decelerate under the pressure of a new capitalist "frontal assault." Fordism's mass consumption capacity was thus eroding. Further, the booming accumulation process of the postwar years – which for a time had reflected a rough balance between the capital goods and wage goods sectors – compelled capitalists to seek continually to revolutionize the social "forces of production" and thus generated tendencies toward uneven development. The Fordist virtuous cycle of mutual reinforcement between expansion of the capital goods sector and the growth of the wage goods sector became increasingly problematic. As Fordism approached its limits, the danger of disproportionality and capitalist crisis began to reassert itself: the degenerating regime of intensive accumulation became less able to offset the basic crisis tendencies of capitalism through steadily intensified exploitation, increasing productivity and mass consumption of mass produced commodities.[14]

The evidence in table 8.1 supports an historical interpretation which suggests that Fordism was alive and well in the two postwar decades,

Table 8.1 *Growth of real wages and productivity: average annual rates of change during postwar economic phases* (percent)*

| phase | All non-farm business | | Manufacturing | |
	productivity	wages	productivity	wages
1948–66	2.51	2.38	2.97	2.28
1966–73	1.53	1.60	2.49	1.34
1973–79	0.66	−0.59	1.97	0.17
1979–89	0.96**	−0.85	3.04**	−1.01

Note: Calculations based on constant (1982) dollars. * 1948–66 subsumes four business cycles into a single "postwar boom" phase. ** Average rate for 1979–88.
Sources: Average hourly earnings of production and non-supervisory workers from *Economic Report of the President, 1991*, table B-44, p. 336; and Consumer Price Index from table B-58, p. 351. Output per hour from *Handbook of Labor Statistics, 1989*, table 98, p. 348.

but thereafter became progressively enfeebled until, in the 1980s, it was mortally wounded in a violent assault. During the postwar golden era (1948–66) real output per hour in manufacturing, and in the non-farm business sector more generally, was rising rapidly; real hourly wages of production workers were increasing too, albeit at a somewhat less rapid rate. The growth of productivity and wages, more or less in tandem, enabled the linkage of mass production and mass consumption – the central economic relationship of postwar Fordism. After 1966, productivity growth dropped off markedly in the non-farm business sector and, to a lesser degree, declined in manufacturing as well. The brakes were applied to the growth of real wages, which during 1966–73 grew at roughly two-thirds of their former rate. While in the non-farm business sector this wage deceleration became a downward spiral in the 1970s, real wages simply stagnated in the manufacturing sector, where neoliberal industrial unionism was relatively stronger and the continuing decline of productivity was not quite as drastic. During the corporate and governmental anti-labor offensive of the 1980s the deterioration of productivity was apparently halted – with a dramatic turnaround in manufacturing – but real wages were now in free fall, showing a negative rate of growth even in the reinvigorated manufacturing sector. By the 1980s, even in the old Fordist industrial core, workers were being compelled to work much harder for a shrinking paycheck. That productivity and wages were no longer rising in tandem, and indeed by the 1980s were moving in opposite directions, signals the passing of Fordism and its social consumption norms: it suggests that wage workers were no longer being viewed as potential consumers but rather primarily as economic inputs whose cost – in an increasingly competitive world economy – was to be ruthlessly suppressed.

Capitalist restructuring and neoconservative political economy

Corporate capital and the state responded to the pressures of "the Fordist climacteric" and a declining rate of profit with deliberate strategies aimed at reducing or breaking even the limited power which organized labor had achieved within the neoliberal order.[15] Together, corporate restructuring and right-wing state policy have attempted to restore corporate profitability by directly and indirectly attacking the standard of living which many working people had been able to attain within the neoliberal regime.

From the early years of the neoliberal order, corporate capital had exhibited tendencies toward decentralization and internationalization of production, tendencies which eroded the ability of unionized workers to shut down operations or damage corporate profitability by withholding their labor within any particular node in the organization of production.[16] Thus the bargaining power of organized labor was diminished and – as the organization of production expanded to encompass a wider variety of locations and a greater variability of local conditions (including less-unionized workforces in the right to work states of the southern and western USA, and the developing world) – the unions' task of establishing or sustaining large-scale pattern bargaining within particular industries became very much more difficult. Further, since the late 1960s when the Fordist regime of mass production and mass consumption began to unravel and the profitability of productive investment declined, corporate capital has responded by auotomating production or seeking out lower-wage sites for more labor-intensive manufacturing operations, diversifying its organization through mergers and acquisitions, becoming increasingly bound up in financial and speculative forms of investment, and changing the organization of work, all in order to improve corporate profit margins by increasing the "flexibility" of firms.[17]

As part of this process of restructuring, the characteristic labor process associated with Fordism has in a number of industrial settings undergone mutation and change, to the point that some scholars now argue (controversially) that a qualitatively new organization of production is emerging. Variously described in terms of "flexible specialization," "post-Fordism" or "lean production," the new industrial paradigm (if such it is) is said to have left behind Fordism's single-minded emphasis upon economies of scale achieved with dedicated machines and highly detailed labor working over huge production runs of a standardized product. Rather, flexible manufacturing is said to offer unprecedented "economies of scope" in which a range of customized products may be efficiently produced in relatively smaller batches. This transition is made possible by changes in the social organization of the production process and by new computer-controlled manufacturing technologies. Numerically controlled machine tools and flexible manufacturing systems – integrated constellations of machines and materials-handling systems, coordinated by computer – hold the potential to allow producers quickly and easily to modify particular products and to produce a variety of different items with the same equipment, thus tailoring their products more closely to the desires of their customers and adjusting rapidly to changes in their product markets. In its Japanese avatar, this system involves the manufacturer in closer relationships with both suppliers and customers so that the needs and wishes of the latter may be promptly incorporated into product design and manufacture, a process in which the former is expected to play an active and ongoing role.[18]

Achieving this goal of flexibility is also said to require a more versatile and adaptable workforce, able to perform a range of tasks and to participate creatively in the restructuring and debugging of the continually changing production process. This, in turn, entails changes in industrial relations: in particular, the redefinition or dissolution of the wage formulas, work rules and relatively narrow job categories which have been institutionalized in American collective bargaining practices, and the institution of various sorts of employee participation or teamwork schemes with which to establish and sustain among workers an identification with the firm or the plant and a commitment to strive toward continual improvements in productivity and quality. Proponents claim that this reorganization of work implies that workers are no longer reduced to the status of Taylorist automatons, mindlessly repeating simple mechanical operations designed and closely supervised by management. Instead, in a workplace culture of "reciprocal obligation," workers are enabled to learn and exercise a variety of skills, and to bring their judgment and expertise to bear on the collective resolution of problems confronting their work team or their plant.[19]

There is cause for some skepticism as to whether new workplace innovations indeed represent a qualitative break with the form of capitalist organization of production which underlay the Fordist regime. In the auto industry, overall economies of scale and the pacing mechanism of the assembly line continue to be important, even in those plants which have instituted production teams in pursuit of flexibility. Further, empirical studies of a variety of American industrial settings – ranging from smaller metalworking shops to aerospace, agricultural implement, and auto assembly plants – suggest that the new production technology is being used in ways which augment overall managerial control and increase the intensity of work. In those workplaces where programmable machining technologies have been introduced, management has tended to centralize control over programming in order to reduce their dependence on skilled labor, to limit the extent to which workers are able to control their own work pace, and to improve (through electronic programming and monitoring) management's ability to supervise and regulate work. Observed in a larger manufacturing plant, workers tending flexible manufacturing systems appeared to have responsibilities little different from those who work on the transfer lines of mass production plants. The vaunted Japanese-style "Just In Time" system of inventory management was found to impose a more uniform pace of work by minimizing buffer stocks throughout the production process. In interviews with managers who had adopted more flexible production methods, researchers found a fundamental continuity with the traditional managerial ideologies of Taylorism and Fordism: the bottom-line belief that "greater managerial control" is the key to profitability – justified in the contemporary context because it allegedly "increases firm responsiveness to the market as well as improving product quality, productivity, and other performance measures."[20]

Studies of work reorganization in the automobile industry suggest that the primary managerial motivation for adopting new methods is to compete more effectively with Japanese levels of productivity and quality, and to get workers to cooperate in this effort. Under pressure of Japanese import competition, and with Japanese "transplants" demonstrating that the new production methods can achieve dramatic results with American workers, US auto makers have become increasingly interested in the reorganization of work along lines suggested by the Japanese exemplar. Critics point to the fundamental imbalance of power which underlies the Japanese production regime: the early postwar destruction of independent unionism in the Japanese auto industry and the subsequent use of company unions and work groups as a means to motivate workers and to limit and channel their participation in ways which serve the interests of the firm; the relentless intensification of work which results from the deliberate managerial strategy of continually stressing the entire production system through systematic understaffing and the elimination of buffer stocks; incentive pay linked to individual and group performance, and individual advancement based upon managerial valuation rather than seniority; and the ideology of identification with the work team, the plant, and the firm. Militant union activists and critics in the USA fear that such a "flexible" workplace regime would undermine the hard-won protections institutionalized in the workplace rule of law and facilitate a generalized speed-up of work, that it would weaken the solidarity and bargaining power of unions through plant-level bargaining and a pervasive "ideology of competition" which encourages workers to identify with the interests of the firm or plant in competition with others, that it would intensify pressures of inter-plant competition and "whipsawing" by management and, ultimately, that it would lead to the effective replacement of industrial unionism with captive enterprise unionism. For these critics, "the new participatry management schemes constitute an intensification, not an abandonment, of the essence of classical Taylorism."[21]

Viewed from this perspective, the new managerial emphasis on "flexibility" appears to fit into an array of corporate strategies aimed at decreasing the extent to which the corporate bottom line is sensitive to the needs, desires or demands of labor. Especially during the last decade, corporate managers have divided their workers through two-tiered wage systems in which new workers are paid at a lower scale than more senior workers, and through the increasing use of contingent labor – part-time and temporary workers whose wage–benefit costs are much lower than those of year-round full-time workers, among whom union organization is more difficult, and who are more readily disposable. They have used subcontracting and "outsourcing" to non-union suppliers as ways to suppress costs.[22] And they have directly attacked unions and collective bargaining patterns which had established norms for entire industries.

Concessionary bargaining became widespread during the 1980s in part because of a demonstration effect. Under pressure from the federal government as well as Chrysler Corporation, the UAW made a series of substantial wage and benefit concessions during the Chrysler bailout of 1979–80, and the union sold these to workers on the grounds that they were necessary to save jobs: "without the sacrifices," the UAW told auto workers, "there will be no loan for Chrysler and those jobs will go under along with the company." By Kim Moody's reckoning, "This [set of concessions] put Chrysler workers about $3 an hour behind workers at Ford and GM, introducing a new economic element in Big Three bargaining. The pattern, established four decades earlier, was broken." The broken pattern meant that wage differentials were subject to competitive pressures, and the UAW concessions to Chrysler were soon followed by similar give-backs at Ford (worth $1 billion), General Motors ($3 billion), and American Motors ($115 million). This episode was a highly visible demonstration of the way in which the threat of job loss could be used to wring concessions from even the strongest industrial unions, to undermine even long-established patterns of bargaining, and to reap non-trivial corporate windfalls thereby. Concessionary bargaining rapidly spread to other industries, with profitable and unprofitable firms alike using the threat of plant closure and job loss (whether through bankruptcy or capital mobility) as a coercive lever with which to extract concessions and break bargaining patterns. Such threats carried extra weight in the context of the early 1980s recession, when massive job losses in manufacturing threatened even union workers who had attained moderate levels of seniority. After several rounds of concessionary bargaining, the result was a marked deceleration in wage gains in new collective bargaining agreements (see figure 8.4). In addition to wages, concessions struck benefit packages and cost of living adjustments, and were also extended to such aspects of the neoliberal factory regime as working conditions and union-sanctioned company work rules and production standards.[23]

Contributing further to the curtailment of labor's bargaining power, following Ronald Reagan's dramatic example in the breaking of the air traffic controllers' strike of 1981, the use of "permanent replacements" to deprive striking unionists of their jobs and disarm their unions seems to have become more common. Employers have used permanent replacements to break a number of highly visible strikes – including the UAW's 1992 strike at Caterpillar in which the (profitable and internationally competitive) company used the threat of permanent replacements to break an established bargaining pattern in the heavy equipment industry. Whereas the practice is thought to have been less common before the Reagan era, a 1991 General Accounting Office study found that it was widespread in the 1980s: the GAO estimated that in 1985 and 1989 employers actually hired permanent replacements in 17 percent of strikes, and threatened to do so in about a third. Testifying before the Senate Subcommittee on Labor in March, 1991, Lynn Williams, president of the United Steel Workers, explained how established union leaderships view the consequences of this tendency:

> Increasingly, we have to advise our members that they dare not strike because of the risk of permanent replacement. And, what is crucial is this: the employers know as well as we that we are left without any meaningful strike weapon, and therefore felt no compulsion to negotiate seriously toward a mutually acceptable agreement. In this way, the use of permanent replacements by only a few employers has been sufficient to alter the balance of collective bargaining with many others.

Partly as a result of the increasingly visible and effective use of this tactic by employers, unionists have come to see the strike as a last ditch defense, and the incidence of major strikes (involving a thousand or more workers) has declined dramatically from an average level of 344 per year during the business cycle 1966–73, and 280 during the 1973–79 cycle, to 92.5 between 1979 and 1990. In the subset of this latter period which is often identified as the "Reagan recovery" (1984–90), there were on average only about fifty-two major strikes per year.[24]

The bargaining power of organized labor within the neoliberal order had been based upon its ability collectively to withhold its labor from an employer, and the use of this leverage to establish negotiated wage and benefit patterns which served to limit what would otherwise have been mutually undercutting competition among workers and plants within an industry. This power has been effectively suppressed by the joint counter-offensive of government and corporate capital. Assuming that collective bargaining wage settlements reflect the rough "correlation of forces" between capital and organized labor, figure 8.4 appears consistent with the argument that the bargaining power of unionized labor was at relatively high levels during the late 1960s and

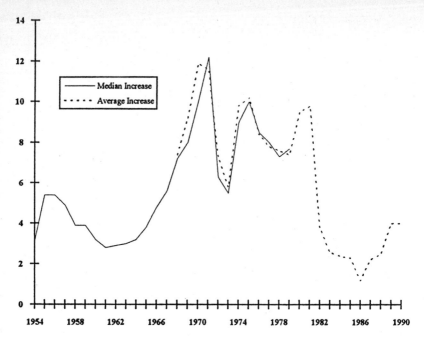

Figure 8.4 Pay increases through collective bargaining, 1954–90 (percent)

Sources: Median first year wage adjustments for major collective bargaining units (1,000 or more workers) in private non-farm industry 1954–79 from *Handbook of Labor Statistics, 1980*, table 128, p. 303; average first year wage adjustments, 1968–90 from *Monthly Labor Review*, various issues.

1970s – to some extent insulating more unionized sectors such as manufacturing from the downward wage pressures strongly operative in the rest of the economy by the 1970s – but that this union power was reduced to a dramatically lower level during the 1980s. Indeed, negotiated first year wage increases during the business cycle 1973–79 averaged about 8.14 percent, whereas the average during the subsequent cycle, 1979–89, was almost halved – to about 4.36 percent. Insofar as union pay scales act to reduce wage inequality, and may "spill over" into non-union workplaces if employers have reason to fear an organizing campaign, the decline of union power has economic implications for much broader segments of the working class than those directly affected by concessionary bargaining.[25]

Of course a vibrant and growing union movement, responsive to the needs and aspirations of rank and file American workers, might have been better able to resist these assaults, but organized labor had been weakened by a long-term process of ossification within and intensifying capitalist opposition without. Labor union membership as a percentage of the non-agricultural workforce reached its postwar peak in 1954, just shy of 35 percent; thereafter it declined to about 27 percent in 1970, and dropped to around 16 percent by 1990.[26] Further, there has been a steady, almost linear decline in rates of union success in NLRB certification elections, the main method for organizing previously unorganized workplaces. While unions typically won 65 to 75 percent of such elections during the 1950s, by 1970 they were winning about 55 percent, and this figure declined still further to 45 percent by the end of the 1970s. By the 1980s, then, unions were facing a less than even chance of success in their efforts to organize new workplaces.[27]

Although many large industrial employers were compelled to deal with labor unions which were legally protected under the neoliberal regime, they have (especially since the 1960s) engaged in various kinds of practices designed to hinder new union organizing and to weaken unions where they already existed. They have propagandized employees in order to defeat unions in NLRB elections, formed anti-union trade associations, and hired union-busting consulting firms to harass and intimidate union activists and sympathizers. Such anti-union activities, never entirely absent even during the postwar golden era, have increased dramatically since the 1970s. There has been an accelerating growth in the incidence of legally proscribed "unfair labor practices" (such as the firing of union activists or sympathizers, charges of which doubled between 1970 and 1980) and various other union-busting techniques designed to prevent unions from winning NLRB elections, or to de-certify existing unions. Under the Reagan administration, the National Labor Relations Board was packed with anti-labor ideologues who overturned a number of established labor protections, precedents and norms in the name of restoring the priority of individual rights, and who showed little enthusiasm for punishing corporate violators of labor law: according to NLRB documents obtained by the journal *Multinational Monitor*, between 1982 and 1990 the Board ruled that unfair labor practices occurred in only 2 percent of the cases brought before it which involved the fifty largest US corporations. Further, Board rulings during the 1980s effectively facilitated corporate strategies which involve plant closures and/or concessionary bargaining.[28]

While corporate capital and the state have been diligently working to effect corporate restructuring and increase the obstacles facing organized labor, the major unions themselves have been remarkably inert. In general, AFL–CIO unions have proven themselves unable or unwilling aggressively to organize new constituencies (with the significant exception of white collar unions and especially public sector workers), and have failed especially to organize large numbers of workers in relatively low-paying and rapidly proliferating private service sector jobs. Together, the conservatism and lethargy of AFL–CIO business unionism and the increasingly aggressive opposition of employers go a long way toward explaining the underlying weakness of unions in America, and their inability to respond effectively to the 1980s attack on their place within the neoliberal order.[29]

The social position and bargaining power of labor has been further weakened by macroeconomic state policy, which has sought since the late 1970s to restore productivity growth and profitability by lavishing carrots upon business and the wealthy (especially through deregulation and the regressive tax reforms of the 1980s), and by beating the working class with the stick of unemployment and economic insecurity.[30] The state applied what Bowles, Gordon and Weisskopf call the "cold bath": immersions of recession and unemployment designed to weaken labor and impose maximum wage flexibility – in the language of the economists, to "squeeze inflation out of the economy." In 1979 Federal Reserve Board chairman Paul Volcker inaugurated a policy which tightened the money supply and effectively raised interest rates. A deep and painful recession was thereby induced which lasted from 1980 into 1983, and brought the officially measured unemployment rate from 5.8 percent in 1979 to 9.5 percent in 1981–82. The "Reagan recovery" which ensued brought the unemployment rate down only to 5.3 percent by 1989 – a figure which, while lower than that of 1979, is higher than that of comparable business cycle peaks in 1966 and 1973, near the end of the postwar golden era (see table 8.2).

At the same time, the class-based coercive effects of recession were magnified and focused by minimizing the effectiveness of unemployment insurance programs which might have served to lessen the dependence of workers upon the wage relation. The Reagan administration redefined unemployment benefits as taxable income, tightened the requirements for federally funded unemployment insurance programs, and encouraged state governments to adopt more restrictive eligibility guidelines for the programs which they administer.

Between 1981 and 1987, forty-four states did so. As a result of these policies, the number of unemployed who are eligible to receive benefits declined from more than 42 percent in 1979 to fewer than 33 percent in 1989 (table 8.2). However, as Bowles, Gordon and Weisskopf point out, a comparison of business cycle peaks substantially understates the effect of these changes, which are most pronounced in the depths of recession: in 1975, more than 62 percent of unemployed workers received benefits, while in 1983 the figure was 35 percent.[31] As a matter of policy, then, workers were more directly vulnerable to the violence of the job market.

Moreover, those jobs which were created during the Reagan era were typically not the high-paying manufacturing jobs upon which the neoliberal regime had been based, but rather were predominantly lower-paying service sector and retail jobs. According to the Economic Policy Institute, there was a net gain of 14.4 million service and retail jobs between 1979 and 1989, whereas more than 1.4 million manufacturing jobs (nearly 7 percent of all manufacturing jobs) were lost. During these years, manufacturing jobs declined from 23.4 to 18.1 percent of employment, while the proportion of service and retail jobs grew from 35.8 to 42.8 percent. Reflecting on evidence from the first half of this period, Bennett Harrison and Barry Bluestone suggest that it represents a significant turning point: "nearly three out of five (58 percent) of the net new jobs created between 1979 and 1984 paid $7,400 or less a year (in 1984 dollars). In contrast, less than one in five of the additional jobs generated between 1963 and 1979 had paid such low wages." Correspondingly, there has been a resurgence of the "working poor." The US Census Bureau reports that the proportion of year-round full-time workers whose wages did not exceed the official poverty level (for a family of four) increased by half between 1979 and 1990 – from 12.1 percent to 18 percent. So, even for those who have escaped the dangers of unemployment, it seems, it has become more difficult for working people to make a minimally decent living.[32]

In summary, American unionism has been in a long-term decline by some measures since the middle 1950s, but the state and capital have responded to the crisis of Fordism by attacking an already weakened union movement and destroying what was left of its ability to defend neoliberal collective bargaining regimes and wage levels in core industry. The basic strategy, then, has been to exploit this weakness in order to shore up profitability at the expense of the American working class.

Table 8.2 *Economic insecurity and inequality, 1966–89*

	1966	1973	1979	1989
(1) Real after-tax hourly earnings of production workers (1988 $)	8.07	8.75	8.33	7.73*
(2) Real median family income (1988 $)	27,860	32,109	31,917	32,191*
(3) Hours worked per capita	682	707	742	790
(4) Unemployment rate (percent)	3.8	4.9	5.8	5.3
(5) Percentage of unemployed receiving unemployment insurance	39.3	41.1	42.2	32.6
(6) Mortgage foreclosure rate (per 10,000 mortgages)	n.a.	38	38	106**
(7) Percentage of people living in poverty	14.7	11.1	11.7	13.1*
(8) Household income inequality ratio (top 5%/bottom 40%)	0.87	0.89	0.94	1.12*

Note: * Figures for 1988; ** figures for 1987.
Source: S. Bowles, D. Gordon, and T. Weisskopf, *After the Waste Land* (Armonk, NY: Sharpe, 1990), tables 9.1, 9.2, 9.3, pp. 139, 141, 144.

In terms of the lives of American working people, the results of the governmental and corporate counter-offensive have been severe. Overall in the US economy, the real hourly earnings of production workers – in decline since 1973 – fell more rapidly during the 1980s (see table 8.2, row 1). Wage erosion became dramatically evident even in the relatively privileged manufacturing sector, where the growth of real wages, which had been slowing over previous postwar business cycles, became *negative* between 1979 and 1989 (see table 8.1). As a result families have had to work harder, longer, just to keep up. Real family income has held more or less steady only through an increase in the number hours worked by household members – working women, often in lower-wage service sector jobs, generally making up the difference (table 8.2, rows 2–3). A higher level of unemployment has become the norm, along with a decline in the proportion of workers who are shielded from its worst effects through eligibility for even minimal unemployment benefits (rows 4–5). The economic insecurity of families aspiring to "middle-class" status is reflected in a dramatic rise in the rate of mortgage foreclosures (row 6). The proportion of the population living in poverty, which had declined through the early 1970s, began to increase thereafter and expanded sharply during the

1980s. While the income share of the lowest quintiles of the population declined, the rich were getting richer: by the end of the Reagan era, the income share of the top 5 percent of households was substantially larger than that of the bottom 40 percent (rows 7–8). Most of this income growth was concentrated in the top 1 percent.[33]

The neoliberal regime had been based in part upon the construction of a broad "middle class" encompassing unionized industrial workers as well as technicians, professionals, and managers; it would seem, however, that the counter-offensive of capital and the state has made it more difficult for many families to sustain a "middle-class" standard of living. Not only does all of this signal the onset of hard times and chronic insecurity for working-class families, even as the wealthy luxuriate in their Reaganite windfall; but the weakening of mass consumption capacity also implies that a central aspect of the Fordist regime and its stabilization mechanism has been undermined. But the implications of this extend beyond renewed dangers of underconsumption and economic crisis. The political foundations of the postwar regime may have been severely damaged as well. In response to the weakening of core Fordism and the attendant global pressures, the state and capital in the USA have attacked the social position and living standards of the industrial working class in order to focus upon it the coercive effects of the labor market, imposing more "flexible" workplaces and driving workers to greater productivity at reduced wages. In so doing, they have not only undermined Fordist mass consumption but also fragmented the neoliberal historic bloc, effectively expelling industrial labor from its former position as relatively privileged junior partner and potentially creating thereby the preconditions for a political crisis of hegemony. Of hegemonic crisis, Gramsci wrote:

> If the ruling class has lost its consensus, i.e., is no longer "leading" but only "dominant," exercising coercive force alone, this means precisely that the great masses have become detached from their traditional ideologies, and no longer believe what they used to believe previously, etc. The crisis consists precisely in the fact that the old is dying and the new cannot be born; in this interregnum a great variety of morbid symptoms appear.[34]

Has capital's increasing reliance on coercion undermined the ideological affiliations of the American working class? Do industrial workers "no longer believe what they used to believe previously"? Have we arrived at such a crisis of hegemony?

A crisis of neoliberal Americanism?

It is my contention that the hegemony of neoliberal capitalism in the United States and in the core of the world economy is expiring; but no new system of capitalist (or other) organization has yet emerged to replace it. The mode of social organization which succeeds the neo-liberal order – whether capitalist or non-capitalist, hegemonic or non-hegemonic – will be determined by political struggles in which ideo-logical frameworks delimit or extend the horizons of possible collective action. The meanings of "Americanism," central to the historical self-understandings of the industrial working class in the USA, will be important in that aspect of the struggle which unfolds in the nexus between the world economy and the USA.

The politics of productivity formula which had been at the heart of the neoliberal regime has been opened to question by the vicious anti-labor offensives of the 1980s, but also by long-term tendencies fostered by the neoliberal world order: in particular, the rise of multi-national corporations (MNCs) and transnational production networks in the decades after World War II. Whereas the whole ideological thrust of Taylorism and Fordism had been an identification of the interests of workers with productivity and the profitability of their employer – and, with the assistance of industrial unions, the linking of this identity with a conception of "Americanism" which validated liberal capitalism as a universal model of individual opportunity and freedom – this identification has become problematic as US-based multinational firms have pursued global profits at the expense of American workers, and as the consequences for Fordist mass con-sumption in America have become more painfully apparent.[35]

Table 8.3 suggests that even while the USA (as a territorial entity) lost around one-third of its share of world exports of manufactures between 1957 and 1984, US multinationals maintained their global share by shifting their production for world export markets toward majority-owned foreign affiliates (MOFAs), whose export share increased over this period. Evidence such as this seems to suggest that over the last several decades transnational production for world markets has to a significant degree displaced export production from within the territorial USA. Nominally American multinational firms have maintained their global competitive position, but their US workers now produce less for world markets while workers employed by their foreign affiliates produce more. Further indicative of this

Table 8.3 *Percentage shares in world exports of manufactures: USA, US multinationals, and foreign affiliates, 1957–84*

	1957	1966	1977	1984
Territorial USA	21.3*	17.5	13.3	14.0
		(−18%)	(−24%)	(+5%)
US MNCs	n.a.	17.7	17.6	18.1
			(−0.5%)	(+3%)
Foreign Affiliates	5.8*	8.2	9.7	10.3
of US MNCs		(+41%)	(+18%)	(+6%)

Note: Figures in parentheses are percentage changes from the previous data point. * Figures for 1957 are not strictly comparable to later figures, and changes between 1957 and 1966 are probably slightly overstated.
Source: Robert E. Lipsey and Irving B. Kravis, "The Competitiveness and Comparative Advantage of US Multinationals, 1957–1984" *Banca Nazionale del lavoro Quarterly Review* 161 (1987), p. 151.

tendency, employment in the manufacturing MOFAs of US-based firms grew from 2.4 million in 1966 to almost 4.1 million in 1987, an increase of about 70 percent (there was, however, an 8 percent decline of MOFA manufacturing employment between 1982 and 1987). Further, although direct foreign investment by US-based firms has remained heavily concentrated in the developed market economies, after 1966 employment by US MNCs engaged in manufacturing in the newly industrializing countries – especially in Brazil, Mexico, and Asia – grew almost five times as rapidly as did such employment in the developed countries. This suggests that US-based MNCs may have sought to transfer some of their more labor-intensive manufacturing activities to these areas after the crisis of Fordism had set in.[36] While the process of shifting world market production overseas from the USA appears to have slowed down somewhat relative to earlier decades, its tangible effects upon American workers have been magnified by the crisis of Fordism in the industrial core and the intensified anti-labor climate of the 1980s.

In some industries, multinational production has involved overseas processing or assembly of components or entire commodities for import back into the US market.[37] For example, from relatively modest beginnings in the 1960s, all three major American auto makers now have major plants across the Mexican border employing altogether around 100,000 Mexican workers. These plants produce parts and assemble finished cars (using Mexican and American-made parts), about one-third of which are sent back into the US market for sale (this proportion is expected to grow). In addition to its geographical proximity to the USA market, a large part of the attraction for American capital is the dramatic wage gap between the USA and Mexico: the average manufacturing production worker in the US was paid about $14.83 per hour in 1990; whereas the Mexican counterpart earned $1.85, just over 12 percent of the US level. In maquiladora manufacturing plants, the differential has been even more dramatic: on average in 1990, a Ford production worker in the United States earned about $16.50 per hour; at Ford's plant in Hermosillo, Mexico, workers were paid an average hourly wage of $1.03, a little more than 6 percent of the US Ford workers' wage. In addition to dramatically lower wages, Mexican workers face institutionalized obstacles which inhibit attempts to exercise any significant measure of democratic control over their working lives: major union federations in Mexico are dominated by the state and the ruling Institutional Revolutionary Party (PRI), and the Mexican state has an established track record of suppressing the kind of independent unionism which might foster activism among rank and file workers. The North American Free Trade Agreement (NAFTA) is unlikely to make any substantial improvement to the hostile climate facing independent labor organizers in Mexico.[38]

Further heightening the attractiveness of Mexico for transnational production, the performance of MNC manufacturing plants in Mexico can be very good. In electronics and transportation equipment, the difference between productivity in US plants and MNC plants in Mexico is much smaller than the gap in wage levels. In some cases, performance is world class: Ford's Hermosillo plant achieved the best quality (lowest defect rate) of eighty high-volume assembly plants surveyed worldwide by MIT's International Motor Vehicle Project in 1989. Ford's Chihuahua engine plant, and the General Motors plants at Toluca and Ramos Arizpe, have each been recognized as being among the best-quality producers within their parent firms' global manufacturing networks. In these new automobile plants – constructed in northern Mexico in the early 1980s as part of an increasingly export-oriented strategy – labor contracts highly favorable to management and its control of the factory floor have been negotiated with local unions, allied with enterprise unions and the compliant, government-affiliated Confederation of Mexican Workers (CTM). This has allowed the MNCs to adapt and operate Japanese-style "flexible" production systems without significant resistance from organized workers. The multinationals' automobile plants in northern Mexico have thus established a remarkable record of high-quality, low-cost production which promises to exert a long-term attraction over firms producing motor vehicles for the North American market.[39]

The tendency toward transnational production has the effect of placing American industrial workers in direct competition with their Mexican counterparts, and provides the multinational firm with terrific bargaining power relative to its American workers: as an American auto worker explained, "When they start sending big-ticket items down there [for production], it puts the fear in you." NAFTA suggests that transnational manufacturing has a bright future on the American continent, but this future may not be shared by unskilled or semi-skilled American industrial workers, some of whose jobs may be endangered and many more of whom will certainly face increasingly intense wage and work rule competition.[40] To the extent that multinational producers seek to manufacture products for the US market in locations with lower costs or a more management-friendly labor climate, and to use these competitive advantages to obtain bargaining leverage against US workers, their abandonment of the Fordist regime and its equation of mass production and mass consumption becomes increasingly transparent. In these circumstances, the ideological basis of neoliberalism may – like the emperor's new clothes – lose its power over popular imagination.

Under the pressure of late Fordist transnational capitalism, the common sense of industrial workers is once again being contested and reconstructed: although contradictory tendencies are clearly in evidence, among some elements of the labor movement the identity of interest between workers and their corporate employer – presumed by neoliberal ideology and its associated vision of "Americanism" – is being opened to question. Despite its basically conservative political commitments and its historic role of upholding the American imperial order, the AFL–CIO itself may have contributed to this questioning by explicitly (if not unambiguously) recognizing the growing tension between American unionism and transnational capitalism, and by backing away from its earlier support of free trade, beginning in the late 1960s and early 1970s. Even those AFL–CIO foreign policy statements of the late 1980s which continued to insist upon the overriding importance of global anticommunism also acknowledged that the world was changing in significant ways, ways which threatened to do further violence to core Fordism and the unions it had supported. In the words of an AFL–CIO foreign policy pamphlet, "The exploitation of foreign workers by their employers – often multinational corporations – hurts American workers, too." It hurts them, the AFL–CIO explained, because low-wage foreign workers will not be able to afford to buy their own products, much less American exports. Thus, not only is the growth of such employment overseas unlikely to contribute to the prosperity of American labor by expanding the global basis of Fordist mass consumption, but the products of foreign exploitation are likely to be exported to wealthier countries such as the USA where they will undercut American wages and endanger union jobs. On similar grounds, the AFL–CIO along with the UAW and other member unions opposed NAFTA as exploitative of Mexican labor, and a threat to American workers and what remains of their Fordist standard of living. In addition, the AFL–CIO has sought to protect itself against "downward harmonization" in the global economy by placing greater emphasis on the international enforcement of worker rights through multilateral institutions (such as the GATT) and through US trade policy, and has also called for debt relief for Third World countries whose standard of living is being held down by massive debt service burdens and IMF austerity plans. The American union movement no longer lends its unequivocal support to the neoliberal agenda of international openness and the expansion of transnational capitalism.[41]

There are, however, basic ideological continuities which coexist with these seemingly dramatic departures. The AFL–CIO's longstanding anticommunism, and its more recent gestures toward international solidarity and the protection of worker rights, have both been grounded in an ideological commitment to liberal capitalism and its civil society of autonomous individuals, out of which "free trade unions" are understood to emerge. From this perspective, transnational capitalism is to be accepted as a "fact of life that trade unions cannot wish away" (in the words of AFL–CIO president Lane Kirkland); so the purpose of international solidarity is not to contest that reality, but to adapt it – through collective bargaining – so that workers are able to live a less precarious existence. Accordingly, AFL–CIO foreign policy statements of the late 1980s reveal a world view in which the primary political task is "to secure the rights that unions and all people want *and* need to survive: freedom of association, and of free speech, the right of a people to select its own government, and so on."

In the context of this vision, the central political struggle is between autonomous individuals and the state. The basis of international solidarity is not a shared class position in relation to transnational capital, but the presumed universality of individual rights, including the right to organize. The future of unionism is seen to depend upon the extension of this narrowly political Americanism: unless such rights are recognized and safeguarded internationally, individual workers will be unable to come together and engage in the collective action necessary to realize their common economic interest in taking wages out of competition and humanizing global capitalism. Such a failure of political vision, the AFL–CIO warns, would bring in its wake a grim economic future for the world's workers.[42]

Perhaps ironically, then, even as it departed from its former commitment to the free trade component of the neoliberal order, and suggested that what is good for General Motors and other multinationals might not always be good for the rest of America, the AFL–CIO was reaffirming its ideological commitment to an international community based upon norms of liberal individualism and a mildly reformed transnational capitalism in which workers might secure an improved standard of living. Core elements of neoliberal Americanism thus remain firmly anchored in AFL–CIO ideology, in uneasy tension with the recognition that the world created by that vision is increasingly inhospitable for American unions. As a consequence, in a period when Fordism is in decline, possibilities for transnational solidarity are overshadowed by the apparent threat of zero-sum economic competition from foreigners. The result is a contradictory agenda. The AFL–CIO's official foreign policy statements proclaim the universal relevance of Americanism as a political model, emphasizing the protection of the individual rights of all workers; while its increasing willingness to resort to protectionist policies and "buy American" campaigns suggest that the AFL–CIO's brand of Americanism views foreign workers primarily as competitors in the world market, that it values the economic well being of American workers more highly than cosmopolitan labor solidarity, and is prepared to make common cause with "American" corporate employers in order to protect American jobs from foreign competition.

Despite official declarations suggesting intensified efforts to strengthen international union solidarity and resist global corporate exploitation, in the late Fordist period American unions and their hobbled neoliberal vision have been on the strategic defensive and have had difficulty sustaining even their historically strongest trans-national ties. The American and Canadian auto industries have been effectively integrated for decades, and so too have their auto workers' unions, which were organizationally united in the International UAW and whose bargaining strategies were closely coordinated. Despite differences in the culture and politics of unionism in the two countries, the International UAW sustained this transnational alliance until the early 1980s, when American unions – confronting historically deter-mined socio-political limitations which the Canadians did not share, more closely identified with the economically oriented world view of their corporate employers, and largely unable to conceive of more militant and socially solidaristic strategies to meet the anti-labor offensive – began to submit to successive rounds of concessionary bargaining. While American unions were giving up wage gains and work rules in favor of corporate competitiveness, the more socially activist-oriented Canadian unionists were determined not to accept the defensive posture of American economistic unionism and could not, therefore, remain within the International union, dominated as it was by the Americans. The result of this strategic divergence was an organizational split in 1984: the Canadian Auto Workers constituted themselves as an independent union. Thus, just when the corporate and neoconservative counter-offensive was reaching its greatest inten-sity, and when transnational solidarity was more important than ever, the UAW failed to articulate a vision of industrial unionism to which the Canadians could subscribe: an Americanism which seemed to bring the UAW to identify with corporate profitability and to side with MNC employers in opposition to foreign "competitors" was not an identity which Canadians were willing to accept as defining the limits of their own practice of industrial unionism.[43] This inability of American neoliberal unionism to sustain common ground with its closest international ally does not bode well for official labor solidarity on a continental- much less global – scale.

Rank and file unionists in the USA have also struggled with the contradictions and ambiguities of neoliberal Americanism in an increasingly harsh global capitalism. Paul Garver – a local union officer in Pittsburgh – sketches different kinds of reactions among rank and file workers to the declining fortunes of local steel plants. One kind of reaction has involved a reassertion of Americanism, along with a heightening of its nativist strains: blaming foreigners for unfair trade practices, joining with employers to call for increased protectionism, and appealing to consumers to circle the wagons and "buy American." As Garver explains, this kind of reaction has often had "an ugly chauvinist edge":

> In 1985 the Pittsburgh labor movement held its first Labor Day Parade in many years. Organized around the slogan "Put America Back to Work: Buy American-Made Products," the most popular float portrayed a brawny American steelworker smashing a Japanese-made car and its buck-toothed passengers.[44]

Similar kinds of reactions are evident among automobile workers at Ford's Michigan truck plant, interviewed by Richard Feldman in 1986–87 as part of an oral history project. Ford, which had employed 2,800 people working two shifts in the plant, reduced its workforce in 1980 to 1,100 people working a single shift plus overtime, increased the intensity of work and introduced greater automation along with an "employee involvement" program designed to improve productivity and quality. The mass layoffs and their apparent permanence induced pervasive fear among the surviving employees, many of whom expressed dissatisfaction with the union's apparent inability to protect them.[45] A number of them blamed foreign competitors and disloyal consumers for the situation of their industry and the threat to their jobs. The following comments – each of which presupposes a zero-sum world in which foreign workers can gain only at the expense of American workers – are from three different auto workers:

> There's too many Japanese invading. They should be shipped home. We shouldn't have as many imports and exports. Keep it in the country ... I got one of the [job] applications for the [Flat Rock, Michigan] Mazda plant in the mail, but I won't apply because I'm not working for any Japs. I don't understand how people could work for them. The more Japanese who come over, the less Americans are going to have because the Japs will work cheaper and harder. But if we go over there, we won't be treated as well as we treat them ... If I had anything to do with it, I'd ship everybody home: the Japs, the Arabs, all of them. Go back where you came from ... They're taking our jobs, and that's not right.

> If I saw someone with a broken-down foreign car on the road and it was raining snowballs, I wouldn't stop to help them. Not here in the Detroit area, no way in hell. I was at a picnic at my wife's uncle's house the other day. He was driving a damn Toyota. He is making American bucks and buys a foreign product, and I resent that.

> If we don't buy, within reason, as many American-made products as we can, we're going to lose our way of life ... It's not just the

> company that benefits when people buy American. It's every guy on the assembly line who is supporting his family ... If we don't buy American, we'll lose jobs, and jobs are not easy to come by. I'd hate to work at McDonald's for $3.50 an hour. Having to take that cut in pay would destroy me.[46]

Exploiting such currents of xenophobic Americanism, and the fear which underlies them, Ford has attempted to reassert the identity of interest between the company and its workers. Through its "employee involvement" (EI) program, the company has sought to recast its relationship with labor in less adversarial terms by focusing instead on the putatively common threat which management and labor face from foreign competition. According to a local union officer, "The Employee Involvement concept came along when management decided they wanted people more involved in the process of obtaining quality, of being competitive through cutting costs." A worker involved in the EI program explained it to his fellow workers in terms which clearly imply that jobs are at stake: "In our training sessions I tell people we should do what we can to make Ford viable because these are our jobs." Another says: "profits are good for all of us. The better Ford Motor Company does, the more people have jobs, the better our salaries are, and the easier it is for our union to negotiate benefits ... [W]e are the company. We are the people who determine whether profits are made."[47] The corporate strategy at Ford's Michigan truck plant appears to be based on combining the implicitly coercive force of the transnational labor market with the apparently consensual regime of "employee involvement" in order to maximize productivity and minimize labor resistance to the speed-up and to increasing automation.

But xenophobic and pro-corporate reactions such as these are not universal among industrial workers. In the Pittsburgh area, Paul Garver noted another kind of reaction which contrasted the multinational profit-seeking of US Steel (now USX) and the Mellon Bank with declining investment, closing plants and rising unemployment in local communities: "Steelworkers and other unionists began to question whether American companies were committed to the patriotic 'Americanism' that was as traditional in these valleys as mining coal and making steel." Those who raise such questions, Garver suggests, may be led to the conclusion that in a world where transnational production is an option available to corporate employers, effective international labor solidarity will be necessary in order to defend the living standards achieved by American workers and to elevate those of (potentially competing) workers in more directly oppressive, low-wage environments.[48]

In the Michigan truck plant interviews, such cosmopolitan class-based perspectives were not as common as Japan-bashing, but neither were they entirely absent. One worker expressed skepticism about corporate representations of the need for a unified American labor–management front against foreign competition: "The companies say the lower wages are necessary to compete with foreign industry. I think that's a big farce. Big corporations have no loyalty to any country. Their loyalty is to the dollar." Sometimes the xenophobic and the cosmopolitan tendencies are present in the same statements. One worker who was using a computer to keep track of parts inventories saw "buy American" appeals as misleading in an industry where production is transnational, but appears to believe that lower-paid foreign workers are not capable of meeting American-level quality standards, implying that they are not serious competitors and that raising their wages may therefore be a less urgent task:

> I've learned a lot about parts. When the Ford Escort was first introduced, Ford's PR people called it the world car. It's a world car all right because the parts come from all over the world. It's just assembled in the United States. The whole front-end technology comes from Japan. The wiring looms were shipped out from California to Mexico [for production] about four years ago and it's all junk now. What do you expect? The workers down there get a buck and a half an hour. They get parts from Brazil and even Argentina. "Buy American" is a joke. These vehicles aren't American.

In another instance, a production worker expressed solidarity with foreign counterparts, and yet also supports the "buy American" campaign:

> I'm not against people bringing their products here at a fair price. But the autoworkers in other countries are exploited worse than we are. In Mexico, guys are getting a dollar an hour to produce the same stuff we do. There should be a law that says we don't want goods in this country that are produced by workers who are being exploited. If they have to live in substandard conditions and do the same job I'm doing, I don't want to buy the cars they make.
>
> Everybody who builds cars worldwide should be in the same union and get the same amount of money, so it wouldn't matter where the cars are sold. They'd all get a good wage.
>
> There will always be automobiles, but they may be made some-

where else. If people in this country let that happen, they are as much
to blame as anybody. We've lost the feeling of nationalism. I think
"buy American" because you'll keep somebody working. It's not that
you hate somebody else in another country; but hey, we have to
make our own, and they should make their own.[49]

Such evidence appears to suggest that the common sense of
American industrial workers harbors some possibility of cosmopolitan
labor solidarity as well as tendencies toward parochialism, xenophobia, or racism. In order to build a more cosmopolitan, transnational
unionism, the struggle over the common sense of American workers is
being renewed: among various communities of unionists and activists,
racist and xenophobic forms of "Americanism" – the nativist strain
familiar since before the days of the first Henry Ford – are being
supplanted by a broader vision of community in which workers and
allied groups across a number of countries can make common cause
against the corporations whose global powers affect their lives and
communities. This ideological task involves the development of those
strains of common sense "Americanism" which are inclusive rather
than exclusive, and which stress effective equality and the participation of all in the affairs which affect their lives. If American unionists
are to participate in a transnational counter-hegemonic movement,
these aspects of common sense will need to be framed in such a way
that they do not appear to be circumscribed by the territorial boundaries of the USA: "Americanism" will need to transcend America.

This kind of vision is evident in increasing transnational linkages
among rank and file unionists, and in emerging dissent about labor's
support for American foreign policy in areas of intense labor exploitation such as Central America. In examples of the former tendency, auto
workers, frozen-food workers, and farm workers have established
direct contact with Mexican counterparts, in at least one case assisting
them to win significant contract improvements from their multinational employer and to that extent at least diminishing the vulnerability of the American workers. Ford workers from St. Paul, Minnesota exchanged delegations and expressed solidarity with striking
workers at the Ford plant in Cuatitlan, Mexico. There have been
transnational conferences of auto workers employed by General
Motors, and similar conferences of Ford workers, designed to coordinate bargaining goals, strategies and timing. Transnational organization among networks of grassroots unionists is a nascent tendency
which may extend the limits of official union solidarity and thus

become crucially important for the survival of effective unionism in the late twentieth century.[50]

During the 1980s, a labor insurgency also broke out in the area of foreign policy. Traditionally the preserve of top labor bureaucrats ensconced in the AFL–CIO's Department of International Affairs (DIA), the federation's foreign policy had been closely aligned with that of the US government, and indeed the DIA and its overseas activities were largely funded by the US Agency for International Development, and in the 1980s by federal funds disbursed through the National Endowment for Democracy. With such funding, DIA and its regional institutes (AIFLD in Latin America, AALC in Africa, AAFLI in Asia and, since 1977, the FTUI in Europe) endeavored to help organize, train and equip "free" trade unions around the world. Operationally, this was understood to entail opposition to leftist or radical forces and support for "apolitical" unions: pro-capitalist, productivity-oriented unions which were not inclined to rock the boat by advocating radical political programs or by fomenting hostility towards the United States or multinational corporate capitalists. During the period of neoliberal hegemony, such union activities could be assimilated within the framework of popular common sense: they were understandable in terms of the propagation of liberal capitalism as the social system best able to secure generalized prosperity along with individual rights and liberties; and they were part of the defense of that system against the totalitarian menace. Although some unionists, and especially the UAW leadership, had dissented from the AFL–CIO's unquestioning support for US imperial foreign policy during the Vietnam War years, they had not renounced the neoliberal vision of a capitalist world order in which free labor unions had an important part to play.[51]

By the 1980s, however, major elements within the union movement had become painfully aware that a foreign policy premised upon the defense of international capitalism was not necessarily in the interests of either foreign or American workers, and there occurred extraordinary instances of dissent from the fundamental policy goals of the AFL–CIO. In contrast to the DIA's continuing commitment to anticommunism in the guise of "free trade unionism," in 1981 a group of twenty-four union officials formed the National Labor Committee in Support of Democracy and Human Rights in El Salvador. The Committee opposed Reagan administration policies of support for oppressive right-wing governments in Central America, and the Contra war against Nicaragua. (It is, I think, noteworthy that this dissenting group chose to frame their objectives in terms valorized by popular liberal common sense: support for "democracy" and "rights.") In 1983 and again at the 1985 AFL–CIO convention, dissenters questioned the federation's uncritical stance toward these policies, in the latter instance this involved an unprecedented floor debate over the federation's official foreign policy. During that debate, Kenneth Blaylock, of the American Federation of Government Employees, shared with the convention his reflections on experiences during a visit to Central America, and challenged the official narrative of US foreign policy: "when I look at Iran, I look at Vietnam, I look at Nicaragua, I look at El Salvador, Guatemala, I would like for one time for my government to be on the side of the people, not on the side of rich dictators living behind high walls." Following dissidents such as Blaylock, large numbers of unionists began to speak out against a foreign policy which was explicitly based upon the model of American-style liberal capitalism as global panacea, while implicitly accepting complicity with oppressive forces in the defense of privilege. Despite official discouragement from AFL–CIO president Lane Kirkland, some 30–50,000 unionists joined in a 1987 demonstration in Washington DC, calling for "peace, jobs and justice in Central America and South Africa." This persistent undercurrent of opposition within the AFL–CIO signaled that even before the collapse of the Soviet empire in Eastern Europe, the official rationale of anticommunism was increasingly threadbare, no longer able to command the near-universal assent of labor for the basic goals of US foreign policy.[52]

Foreign policy dissension was also evident in labor's response to George Bush's "new world order." Before to the 1991 US attack against Iraq, strong pro-war positions were taken by a number of the traditionally more conservative unions. For example, Robert Georgine of the AFL–CIO Building and Construction Trades Department expressed his support for the war in the familiar terms of neoliberal opposition to totalitarianism, echoing President Bush's comparison of Saddam Hussein's aggression to that of Hitler (and adding Stalin and Mussolini for good measure). There was, however, significant dissent from this orthodoxy: before the start of the war, eleven major US unions announced their opposition and there was a flurry of anti-war organizing by unionists at the regional and local levels. Significantly, some unionists who opposed the war did so on grounds which explicitly rejected the neoliberal identity: a coalition of anti-war unionists from Oregon explained that they opposed foreign policy actions designed to make the world safe for corporations "who are closing union shops here while opening sweatshops in the Third World."[53]

The debate over the North American Free Trade Agreement (NAFTA) further revealed the extent to which the popular common sense of American working people is now again being actively contested. Whereas NAFTA's supporters tended to cast the treaty as politically neutral, a technical instrument enhancing the functioning of international markets and contributing thereby to the general welfare of North American consumers, NAFTA's opponents more often rejected the homogenizing liberal vision of a world of individual market actors. In a post-Fordist world where global competition turns on the reduction of labor costs, this consumer-oriented vision may no longer find an easy resonance with the lives of many Americans fearing wage reductions, benefit cutbacks, downsizing, layoffs and plant closings. Accordingly, the treaty's critics have represented the world as divided by fundamental political-economic inequalities. They have depicted NAFTA as augmenting the power of multinational capital relative to workers, unions, and local communities. Framing an alternative vision of global political economy based on democratic self-determination and transnational linkages among working people and citizens – rather than allowing markets and the criterion of private profit to make our social decisions for us – they counterposed the common sense value of "democracy" to liberalism's traditional valorization of private property. This ideological tension is crystallized in anti-NAFTA formulations such as the following (by John Cavanagh of the Institute for Policy Studies): "The key to genuine democracy in this decade will be the struggle by communities and citizens' organizations to control their own destinies, to take control of their own lands and natural resources, to collectively make the decisions that affect their futures. The free trade agreements that are currently on the table appropriate these decisions and toss them to the private sector." That this tension now implies a global struggle is made explicit by William Greider:

> For ordinary Americans, traditionally independent and insular, the challenge requires them to think anew their place in the world. The only plausible way that citizens can defend themselves and their nation against the forces of globalization is to link their own interests cooperatively with the interests of other peoples in other nations – that is, with the foreigners who are competitors for the jobs and production but who are also victimized by the system. Americans will

have to create new democratic alliances across national borders with the less prosperous people caught in the same dilemma.

Fears of a continental, hemispheric, or global political economy dominated by the institutionalized and ideologically disguised power of corporate capital, and the desire to construct a more democratic and participatory vision of the world, provided the common ground on which NAFTA's labor critics could be joined by environmental activists, consumer advocates, left-oriented intellectuals, and others. While they did not win their battle to defeat the treaty in the US Congress, they did mount a serious challenge to the agenda of transnational corporate capital and, in the process, began to articulate an alternative political vision.[54]

The kinds of developments reviewed above suggest that the hegemony of neoliberalism is expiring, its identification of liberal capitalism with universal aspirations no longer generally credible, its "historic bloc" of corporate capital and industrial labor fragmenting. The "morbid symptoms" of hegemonic crisis – deepening global inequality and recurrent wars in the periphery of the world economy, right-wing reaction at home and abroad, deindustrialization, homelessness and poverty juxtaposed to unprecedented concentrations of wealth, the exhaustion of established political ideologies and the meteoric rise of charismatic and unorthodox figures such as Ross Perot – signal that neoliberalism too has been unable to fulfill its promises to the masses of people in America, or to create the world of generalized peace and prosperity envisioned during the years of hubris after World War II. The failures of neoliberalism have not been socially uniform in their incidence, however: this is not an instance of *national* decline, as some scholars of international relations would have it.[55] US-based multinational corporations and the wealthiest individuals in American society have continued to profit even as formerly privileged industrial workers have been squeezed out of their status as "middle class" Americans. These workers now join in increasing numbers – and still more fear that they will soon join – those groups excluded from the neoliberal accommodation: the non-unionized, those unable to find full-time year-round employment, those working in the low-paying service sector, women, African-Americans and other systematically disadvantaged groups, as well as the great masses of people who reside in post-colonial societies. The "fusion of power and purpose" (in John Ruggie's phrase) which had constituted the national interest and which laid claim to the allegiance of the entire "free world" has demonstrably left these people behind. If they are able to find the terms in which to frame a common interest, a formidable counter-hegemonic movement could be constructed in ways which might not be constrained by state-based conceptions of politics, or individualistic visions of social reality. One task which must be on the agenda of critical international relations research is to explore further the possibilities of such movements, and the concrete conditions in which they might emerge and grow.

Notes

1 Introduction

1 Robert Cox, "Social Forces, States, and World Orders" *Millennium* 10 (1981), pp. 126–55.

2 *Ibid.*; Richard Ashley, "The Poverty of Neorealism" *International Organization* 38 (1984), pp. 225–86; Alex Wendt, "The Agent-Structure Problem in International Relations Theory" *International Organization* 41 (1987), pp. 335–70.

3 Hayward Alker, "The Presumption of Anarchy in World Politics", manuscript, Massachusetts Institute of Technology, 1986.

4 Steven Lukes, *Individualism* (Oxford: Blackwell, 1973), p. 73. See also Anthony Arblaster, *The Rise and Decline of Western Liberalism* (Oxford: Blackwell, 1984), pp. 15–54.

5 Robert Gilpin, *US Power and the Multinational Corporation* (New York: Basic Books, 1975), p. 39.

6 Charles Kindleberger, *The World in Depression, 1929–1939* (Berkeley: University of California Press, 1973); "Dominance and Leadership in the International Economy" *International Studies Quarterly* 25 (1981), pp. 242–54; Gilpin, *US Power*; and *The Political Economy of International Relations* (Princeton: Princeton University Press, 1987).

7 Stephen Krasner, "State Power and the Structure of International Trade" *World Politics* 28 (1976), pp. 317–47; Robert Keohane and J. Nye, *Power and Interdependence* (Boston: Little, Brown, 1977); Robert Keohane, "The Theory of Hegemonic Stability and Changes in International Economic Regimes, 1967–77" in O. Holsti, R. Siverson and A. George, eds., *Change in the International System* (Boulder: Westview, 1980), pp. 131–62; "Hegemonic Leadership and US Foreign Economic Policy in the 'Long Decade' of the 1950s" in W. Avery and D. Rapkin, eds., *America in a Changing World Political Economy* (New York: Longman, 1982), pp. 49–76.

8 Timothy McKeown, "Hegemonic Stability Theory and Nineteenth Century Tariff Levels in Europe" *International Organization* 37 (1983), pp. 73–92;

Keohane, "The Demand for International Regimes" in S. Krasner, ed. *International Regimes* (Ithaca: Cornell University Press, 1983), pp. 141–71; and *After Hegemony* (Princeton: Princeton University Press, 1984); John Conybeare, "Public Goods, Prisoners' Dilemmas, and the International Political Economy" *International Studies Quarterly* 28 (1984), pp. 5–22; Arthur Stein, "The Hegemon's Dilemma" *International Organization* 38 (1984), pp. 355–86; Bruce Russett, "The Mysterious Case of Vanishing Hegemony or Is Mark Twain Really Dead?" *International Organization* 39 (1985), pp. 202–31; Duncan Snidal, "The Limits of Hegemonic Stability Theory" *International Organization* 39 (1985), pp. 579–614; Susan Strange, "The Persistent Myth of Lost Hegemony" *International Organization* 41 (1987), pp. 551–74.

9 Thus, for example, even Keohane – who counts himself a critic of "neorealism" – can explicitly acknowledge the limitations of system-level analyses, and still define the fundamental objectives of his research program in terms of the atomistic ontology in which these limitations inhere: see his "Theory of World Politics" in R. Keohane, ed. *Neorealism and its Critics* (New York: Columbia University Press, 1986), pp. 158–203.

10 Cox, "Social Forces"; Ashley, "Three Modes of Economism" *International Studies Quarterly* 27 (1983), pp. 463–96; and "Poverty of Neorealism"; Alker, "Presumption of Anarchy"; R. B. J. Walker, "Realism, Change, and International Political Theory" *International Studies Quarterly* 31 (1987), pp. 65–86; Wendt, "Agent-Structure Problem".

11 Jacob Viner, "Power versus Plenty as Objectives of Foreign Policy in the Seventeenth and Eighteenth Centuries" *World Politics* 1 (1948), p. 10. Compare Gilpin, *US Power*, p. 37; and Keohane, *After Hegemony*, pp. 18–25.

12 Gilpin, *US Power*, p. 182.

13 Keohane, *After Hegemony*, p. 22.

14 *Ibid.*, p. 23.

15 Immanuel Wallerstein, *The Modern World System I* (New York: Academic Press, 1974); *The Capitalist World-Economy* (Cambridge: Cambridge University Press, 1979); *The Modern World System II* (New York: Academic Press, 1980); *The Politics of the World-Economy* (Cambridge: Cambridge University Press, 1984). Helpful critiques include Robert Brenner, "The Origins of Capitalist Development: A Critique of Neo-Smithian Marxism" *New Left Review* 104 (1977), pp. 25–92; Theda Skocpol, "Wallerstein's World Capitalist System" *American Journal of Sociology* 82 (1977), pp. 1075–90; and Wendt, "Agent-Structure Problem", pp. 340–9.

16 Wallerstein, *Capitalist World-Economy*, p. 5.

17 *Ibid.*, pp. 17–21, 25; and *Politics of the World-Economy*, pp. 1–46.

18 Wallerstein, *Modern World-System I*, p. 84.

19 Wallerstein, *Politics of the World-Economy*, p. 29.

20 Compare, for example: *Modern World-System I*, pp. 87, 136, 146–51; *Capitalist World-Economy*, p. 21; *Modern World-System II*, p. 114; *Politics of the World-Economy*, pp. 14, 33, 36, 43, 46.

2 Marx, Gramsci, and possibilities for radical renewal in IPE

1 Wendt, "Agent-Structure Problem".
2 Cox, "Social Forces"; "Gramsci, Hegemony, and International Relations" *Millennium* 12 (1983), pp. 162–75; and *Production, Power and World Order* (New York: Columbia University Press, 1987); also Kees van der Pijl, *The Making of an Atlantic Ruling Class* (London: Verso, 1984); Enrico Augelli and Craig Murphy, *America's Quest For Supremacy and the Third World* (London: Pinter, 1988); and Stephen Gill, *American Hegemony and the Trilateral Commission* (Cambridge: Cambridge University Press, 1990).
3 A concept of internal relations is central to dialectical methodologies. In brief, an internal relation is one in which the inter-related entities take their meaning from (or are constituted within) their relation, and are unintelligible (or non-existent) outside of the context of that relation. Classic examples include master–slave, parent–child and teacher–student relations. Carol Gould contrasts these with external relations, "in which each *relatum* is taken as a separate self-subsistent entity, which exists apart from the relation and appears to be totally independent of it." Gould, *Marx's Social Ontology* (Cambridge, MA: MIT Press, 1978), p. 38. See also Bertell Ollman, *Alienation* 2nd edn. (Cambridge: Cambridge University Press, 1976), pp. 12–40, 256–76.
4 Karl Marx, "Economic and Philosophical Manuscripts" in *Early Writings* (New York: Vintage Books, 1975), p. 328. See, more generally, *Ibid.*, pp. 322–34, 349–50, 355–8, 389–91; Karl Marx and Friedrich Engels, *The German Ideology*, C. J. Arthur, ed. (New York: International Publishers, 1970), pp. 48–52, 59–64; and Marx, *Capital, Volume I* (New York: Vintage Books, 1977), pp. 133–4, 173.
5 Marx, *Capital I*, p. 290.
6 The "violence of things" is from Marx and Engels, *German Ideology*, p. 84. On "alienation," see pp. 52–4, 84, 91–3; also Marx, "Manuscripts," pp. 322–79; and Marx, "Appendix: Results of the Immediate Process of Production", in *Capital I*, pp. 990, 1003–4, 1016, 1054, 1058. For discussions of the related notion of "fetishism," see *Capital I*, pp. 164–5, 167–8, 174–5; also "Appendix," pp. 980–90, 998, 1003, 1005–8, 1052–8.
7 See Istvan Meszaros, *Marx's Theory of Alienation*, 4th edn. (London: Merlin Press, 1975), pp. 78–84; and C. J. Arthur, *Dialectics of Labor* (Oxford: Blackwell, 1986), pp. 5–19.
8 Marx, "Manuscripts," pp. 324–34; also Marx and Engels, *German Ideology*, pp. 52–4.
9 Marx, "Manuscripts," p. 324.
10 *Ibid.*, p. 326.
11 Ollman, *Alienation*, p. 19.
12 According to Marx's analysis of the two-fold character of commodities in capitalist society, "labor-power" denotes the abstract, commodified form of labor – i.e., the capacity to work – which is sold at its "exchange value" for wages. This is rigorously distinguished from "labor," which denotes the

actual work performed for the wages paid by the capitalist. Labor is then the "use value" which the capitalist may derive from his purchase of labor-power. In Marx's theory of value, human labor-power is unique among commodities in that the value of the commodities generated by labor is potentially much greater than the value of labor-power itself (that is, the labor time socially necessary to produce the workers' means of subsistence and reproduce labor-power). The use value of labor-power, then, is greater (by some variable magnitude) than its exchange value. It is this difference – "surplus value," the product and in turn a precondition of the process of alienated labor – which serves as the centerpiece of Marx's theory of exploitation in capitalist society, and which represents the daily reality of class struggle.

13 Capitalists, too, are governed by the operation of seemingly objective economic laws, and in this sense may be understood as experiencing their own kind of alienation (Marx, "Appendix," p. 990). They confront the market as individuals in mortal competition with one another, and hence are driven to intensify the extraction of surplus value by increasing their control over the organization and performance of work. It is this "real subsumption of labor" which enables the continual incorporation of new technologies and processes into the capitalist labor process, and which underlies the unique economic dynamism of capitalist social formations. See *ibid.*, pp. 1023–5, 1034–8; also *Capital I*, part four.

14 Marx, "Appendix," p. 1027 (emphases in original).

15 Marx and Engels, *German Ideology*, pp. 53–4, 57–8, 79–81, 83; Marx, "Manuscripts," p. 369; *Capital I*, pp. 874–5; and "Appendix," p. 1027. See also "Critique of Hegel's Doctrine of the State" in *Early Writings*, pp. 57–198; and "On the Jewish Question" in *Early Writings*, pp. 211–41.

16 Marx, *Capital I*, p. 280. The historical grounding of the Smithian competitive market and its egoistic individual in capitalist relations of production is a central theme in the works of Robert Brenner, for example, "The Social Basis of Economic Development" in J. Roemer, ed. *Analytical Marxism* (Cambridge: Cambridge University Press, 1986), pp. 23–53.

17 Derek Sayer, "The Critique of Politics and Political Economy" *Sociological Review* 33 (1985), pp. 231, 233.

18 Marx and Engels, *German Ideology*, p. 80. The manner of this interdependence is a matter of vigorous debate among Marxian political theorists: see Bob Jessop, *The Capitalist State* (New York: New York University Press, 1982); and Martin Carnoy, *The State and Political Theory* (Princeton: Princeton University Press, 1984).

19 Gramsci's primary theoretical legacy is contained in his prison writings: *Selections from the Prison Notebooks* Q. Hoare and G. Smith, eds. (New York: International Publishers, 1971). Among the interpretations from which I have learned most are Walter Adamson, *Hegemony and Revolution* (Berkeley: University of California Press, 1980); and Ann S. Sassoon, *Gramsci's Politics*, 2nd edn. (Minneapolis: University of Minnesota Press, 1987).

20 Gramsci, *Prison Notebooks*, p. 352.

21 *Ibid.*, pp. 34–5.

22 *Ibid.*, p. 171; also pp. 9, 34–5, 133–4, 323–5, 332–4, 344, 351–7, 360–1, 445–6.

23 *Ibid.*, p. 172. Gramsci clearly implies that the philosophy of praxis can claim no validity as absolute, transhistorical truth, but is rather specific to a particular historical social reality and will itself be transcended along with that reality; on the historical embeddedness of knowledge see pp. 364–6, 404–7, 446. For discussions of the tension between Gramsci's dialectical openness and a Marxian teleology of proletarian revolution, see Adamson, *Hegemony and Revolution*, pp. 130–9; and Martin Jay, *Marxism and Totality* (Cambridge: Polity Press, 1984), pp. 150–73. When I first wrote this chapter, I regarded this as a healthy dialectical tension to be worked out through historically concrete practice; but I now find myself increasingly troubled by this, insofar as the Marxian teleology may entail too narrow an understanding of the possibilities of such practice.

24 Gramsci, *Prison Notebooks*, pp. 12, 54, 235–9, 242–3, 244, 258–63.

25 *Ibid.*, pp. 164–5, 326, 328, 375–7.

26 *Ibid.*, p. 244; see also pp. 12–13, 52, 56, 239, 257–63, 268. The preceding quotation is from p. 263.

27 *Ibid.*, pp. 229–39, 242–3.

28 *Ibid.*, pp. 139–40, 144–57, 2 258–60, 263, 267, 332–5, 350–1, 382, 418.

29 *Ibid.*, pp. 158–68, 175–85, 229–39, 257–60, 381–2, 407–9.

30 My interpretation here diverges from that of such commentators as Adamson, who contends that Gramsci's concrete "pragmatological dialectic" could hardly accommodate such notions as alienation: *Hegemony and Revolution*, pp. 130–5.

31 Gramsci, *Prison Notebooks*, pp. 9, 158–68, 175–85, 229–39, 268, 323–7, 332–5, 344, 366–7, 407, 419–21.

32 *Ibid.*, pp. 184, 233, 407.

33 *Ibid.*, pp. 12, 136–7, 161, 167–8, 180–3, 365–7, 375–7, 418.

34 See Adamson, *Hegemony and Revolution*, p. 178; and Sassoon, *Gramsci's Politics*, pp. 121–2.

35 Gramsci, *Prison Notebooks*, pp. 328, 420.

36 *Ibid.*, pp. 58–9, 106–14.

37 *Ibid.*, pp. 144, 152, 253, 257–60, 263, 267, 332–5, 382.

38 Gilpin, *US Power*, pp. 26–33; Keohane, "Theory of World Politics". More formidable criticisms of Marxian theory are offered by Skocpol, *States and Social Revolutions* (Cambridge: Cambridge University Press, 1979), pp. 26–31; Anthony Giddens, *The Nation-State and Violence* (Berkeley: University of California Press, 1985); and Andrew Linklater, "Realism, Marxism and Critical International Theory" *Review of International Studies* 12 (1986), pp. 301–12.

39 Sayer, *Marx's Method* 2nd edn. (Atlantic Highlands: Humanities Press, 1983), p. 8.

40 This argument draws inspiration, but departs substantially, from R. N. Berki, "On Marxian Thought and the Problem of International Relations"

in R. Walker, ed. *Culture, Ideology, and World Order* (Boulder: Westview, 1984), pp. 217–42; and James Der Derian, "Mediating Estrangement: A Theory for Diplomacy" *Review of International Studies* 13 (1987), pp. 91–110.

41 Gramsci, *Prison Notebooks*, p. 240.

42 *Ibid.*, p. 176.

43 *Ibid.*, p. 182, see also p. 116.

44 *Ibid.*, p. 350, see also pp. 240–1.

45 On division of labor in the workshop vs. that in society, see Marx, *Capital I*, pp. 470–80. On globalization of capital, see Peter Dicken, *Global Shift* 2nd edn. (New York: Guilford Press, 1992); Cox, "Social Forces," pp. 146–7, and *Production*, pp. 244–53; Gill, *American Hegemony*, pp. 90–3. But compare David Gordon, "The Global Economy" *New Left Review* 168 (1988), especially pp. 41–2.

46 Cox, "Social Forces," pp. 144–6; and *Production*, pp. 253–65; van der Pijl, *Ruling Class*; Gill, *American Hegemony*.

3 The quality of global power: a relational view of neoliberal hegemony

1 Cox, "Social Forces," p. 141. See also "Gramsci"; and *Production*. For a more general discussion of power as embedded in historical social relations, see Jeffrey Isaac, *Power and Marxist Theory* (Ithaca: Cornell University Press, 1987).

2 See Cox, "Social Forces", p. 153; and *Production*, pp. 6–8, 409–10.

3 Compare, for example: Gilpin, *US Power*, pp. 33–8; Keohane, *After Hegemony*, p. 32; Wallerstein, *Modern World-System II*, pp. 38–9; Wallerstein, *Politics of the World-Economy*, pp. 17, 38–41; Cox, "Gramsci," pp. 171–2; and *Production*, pp. 4–9.

4 Cox, *Production*, p. 109.

5 *Ibid.*, pp. 111–50.

6 *Ibid.*, pp. 151–210.

7 *Ibid.*, pp. 219–20. Cox's notion of neoliberalism has some significant commonalities with John Ruggie's concept of "embedded liberalism," for which see "International Regimes, Transactions, and Change" in S. Krasner, ed., *International Regimes* (Ithaca: Cornell University Press, 1983), pp. 195–231.

8 Cox, *Production*, p. 215.

9 Charles S. Maier, "The Politics of Productivity" in his *In Search of Stability* (Cambridge: Cambridge University Press, 1987), pp. 121–52. See also "The Two Postwar Eras and The Conditions for Stability in Twentieth-Century Western Europe," *ibid.*, pp. 153–84.

10 This is Maier's abstract of "The Politics of Productivity" as it appears in P. J. Katzenstein, ed., *Between Power and Plenty* (Madison: University of Wisconsin Press, 1978), p. 23.

11 Michael Hogan, *The Marshall Plan* (Cambridge: Cambridge University Press, 1987), p. 136.

12 Peter Donohue, "'Free Trade' Unions and the State" *Research in Political*

Economy vol. XIII (Greenwich, CT: JAI Press, 1992), pp. 1–73. The *CIO News* was quoted on p. 21, and Benjamin Haskell of the AFL was quoted on p. 35.

13 On American labor's support for the Marshall Plan and for an anticommunist labor regime in Europe, see Anthony Carew, *Labor under the Marshall Plan* (Detroit: Wayne State University Press, 1987).

14 Ruth L. Horowitz, *Political Ideologies of Organized Labor* (New Brunswick, NJ: Transaction Books, 1978), chapters 1–2.

15 Vivian Fry, Executive Secretary of the ALCIA, speaking in April, 1945; quoted in Carew, *Labor*, p. 62.

16 *Ibid.*, p. 61.

17 Ronald Radosh, *American Labor and United States Foreign Policy* (New York: Random House, 1969), chapter 10; Rhodri Jeffreys-Jones, *The CIA and American Democracy* (New Haven: Yale University Press, 1989), pp. 49–52; Sallie Pisani, *The CIA and the Marshall Plan* (Lawrence: University Press of Kansas, 1991), pp. 99–101, 111–13, 117, 119; Philip Agee, *Inside the Company* (New York: Bantam Books, 1976), pp. 68–71; Carew, *Labor*, pp. 69, 102, 119; also Victor Reuther, *The Brothers Reuther and the Story of the UAW* (Boston: Houghton Mifflin, 1976), pp. 412, 426.

18 V. Reuther, *Brothers Reuther*, quotes the statement by Carey on p. 331. The quotation attributed to British, Dutch and American unionists is from a booklet entitled *Free Trade Unions Leave the WFTU* (London: Trades Union Congress, 1949), p. 3: in the Walter P. Reuther Collection, Box 448, Archive of Labor and Urban Affairs (ALUA), Wayne State University. For a strongly anticommunist interpretation of the breakup of the WFTU, see Carl Gershman, *The Foreign Policy of American Labor* (Beverly Hills: Sage, 1975), chapter 3.

19 V. Reuther, *Brothers Reuther*, p. 332. See also Carew, *Labor*, chapter 5; and Radosh, *American Labor*, pp. 435–8.

20 The first quotation is from a memorandum from the American labor delegates to the Fourth World Congress of the ICFTU, p. 5; the second quotation is from a CIO proposal entitled "Labor's Fund for Freedom," p.2: both in Walter P. Reuther Collection, Box 294, ALUA.

21 See, however, Denis Macshane, *International Labor and the Origins of the Cold War* (Oxford: Oxford University Press, 1992), who argues that stresses internal to European labor movements were more important than American interventions in producing these results.

22 Carew, *Labor*, p. 112.

23 Quoted in *ibid.*, p. 118.

24 V. Reuther, *Brothers Reuther*, pp. 338, 425; also quoted is a letter from Victor to Walter Reuther, dated April 23, 1951: Walter P. Reuther collection, Box 294, ALUA. In *Brothers Reuther*, Victor discusses what he calls the "seduction of AFL–CIO by the Central Intelligence Agency" on pp. 411–27.

25 *Ibid.*, p. 283.

26 Carew, *Labor*, pp. 144, 156. On the various productivity campaigns sup-

ported by the Marshall Plan, see *ibid.*, chapters 9–12; and Hogan, *Marshall Plan*, chapter 4.

27 Reuther quoted in Carew, *Labor*, p. 181.
28 P. Armstrong, A. Glyn, and J. Harrison, *Capitalism Since 1945* (Oxford: Blackwell, 1991), pp. 105, 122–6. See also van der Pijl, *Ruling Class*, chapters 6–8.
29 Carew, *Labor*, p. 223.
30 Maier, "Politics of Productivity," pp. 44–5.
31 Robert Pollard, *Economic Security and the Origins of the Cold War, 1945–1950* (New York: Columbia University Press, 1985); also John Lewis Gaddis, *Strategies of Containment* (Oxford: Oxford University Press, 1982), pp. 3–88.
32 Pollard, *Economic Security*, p. 167. See also Hogan, *Marshall Plan*, pp. 429, 442–3.
33 Thomas Ferguson, "From Normalcy to New Deal" *International Organization* 38 (1984), pp. 41–94; Jeffrey A. Frieden, "Sectoral Conflict and US Foreign Economic Policy, 1914–1940" *International Organization* 42 (1988), pp. 59–90. For an earlier example of this line of "sectoral" research, see J. R. Kurth, "The Political Consequences of the Product Cycle" *International Organization* 33 (1979), pp. 1–34.
34 For Ferguson's categorizations of firms most likely to reach accommodation with organized labor, see "Normalcy to New Deal," p. 66. For his conception of labor militancy as an external constraint on economic "elites," see pp. 49, 88, 93.
35 See, for example, Irving Bernstein, *Turbulent Years* (Boston: Houghton Mifflin, 1970), chapters 10–12; Howell John Harris, *The Right to Manage* (Madison: University of Wisconsin Press, 1982), chapter 1; Stanley Vittoz, *New Deal Labor Policy and the American Industrial Economy* (Chapel Hill: University of North Carolina Press, 1987), chapters 7–8; Rhonda Levine, *Class Struggle and the New Deal* (Lawrence: University Press of Kansas, 1988), chapters 6–7.
36 This vision of "economic security" is a central theme in the works of Maier, Hogan, and Pollard, cited above. For longer-term perspectives on the development of conceptions of economic security in American perceptions of national interest, see the various historical essays in W. H. Becker and S. F. Wells, Jr., eds., *Economics and World Power* (New York: Columbia University Press, 1984); and Walter LaFeber, *The American Age* (New York: Norton, 1989).

4 The emergence of mass production practices and productivist ideology

1 Michael J. Piore and Charles F. Sabel, *The Second Industrial Divide* (New York: Basic Books, 1984), pp. 52–4.
2 In classical Marxist terms, the two-fold dynamic of class struggle and inter-capitalist competition accounts for the technological dynamism of capitalism and its revolutionizing of the production process. Driven by the

imperative for ceaseless accumulation, capitalists will seek ways to increase the exploitation of labor. Extensive increases in exploitation (such as lengthening the working day) will eventually encounter physiological limits and/or political resistance, and so capitalists will be compelled to intensify the exploitation of labor within a given period of labor time – that is, they will attempt to secure "relative surplus value." See Marx, *Capital I*, especially part four, "The Production of Relative Surplus-Value," and "Appendix." Michel Aglietta interprets the rise of a Fordist "regime of intensive accumulation" – which revolutionized both production and consumption – in terms of the interaction of these general dynamics of capitalism and factors specific to the American context: *A Theory of Capitalist Regulation* (London: Verso, 1987). See also H. Braverman, *Labor and Monopoly Capital* (New York: Monthly Review Press, 1974); David M. Gordon, Richard Edwards, and Michael Reich, *Segmented Work, Divided Workers* (Cambridge: Cambridge University Press, 1982), pp. 100–64; David Montgomery, *The Fall of the House of Labor* (Cambridge: Cambridge University Press, 1987), pp. 214–329.

3 Frederick Winslow Taylor, *Scientific Management* (New York: Harper and Brothers, 1947): the quotations are from Taylor's "Testimony," pp. 29–31; but see also therein "Principles of Scientific Management," especially pp. 9–11, 142–4. On the means by which Taylor's scientific management proposed to realize its productivity gains see "Testimony," pp. 40–1, and "Principles," pp. 36–48, 83, 114–5.

4 See Gordon, Edwards, and Reich, *Segmented Work*, pp. 216–18, for evidence of the privileged status of unionized industrial workers in the post-World War II "social structure of accumulation."

5 Aglietta, *Capitalist Regulation*, pp. 73–8; see also Nathan Rosenberg, "Why in America?" in O. Mayr and R. Post, eds., *Yankee Enterprise* (Washington, DC: Smithsonian Institution Press, 1981), pp. 49–61.

6 Gordon, Edwards and Reich, *Segmented Work*, p. 50; see also pp. 79–91.

7 On nineteenth-century labor militancy and struggles over wage reductions, the length of the working day, and control of the production process, see Jeremy Brecher, *Strike!* (Boston: South End Press, 1972), chapters 1–3; also Montgomery, *House of Labor*, chapters 1–4. See also Gordon, Edwards, and Reich, *Segmented Work*, chapters 3–4; and Levine, *Class Struggle*, chapter 2.

8 David A. Hounshell, "The System" in Mayr and Post, eds., *Yankee Enterprise*, p. 127. See also Hounshell's *From the American System to Mass Production, 1800–1932* (Baltimore: Johns Hopkins University Press, 1984).

9 Henry Ford and Samuel Crowther, *My Life and Work* (Garden City, NY: Doubleday, 1922), p. 73. See also David L. Lewis, *The Public Image of Henry Ford* (Detroit: Wayne State University Press, 1976), pp. 43, 494–5.

10 Ford and Crowther, *My Life*, pp. 80, 280.

11 For discussions of the productivity increases which Ford's methods made possible, see Allan Nevins and Frank Ernest Hill, *Ford: The Times, the Man,*

the Company (New York: Charles Scribners Sons, 1954), pp. 472–4, 504; Hounshell, *American System*, pp. 253–6; Stephen Meyer III, *The Five Dollar Day* (Albany: State University of New York Press, 1981), pp. 32–5; and David Gartman, *Auto Slavery* (New Brunswick, NJ: Rutgers University Press, 1986), pp. 141–6. On the problematic day-to-day realization of this potential, see Meyer, *Five Dollar Day*, pp. 71–2, 79–94; and Gartman, *Auto Slavery*, pp. 147–78.

12 Ford conducted factory tours and distributed in-house publications which described its production practices: for example, *Factory Facts from Ford*, 1915 and 1920 editions, Accession 951, Box 11, Ford Archives. The technical press were also welcomed at the Ford plant: see H. L. Arnold and F. L. Faurote, *Ford Methods and the Ford Shops* (New York: The Engineering Magazine Company, 1915). The preceding quotation is from Nevins and Hill, *Ford: The Times, the Man*, p. 488. Price and sales figures are from David L. Lewis, *Public Image*, p. 44; and James J. Flink, *The Automobile Age* (Cambridge, MA: MIT Press, 1988), p. 37. On the connection of mass production, price reduction and sales volume, see also Ford and Crowther, *My Life*, pp. 73–4.

13 See Meyer, "The Persistence of Fordism" in N. Lichtenstein and S. Meyer, eds., *On The Line* (Urbana: University of Illinois Press, 1989), pp. 73–99; also Hounshell, *American System*, chapter 7; and Flink, *Automobile Age*, chapters 4, 5, 7, and 12.

14 Ford and Crowther, *Today and Tomorrow* (Garden City, NY: Doubleday, 1926), pp. 8, 9. On the notion of a partnership between employers and workers, see also Ford and Crowther, *My Life*, pp. 117–21.

15 Ford and Crowther, *Today and Tomorrow*, p. 252.

16 *Ibid.*, p. 111.

17 The criterion of a "clean, sober, and industrious life" is taken from a Ford Motor Company pamphlet, *Helpful Hints and Advice to Employes* [sic] (1915), p. 8; Accession 951, Box 23, Ford Archives. See also the now classic account of Stephen Meyer, *Five Dollar Day*.

18 For evidence suggesting that automobile ownership was not the norm among auto workers, and was still less common among industrial workers more generally, see Joyce Shaw Peterson, *American Automobile Workers, 1900–1933* (Albany: State University of New York Press, 1987), p. 81; Flink, *Automobile Age*, pp. 130–5; Frank Stricker, "Affluence for Whom?" *Labor History* 24 (1983), pp. 29–32; and Lizabeth Cohen, *Making a New Deal* (Cambridge: Cambridge University Press, 1990), p. 103.

19 Hounshell, *American System*, p. 11. Note that Hounshell's use of "Fordism" is a relatively narrow one. In contrast, Aglietta understands Fordism as the regulative principle of a macrosocial "regime of intensive accumulation" entailing transformations of the labor process as well as social consumption norms, thereby expanding the entire circuit of capital – the basis of the accumulation process: see *Capitalist Regulation*, pp. 116–22, 152–61. Understood in this way, Fordism was not "born" in 1913–14 with the assembly line and the five dollar day, but rather was the product of a long period of

socio-political struggle in which Ford himself bitterly opposed such key features of the emerging regime as industrial unionism, collective bargaining, and the New Deal reforms. On the transformation of auto production, see also: Nevins and Hill, *Ford: The Times, the Man*, chapter 18; Jack Russell, "The Coming of the Line" *Radical America* 12 (1978), pp. 28–45; Meyer, *Five Dollar Day*; Gartman, *Auto Slavery*; Peterson, *Automobile Workers*; Flink, *Automobile Age*, chapter 4.

20 Daniel Nelson, *Managers and Workers* (Madison: University of Wisconsin Press, 1975), p. ix. See also: David F. Noble, *America by Design* (Oxford: Oxford University Press, 1977); Alfred D. Chandler, "The American System and Modern Management" in Mayr and Post, eds., *Yankee Enterprise*, pp. 153–70; Piore and Sabel, *Industrial Divide*, chapter 3.

21 For data reflecting the steady increase in size, mechanization, productivity, and capital intensity of US manufacturing between 1879 and 1929, see Gordon, Edwards, and Reich, *Segmented Work*, table 4.4, p. 130.

22 Angus Maddison, *Phases of Capitalist Development* (Oxford: Oxford University Press, 1982), note 20, p. 259.

23 US Bureau of the Census, *Historical Statistics of the United States* (Washington, DC: Government Printing Office, 1975), series D-683, D-685, D-686, p. 162.

24 William H. Becker, "1899–1920, America Adjusts to World Power" in Becker and Wells, eds., *Economics and World Power* pp. 176–8.

25 Chandler, "American System," p. 166.

26 David M. Kennedy, *Over Here* (New York: Oxford University Press, 1980), chapters 2, 6; Nelson, *Managers and Workers*, chapter 8; Jeffrey Haydu, *Between Craft and Class* (Berkeley: University of California Press, 1988), chapter 5.

27 Melvyn P. Leffler, "1921–1932, Expansionist Impulses and Domestic Constraints" in Becker and Wells, eds., *Economics and World Power*, p. 227. On global finance, see Kennedy, *Over Here*, pp. 319–24; and Frieden, *Banking on the World* (Oxford: Blackwell, 1987), pp. 25–9.

28 *Historical Statistics*, series 218, p. 889.

29 *Historical Statistics*, series U-218, p. 889, and series U-287, p. 898.

30 Flink, *Automobile Age*, p.18.

31 *Ibid.*, pp. 19, 43–4.

32 Foreman-Peck, "American Challenge," p. 867; also Flink, *Automobile Age*, p. 251. For US share of world output, see *World Motor Vehicle Data* (Detroit: Motor Vehicle Manufacturers Association, 1991), p. 10.

33 Leffler, "Expansionist Impulses," p. 258. See also Fred Block, *The Origins of International Economic Disorder* (Berkeley: University of California Press, 1977), pp. 14–22; Becker, "America Adjusts," pp. 212–18; and Frieden, "Sectoral Conflict."

34 Hounshell, *American System*, p. 64; see also pp. 4, 17–25, 61–5, 331–2.

35 Judith Merkle, *Management and Ideology* (Berkeley: University of California Press, 1980), pp. 33–4, 148, 178, 221–2; see also Foreman-Peck, "American Challenge," p. 869; and Jean-Pierre Bardou, Jean-Jacques Chanaron, Patrick

Fridenson, and James M. Laux, *The Automobile Revolution* (Chapel Hill: University of North Carolina Press, 1982), pp. 67–8.

36 Patrick Fridenson, "The Coming of the Assembly Line to Europe" in W. Krohn *et.al.*, eds., *The Dynamics of Science and Technology* (Dordrecht: Reidel, 1978), pp. 161–2, 164; Merkle, *Management and Ideology*, pp. 152, 156–8, 161, 177–8, 182–4, 193–6. For a contemporary account, see Paul Devinat, *Scientific Management in Europe*, International Labor Office Studies and Reports, series B, no. 17 (Geneva, 1927).

37 Devinat, *Scientific Management*, p. 160.

38 *Ibid.*, pp. 43–4.

39 Albert Thomas, "Preface" to Paul Devinat, *Scientific Management*, p. vii.

40 *Ibid.*, p. x. For an illuminating comparison, see also the discussions of manufacturing as "service" to the public in Ford and Crowther, *My Life*, especially chapters 4 and 19.

41 Neumaier and Renault quoted in Lewis, *Public Image*, p. 53. See also Flink, *Automobile Age*, pp. 257–60; Foreman-Peck, "American Challenge," pp. 870–2; Bardou, *et. al.*, *Automobile Revolution*, pp. 101–12; Fridenson, "Coming of the Assembly Line," pp. 162–4. The established British industrial culture seems to have been less hospitable to American-style Taylorism and Fordism: see Merkle, *Management and Ideology*, chapter 7; and Wayne Lewchuk, "Fordism and the Moving Assembly Line" in Lichtenstein and Meyer, eds., *On the Line*, pp. 25–6.

42 Devinat, *Scientific Management*, p. 14; see also pp. 41, 45; and Maier, "Postwar Eras," p. 169.

43 Fridenson, "Coming of the Assembly Line," p. 168; see also Merkle, *Management and Ideology*, p. 179; and Maier, *In Search of Stability* (Cambridge, Cambridge University Press, 1987), pp. 19–53.

44 Maier, "Postwar Eras," p. 166, also pp. 163–5.

45 Maier, *Stability* pp. 29–53; "Postwar Eras," pp. 162–8. See also Merkle, *Management and Ideology*, chapters 4–7; Flink, *Automobile Age*, pp. 261–7; Thomas P. Hughes, *American Genesis* (New York: Viking, 1989), chapter 6; David Harvey, *The Condition of Postmodernity* (Oxford: Blackwell, 1989), chapters 2, 16.

46 Brecher, *Strike!*, chapter 4; Montgomery, *House of Labor*, chapter 8; Irving Bernstein, *The Lean Years* (Boston: Houghton Mifflin, 1960), chapters 1–4; James R. Green, *The World of the Worker* (New York: Hill and Wang, 1980), chapter 4; Robert H. Zieger, *American Workers, American Unions, 1920–1985* (Baltimore: Johns Hopkins University Press, 1986), chapter 1; M. J. Heale, *American Anticommunism* (Baltimore: Johns Hopkins University Press, 1990), chapters 4–5; Peterson, *Automobile Workers*, pp. 42–3, 55–6, 94–102; Cohen, *New Deal*, chapter 4; and David Brody, *Workers in Industrial America* (Oxford: Oxford University Press, 1980), chapter 2. For a contemporary account of the American Plan and welfare capitalism written by a radical researcher, see Robert W. Dunn, *The Americanization of Labor* (New York: International Publishers, 1927).

47 Gordon, Edwards and Reich, *Segmented Work*, pp. 130, 163.

48 *Historical Statistics*, series D-685, p. 162; D-802 and D-804, pp. 169–70. Since the productivity index was based on 1958 prices, to provide some comparability earnings figures were standardized with an implicit deflator for 1958 prices: series F-5, p. 224. Insofar as this is a deflator for overall GNP rather than personal consumption expenditure, the resulting figures reflect variation in more than just consumer prices. The deflated wage figures should therefore be interpreted only as rough estimates of the real standard of living which average earnings would have afforded at different points in time.

49 *Historical Statistics*, series G-135 and G-136: these figures reflect the concentration of disposable income: other variants of this measure (series G-131 to 134) show somewhat less dramatic increases. James N. Devine, "Underconsumption, Over-Investment and the Origins of the Great Depression" *Review of Radical Political Economics* 15 (Summer, 1983), pp. 14–15.

50 Stricker, "Affluence." See also Peterson, *Automobile Workers*, pp. 75–83; and Cohen, *New Deal*, pp. 101–4.

51 On the exhaustion of demand for consumer durables such as cars, see Flink, *Automobile Age*, pp. 130, 188–93, 216–20. Aglietta interprets the economic crisis of the 1930s in terms of the uneven development of a "regime of intensive accumulation," a process which after World War I revolutionized social productive powers without as yet transforming social consumption norms and the living conditions of the industrial working class. The result was a growing imbalance as the rapidly developing sector of production goods (Dept. I) outpaced the consumption goods sector (Dept. II), and a tendency toward a crisis of disproportionality as the overall circuit of capital was increasingly vulnerable to disjunction, arrested accumulation, and massive devaluation of capital. Aglietta, *Capitalist Regulation*, pp. 93–5.

52 Bernstein, *Turbulent Years*; Brecher, *Strike!*, chapter 5; Green, *World of the Worker*, chapter 5; Zieger, *American Workers*, pp. 10–61; Peterson, *Automobile Workers*, pp. 130–56; Cohen, *New Deal*, pp. 238–46, 292–321. For the text of the NIRA, see Henry Steele Commager, ed., *Documents of American History*, 6th edn. (New York: Appleton Century Crofts, 1958), p. 453.

53 Figures in these two paragraphs are from *Historical Statistics*, series D-951, D-970 to D-973, D-982 and D-984, pp. 178–9.

54 A. Kenwood and A. Lougheed, *The Growth of the International Economy* (London: George Allen and Unwin, 1983) chapters 11–15; LaFeber, *American Age*, chapter 11; Leffler, "Expansionist Impulses," pp. 225–75; Flink, *Automobile Age*, pp. 261–72.

5 State–society relations and the politics of industrial transformation in the United States

1 Louis Hartz, *The Liberal Tradition in America* (New York: Harcourt Brace and World, 1955); compare Gramsci, *Prison Notebooks*, p. 281.

2 Samuel Bowles and Herbert Gintis, "The Crisis of Liberal Democratic Capitalism" *Politics and Society* 11 (1982), pp. 51–2.

3 Bowles and Gintis, *Democracy and Capitalism* (New York: Basic Books, 1986), p. 3.

4 Bowles and Gintis, "Crisis," pp. 55–62.

5 Michael Burawoy, *The Politics of Production* (London: Verso, 1985), p. 126.

6 Green, *World of the Worker*, p. 11, also pp. 3–66; Montgomery, *House of Labor*; Haydu, *Craft and Class*; Brody, *Workers*, pp. 3–47; and M. Davis, *Prisoners of the American Dream* (London: Verso, 1986), pp. 3–51.

7 Nelson, *Managers and Workers*, pp. 48–121; Bryan Palmer, "Class, Conception and Conflict" *Review of Radical Political Economics* 7 (1975), pp. 31–49; Noble, *America by Design*; Gordon, Edwards, and Reich, *Segmented Work*, pp. 100–64; Montgomery, *House of Labor*, pp. 214–329; and Haydu, *Craft and Class*, pp. 26–59.

8 Brecher, *Strike!*, pp. 53–100; Montgomery, *House of Labor*, pp. 22–44, 269–75; and Haydu, *Craft and Class*, pp. 13–14, 60–4, 73–89.

9 Montgomery, *Workers' Control in America* (Cambridge: Cambridge University Press, 1979), pp. 91–138; and *House of Labor*, pp. 55–6, 171–213; Haydu, *Craft and Class*, pp. 60–124.

10 Montgomery, *House of Labor*, p. 375.

11 Nelson, *Managers and Workers*, chapter 8; Green, *World of the Worker*, chapter 3. On the war economy in general, see Kennedy, *Over Here*, chapters 2, 6; and Ronald Schaffer, *America in the Great War* (Oxford: Oxford University Press, 1991), chapters 3–5.

12 Kennedy, *Over Here*, pp. 258–70; Harris, "The Snares of Liberalism?" in S. Tolliday and J. Zeitlin, eds., *Shop Floor Bargaining and the State* (Cambridge: Cambridge University Press, 1985), pp. 156–9.

13 Montgomery, *Workers' Control*, pp. 91–138; and *House of Labor*, pp. 330–410; Haydu, *Craft and Class*, pp. 90–143, 174–203.

14 Haydu, *Craft and Class*, p. 184.

15 Kennedy, *Over Here*, pp. 266–7; also Haydu, *Craft and Class*, pp. 174–203.

16 Nelson, *Managers and Workers*, chapter 8; Sanford Jacoby, *Employing Bureaucracy* (New York: Columbia University Press, 1985), chapter 5. See also Dunn, *Americanization of Labor*.

17 Jacoby, *Employing Bureaucracy*, pp. 218, 228, 231.

18 Bernstein, *Turbulent Years*; also Green, *World of the Worker*, chapter 5; and "Working Class Militancy in the Depression" *Radical America* 6 (1972), pp. 1–35; Zieger, *American Workers*, chapters 1–2; Brecher, *Strike!*, chapter 5; David Milton, *The Politics of US Labor* (New York: Monthly Review Press, 1982); Davis, *Prisoners*, chapters 2–3; Vittoz, *New Deal Labor Policy*; and Cohen, *New Deal*. Explicitly skeptical about the revolutionary motivations of depression era militancy are Brody, "The Expansion of the American Labor Movement" in S. Ambrose, ed., *Institutions in Modern America* (Baltimore: Johns Hopkins University Press, 1967), pp. 11–36; Brody, *Workers*, chapters 3–4; Vittoz, "The Economic Foundations of Industrial Politics in

the United States and the Emerging Structural Theory of the State in Capitalist Society" *Amerikastudien* 27 (1982), pp. 365–412; Harris, "Snares of Liberalism?"; and Melvyn Dubofsky, "Not So 'Turbulent Years'" in C. Stephenson and R. Asher, eds. *Life and Labor* (Albany: State University of New York Press, 1986), pp. 205–23. For section 7(a) of NIRA, see Commager, *Documents*, vol. II, p. 453.

19 NLRA reprinted in Commager, *Documents*, vol. II, p. 495. See also Bernstein, *Turbulent Years*, chapter 7; Vittoz, "Economic Foundations," p. 392; and Harris, "Snares of Liberalism?" pp. 170–1.

20 Ronald Edsforth, *Class Conflict and Cultural Consensus* (New Brunswick: Rutgers University Press, 1987); see also V. Reuther, *Brothers Reuther*, chapter 13; and Henry Kraus, *The Many and the Few* 2nd edn. (Urbana: University of Illinois Press, 1985).

21 Bernstein, *Turbulent Years*, chapters 10–12; Brecher, *Strike!*, pp. 177–216; Green, *World of the Worker*, pp. 151–73; Milton, *Politics of US Labor*, chapter 4; Vittoz, "Economic Foundations," pp. 393–404; and Davis, *Prisoners*, pp. 55–65.

22 Bernstein, *Turbulent Years*, chapters 13–15; Brody, *Workers*, chapter 3; Milton, *Politics of US Labor*, chapter 5; Nelson Lichtenstein, *Labor's War at Home* (Cambridge: Cambridge University Press, 1982), chapter 2; and Harris, "Snares of Liberalism?" pp. 168–79.

23 Joshua Freeman, "Delivering the Goods" *Labor History* 19 (1978), pp. 570–93; Green, *World of the Worker*, chapter 6; Lichtenstein, "Auto Worker Militancy and the Structure of Factory Life, 1937–1955" *Journal of American History* 67 (1980), pp. 335–53; *Labor's War*; and "Conflict over Workers' Control" in M. Frisch and D. Walkowitz, eds., *Working Class America* (Urbana: University of Illinois Press, 1983), pp. 284–311; Milton, *Politics of US Labor*, chapter 7; Harris, *Right to Manage*, and "Snares of Liberalism?" pp. 179–81. Also: Richard Polenberg, *War and Society* (New York: Lippincott, 1972); and John Morton Blum, *V Was for Victory* (New York: Harcourt Brace, 1976).

24 Lichtenstein, *Labor's War*, p. 51. The preceding quotation is from Harris, "Snares of Liberalism?" p. 179. See also Brody, *Workers*, pp. 108–16, 136, 140, 144; and Davis, *Prisoners*, pp. 110–11.

25 Harris, "Snares of Liberalism?" p. 181.

26 Freeman, "Delivering the Goods," p. 574; see also Davis, *Prisoners*, p. 77; and Frank Marquart, *An Auto Worker's Journal* (University Park: The Pennsylvania State University Press, 1975), p. 97.

27 Lichtenstein, *Labor's War*, chapters 5, 7, 10; Green, *World of the Worker*, pp. 175, 184–7, 205–6; and Davis, *Prisoners*, pp. 74–82.

28 Lichtenstein, *Labor's War*, p. 119. See also his "Auto Worker Militancy" and "Conflict over Workers' Control," p. 291 as well as Harris, *Right to Manage*, chapters 2, 4.

29 Lichtenstein, *Labor's War*, p. 165.

30 On the importance of such mediating elements for the democratic and

participatory character of mass political movements, see Gramsci, *Prison Notebooks*, pp. 150–3, 185–90, 196–200, 340–1, 418.

31 Lichtenstein, "Conflict over Workers' Control," p. 302; also Jacoby, *Employing Bureaucracy*, chapter 8.

32 Lichtenstein, *Labor's War*, p. 202; also "Auto Worker Militancy" and "Conflict over Workers' Control"; Green, *World of the Worker*, p. 205; and Brody, *Workers*, pp. 198–210.

33 Jerold Auerbach, "The La Follette Committee" *Journal of American History* 51 (December, 1964), pp. 449–52; David Caute, *The Great Fear* (New York: Simon and Schuster, 1978), pp. 41–53, 88–108; Harris, *Right to Manage*, pp. 39–40, 95–104, 179, 181, 195–9; and Heale, *American Anticommunism*, pp. 123–32.

34 Richard M. Freeland, *The Truman Doctrine and the Origins of McCarthyism* (New York: Schocken Books, 1974), pp. 70–150; Caute, *Great Fear*, pp. 25–69; and Heale, *American Anticommunism*, pp. 132–44. The Truman Doctrine and the Loyalty Order are quoted from Commager, *Documents*, vol. II, pp. 704–71.

35 For the Taft-Hartley Act, see Commager, *Documents*, vol. II, pp. 716–19. See also Caute, *Great Fear*, pp. 354–8; Green, *World of the Worker*, pp. 198–9; Lichtenstein, *Labor's War*, pp. 238–41; and Zieger, *American Workers*, pp. 108–14.

36 Quotations are from Bert Cochran, *Labor and Communism* (Princeton: Princeton University Press, 1977), pp. 267, 271, 306; see also Roger Keeran, *The Communist Party and the Auto Workers' Unions* (New York: International Publishers, 1986).

37 Caute, *Great Fear*, chapters 18–21; Green, *World of the Worker*, pp. 195–203; Lichtenstein, *Labor's War*, pp. 234–8; and Zieger, *American Workers*, pp. 123–34; as well as the sources cited immediately above. For an account of the purges written by radicals in "sympathetic association" with one of the expelled unions, see Richard O. Boyer and Herbert M. Morais, *Labor's Untold Story* (Pittsburgh: United Electrical, Radio and Machine Workers of America, 1955), chapter 11. The CIO purges were reported in *The New York Times* (November 2, 1949), pp. 1, 3; (November 3, 1949), pp. 1, 33; (November 4, 1949), p. 3: the quotation is from the first of these.

6 Fordism vs. unionism: production politics and ideological struggle at Ford Motor Company, 1914–1937

1 Lukes, *Individualism*, chapter 11; and Arblaster, *Western Liberalism*, chapters 2–4.

2 John Locke, *Two Treatises of Government* (Cambridge: Cambridge University Press, 1988), p. 289.

3 Arblaster quotes John Jay's pithy declaration: "The people who own the country ought to govern it." *Western Liberalism*, p. 197; also pp. 75–9, 84–91, 150–3, 156–61, 162–76, 189–91, 196–202, 264–83.

4 "On the Jewish Question," in Marx, *Early Writings*, pp. 229–31.

5 Gary Gerstle has written pioneering studies of the significance of "Americanism" in the history of the labor movement, but has not grounded his historical accounts in an analysis of the conditions which made it possible for Americanism to become a decisive terrain of social struggle: the contradictions of liberal capitalism and the experience of those contradictions as unfulfilled promises – promises which carry potentially transformative implications. Nor does he interpret the outcome of this struggle in terms of the formation of a hegemonic regime of global significance. See "The Politics of Patriotism" *Dissent* 33 (1986); pp. 84–92; and *Working-Class Americanism* (Cambridge: Cambridge University Press, 1989).

6 Augelli and Murphy argue that liberal individualism, along with Protestant religion and "scientism" (a pragmatic, empiricist outlook), have been the three primary historical elements of American common sense: *Americas Quest*, chapter 2.

7 Gramsci, *Prison Notebooks*, p. 164; also pp. 138, 162.

8 *Ibid.*, pp. 324, 326.

9 Unidentified Ford worker quoted in Robert Cruden, "The Worker Looks at Ford" *Labor Age* (June, 1928), p. 2; Robert Dunn Collection, Box 2, Archive of Labor and Urban Affairs, Wayne State University (hereafter ALUA). For other first-hand accounts of auto work in the interwar years, see Cruden, "The Great Ford Myth" *The New Republic* (March 16, 1932), p. 117; Walter Edward Ulrich, *On the Belt* (New York: League for Industrial Democracy, 1929), ALUA Vertical File: "Ford Motor Company, 1920s"; and Gene Richard, "On the Assembly Line" *Atlantic Monthly* 159 (April, 1937), pp. 424–8.

10 Henry Ford, Transcript of Testimony Before Federal Commission on Industrial Relations, 1915, p. 4: Accession 1, Box 178; Ford Motor Company, *A Brief Account of the Educational Work of the Ford Motor Company*, pp. 2–3, 8–9, 11: Accession 951, Box 3; and *The Ford Profit-Sharing Plan*, pp. 2–3: Accession 293, Box 1: all in Ford Archives. Also John R. Lee, "The So-Called Profit Sharing System in the Ford Plant," *Annals of the American Academy of Political and Social Science* 65 (May, 1916), pp. 299, 301, 304–5, 308.

11 See, for example Ford and Crowther, *My Life*, pp. 80, 258; Ulrich, *On the Belt*.

12 Meyer, *Five Dollar Day*, pp. 85–94; Steve Babson, *Working Detroit* (Detroit: Wayne State University Press, 1986), pp. 32–3. For a more general discussion of various forms of resistance among auto workers, and early unionization efforts, see Gartman, *Auto Slavery*, chapter 8; and Peterson, *Automobile Workers*, chapters 6–7.

13 Meyer, *Five Dollar Day*, pp. 74–9; Babson, *Working Detroit*, pp. 34–7; also Peterson, *Automobile Workers*, pp. 13–20.

14 "The 'Man' in Manufacturing," *Ford Times* (January, 1916), p. 271; Ford Archives; Meyer, *Five Dollar Day*, pp. 71–2.

15 Typed copy of statement on "chief causes for dissatisfaction and unrest among employees": Accession 940, Box 17; typed copy of press release announcing five dollar day: Accession 940, Box 16; Ford Archives. Also *New*

York Times (January 6, 1914), p 1. For overviews of Ford's labor policies in the period roughly covering 1914 to 1921, written from widely different perspectives, see Samuel M. Levin, "Ford Profit Sharing, 1914–1920" *Personnel Journal* 6 (August, 1927), pp. 75–86; and "The End of Ford Profit Sharing" *Personnel Journal* 6 (October, 1927), pp. 161–70; Keith Sward, *The Legend of Henry Ford* (New York: Rinehart, 1948), chapter 4; Nevins and Hill, *Ford: The Times, the Man*, chapters 20–1; Lewis, *Public Image*, chapter 5; and Robert Lacey, *Ford: The Men and the Machine* (New York: Ballentine, 1986), chapter 7. The account upon which I place heaviest reliance is Meyer, *Five Dollar Day*. I have reinterpreted some of Meyer's arguments by viewing them from a Gramscian perspective, and by more explicitly situating Ford profit sharing in the context of a liberal capitalist social formation.

16 These benefits were explained to Ford workers in *Helpful Hints and Advice to Employes*, 1915: Accession 951, Box 23; the company provided an overview of its "educational and profit-sharing" programs in *Factory Facts From Ford*, 1915 and 1917 editions: Accession 951, Box 11: Ford Archives. *Ford Times* touted the services provided by the Medical Department in "The 'Man' in Manufacturing" (January, 1916), pp. 271–3; and those of the Legal Department in "And So the Home Was Saved" (December 1914), pp. 117–18. On the Ford English School, see the sources cited in note 34, below.

17 *Helpful Hints*, p. 8: Accession 951, Box 23, Ford Archives.

18 *Helpful Hints*, pp. 8–9: Accession 951, Box 23; *Factory Facts*, 1917, pp. 49, 51: Accession 951, Box 11; *Brief Account*, p. 5: Accession 951, Box 3; Ford Archives.

19 Typed copy of press release: Accession 940, Box 16; also *New York Times* (January 6, 1914), p. 1; Henry Ford, Transcript of Testimony, p. 3: Accession 1, Box 178; *Detroit News* article, reprinted as "Two Years of Ford Profit-Sharing" *Ford Times* (July, 1916), p. 549; Ford Archives.

20 Ford quoted in Nevins and Hill, *Ford: Expansion and Challenge, 1915–1933* (New York: Charles Scribner's Sons, 1957), p. 508. Also Henry Ford, Transcript of Testimony, pp. 7–8: Accession 1, Box 178; typed copy of press release: Accession 940, Box 16; Ford Archives.

21 Arnold and Faurote, *Ford Methods and the Ford Shops*, p. 43; also Ford and Crowther, *My Life*, pp. 10–11, 19, 77–8, 98–9, 103, 266, 277–80; and *Ford Profit-Sharing Plan*, pp. 6–7: Accession 293, Box 1, Ford Archives.

22 A typed copy of a memorandum laying out explicitly the difference between wages which the company was obligated to pay, and profits which the company might pay at its discretion, is in Accession 940, Box 15, Ford Archives. In a letter to Professor Samuel Levin written by James Couzens in 1927, the former Ford Treasurer affirms that the wage plan was "called profit sharing in order to enable us to control largely the wages paid in excess of the going wage": Accession 940, Box 16, Ford Archives.

23 Quoted passages are from: *Ford Profit-Sharing Plan*, p. 10: Accession 293, Box 1; *Brief Account*, p. 5: Accession 951, Box 3; and *Helpful Hints*, p. 7: Accession 951, Box 23; Ford Archives. On the perceived relationship between dom-

estic life and efficiency on the job, see Lee, "So-Called Profit Sharing System," p. 299; and Samuel S. Marquis, "The Ford Idea in Education" *National Education Association: Addresses and Proceedings* 54 (1916), p. 914.

24 See Meyer, *Five Dollar Day*, chapter 6. A facsimile of a Sociological Department "record of investigation" appears in "Ford Sociological Work" *Ford Times* (November, 1914), p. 81: Ford Archives.

25 Quotations are from *Helpful Hints*, p. 9: Accession 951, Box 23; and five dollar day press release, Accession 940, Box 16; Ford Archives. The change of address policy is conveyed to workers in *Helpful Hints*, p. 11. See also Lee, "So-Called Profit Sharing System," p. 309.

26 Lee, "So-Called Profit Sharing System," p. 307; also Meyer, *Five Dollar Day*, pp. 112–13.

27 "Two Years of Ford Profit-Sharing" *Ford Times* (July, 1916), p. 547: Ford Archives.

28 Lee, "So-Called Profit Sharing System," p. 307.

29 Ford began employing large numbers of African-Americans during World War I: see August Meier and Elliott Rudwick, *Black Detroit and the Rise of the UAW* (New York: Oxford University Press, 1979), chapter 1. Despite Ford's rhetoric of abstract individualism, it would probably be generous to describe his racial attitudes as ambivalent; for he represented the nativist, as well as the liberal, aspects of Americanism, and apparently believed that Anglo-Saxon peoples were superior to all others. This racist presupposition manifested itself in paternalism toward African-Americans as well as southern and eastern European immigrants, and in episodes of venomous anti-Semitism. On the latter, see Lewis, *Public Image*, chapter 9.

30 Henry Ford, Transcript of Testimony, p. 9: Accession 1, Box 178, Ford Archives.

31 Marquis, "Ford Idea," p. 910.

32 Samuel Marquis, "New Industrial Order Is Impossible Until Individuals Improve" *Detroit Saturday Night* (September 2, 1922): excerpt in Accession 940, Box 17, Ford Archives. Henry Ford's 1915 testimony before the Federal Industrial Relations Commission contained a similar statement about the power of individualism to dissolve class conflict (p. 6): Accession 1, Box 178, Ford Archives.

33 "My Future" *Ford Times* (March, 1916), p. 373: Ford Archives.

34 *Ford Profit-Sharing Plan*, p. 8: Accession 293, Box 1; see also the following articles from *Ford Times*: "Assimilation Through Education" (June, 1915), pp. 407–11; "From Codfish to Motor Cars" (August, 1915), pp. 29–31; "A Motto Wrought Into Education" (April, 1916), pp. 407–9; "The Making of New Americans" (November, 1916), pp. 151–2; and "Better Workmen and Citizens" (February, 1917), pp. 315–19: all in the Ford Archives. The best secondary source is Meyer, *Five Dollar Day*, chapter 7. The latter interprets Ford's Americanization program as an attempt to impose upon immigrant workers an effective industrial culture and the "middle class values" of Ford management, but Meyer does not develop its implications in terms of

a wider political culture of abstract individualism, or the structure of liberal capitalism.

35 "New Americans" *Ford Times* (November, 1916), p. 151: Ford Archives.

36 Marquis, "Ford Idea," p. 915.

37 Lee, "So-Called Profit Sharing System," p. 305.

38 "Codfish to Motor Cars" *Ford Times* (August, 1915), p. 31: Ford Archives.

39 Peter Roberts, *English for Coming Americans* (New York: Association Press, 1912), pp. 39, 79; see also Meyer, *Five Dollar Day*, pp. 156–8.

40 "Motto Wrought Into Education" *Ford Times* (April, 1916), pp. 408–9; and "New Americans" *Ford Times* (November, 1916), pp. 151–2.

41 "Motto Wrought Into Education" *Ford Times* (April, 1916), p. 409.

42 "Better Workmen and Citizens" *Ford Times* (February, 1917), p. 319: Ford Archives.

43 Quotations are from *Brief Account*, p. 12: Accession 951, Box 3, Ford Archives; and Marquis, "Ford Idea," p. 915. See also Royal Meeker, "What is the American Standard of Living?" *Monthly Labor Review* 9 (July, 1919), pp. 1–13. This article indicates the currency of this notion in the popular discourse of the time, and suggests that its connotation was "a very superior standard giving all the necessaries, many of the comforts, and a goodly supply of the luxuries of life." Contrary to public mythology (to which Ford was an important contributor), Meeker argued that no uniformly comfortable American standard of living existed, and that working-class families were especially likely to have difficulty in securing the basic necessities of life.

44 *Helpful Hints*, Accession 951, Box 23, Ford Archives; Meyer, *Five Dollar Day*, p. 145. On the implications of Ford's labor policy for the structure of working-class families and the social position of women, see Martha May, "The Historical Problem of the Family Wage" in E. C. DuBois and V. L. Ruiz, eds., *Unequal Sisters* (New York: Routledge, 1990), pp. 275–91.

45 Typed copy of memorandum by A. E. Gruenberg, dated June 3, 1915, entitled "Progress Among Foreigners Since the Proclamation of Profit Sharing Plan": Accession 940, Box 17, Ford Archives.

46 Lee, "So-Called Profit-Sharing System," p. 307–8; also *Factory Facts* (1917) pp. 45–53: Accession 951, Box 11; *Brief Account*, pp. 2, 6, 9, 11: Accession 951, Box 3; and Ford, Transcript of Testimony, pp. 3–4: Accession 1, Box 178: Ford Archives.

47 Klann quoted in Babson, *Working Detroit*, p. 31. Charles Sorenson, one of Ford's top production executives, remembers that during the deliberations which resulted in the five dollar day, he became convinced that the new wage would create more "satisfied, willing workers" and thereby allow the company to increase production and lower costs; *My Forty Years With Ford* (New York: W. W. Norton, 1956), p. 139; see also Marquis, *Henry Ford* (Boston: Little, Brown, 1923), p. 35.

48 National Labor Relations Board, *Decisions and Orders*, vol. IV, November, 1937–February, 1938 (Washington, DC: Government Printing Office, 1938), p. 651.

49 Cox, *Production*, chapters 5 and 6.

50 Excerpt from Reminiscences of William Pioch: Accession 940, Box 17, Ford Archives; see also Chen-Nan Li, "A Summer in the Ford Works," pp. 23–4. Meyer, *Five Dollar Day*, pp. 142–4, 164–6, documents this kind of resentment, but does not develop its implications in terms of struggle over the meaning of common sense Americanism: Ford workers were expressing their resentment in the language of abstract individualism, with its deep commitments to individual autonomy and privacy. The very world view which Ford labor policies had aimed to inculcate was providing grounds for resistance.

51 The company frankly admits this in *Brief Account*, p. 7: Accession 951, Box 3, Ford Archives.

52 Quotations from *The Ford Man*: "Thanks, John Fordon" (March 3, 1919), p. 2; and "What are You?" (December 17, 1917), p. 5: Ford Archives.

53 Marquis, *Henry Ford*, pp. 98–9; also "Ford Idea," p. 911.

54 *Ford Profit-Sharing Plan*: Accession 293, Box 1, Ford Archives.

55 "Changes in Cost of Living in the United States" *Monthly Labor Review* (February, 1925), pp. 65–73; Levin, "End of Ford Profit Sharing," pp. 163, 166; Nevins and Hill, *Ford: Expansion and Challenge*, pp. 325–8, 334. Turnover figures are from *Brief Account*, p. 2: Accession 951, Box 3, Ford Archives.

56 The coming of the Ford company store, and the bonus and investment plans, were announced in the in-house newspaper *The Ford Man* (December 3, 1919), p. 1; (December 31, 1919), pp. 1–2: Ford Archives. The quotation is from an editorial on page 3 of this latter edition.

57 "Dr. Marquis Talks to Eagle Men" (February 3, 1919), p. 4; untitled editorial (January 17, 1919), p. 2; "Individual Effort" (July 17, 1920), p. 1: all in *The Ford Man*, Ford Archives.

58 These themes are ubiquitous in the pages of *The Ford Man*. Typical examples include the following: praising Ford's labor policies and exhorting hard work, the untitled editorial and "Words of Wisdom from a Loyal Ford Worker" both on p. 2 (September 17, 1919); inveighing against employee turnover, "At the End of the Rainbow" and "Sit Tight" (April 3, 1920), p. 2; and, urging Ford Men to be loyal "Boosters" and to disavow agitators, "Lest We Forget" (March 4, 1918), p. 1, and "Bolshevism Not Predominant in the Ford Factory" (February 17, 1919), p. 1: Ford Archives.

59 "Bolshevism Not Predominant in the Ford Factory" (February 17, 1919), p. 1.; also "Some of the Things Henry Ford Has Done" (October 17, 1919), p. 2: *The Ford Man*, Ford Archives. For a recitation of these same themes for a much wider audience, see "Ford Backs His Ideas After Ten-Year Test," *New York Times* (August 10, 1924), section 8, p. 3.

60 Kennedy, *Over Here*, chapter 1; Schaffer, *Great War*, chapters 1, 2, and appendix.

61 Kennedy, *Over Here*, p. 82.

62 Meyer, *Five Dollar Day*, chapter 8. The following paragraph draws heavily upon this work.

63 "Espionage Act" *The Ford Man* (October 17, 1918), p. 1: Ford Archives.

64 "Let Us Curtail Hun Propaganda, You and I" *The Ford Man* (August 17, 1918), p. 1. Other examples of the new, more militant Americanism are "Patriotism" (February 5, 1918), p. 2; and "Now, if Ever, We Should All be Americans" (March 18, 1918), p. 2: Ford Archives.

65 "Hold Steady, Men" *The Ford Man* (October 3, 1918), p. 1: Ford Archives; see also Meyer, *Five Dollar Day*, p. 183.

66 On the AWU and postwar strikes, see Dunn, *Labor and Automobiles* (New York: International Publishers, 1929), pp. 186–93; Meyer, *Five Dollar Day*, pp. 186–7, 193; and Peterson, *Automobile Workers*, pp. 111–21. The brief appearance of pro-union activities among Ford Workers suggests that Ford's earlier policies aimed at homogenizing its workers may have been a double-edged sword: by Americanizing and individualizing a heterogeneous immigrant workforce, Ford sought to integrate these workers into a liberal capitalist society by separating them from ethnic communities and encouraging them to become self-reliant and instrumentally rational, and hopefully thereby more responsive to the constraints and incentives by means of which Ford might control them on and off the job. While such changes could render workers more easily manipulable, they could also have the effect of lessening the linguistic and cultural barriers which separate workers and thus making possible more unified forms of action, such as unionism.

67 Meyer, *Five Dollar Day*, pp. 187–94; and Lacey, *Ford*, pp. 362–4.

68 The anti-Bolshevik quotation is from "Letters and Answers" *The Ford Man* (March 3, 1919), p. 3; A representative letter about non-English speakers is in *The Ford Man* (October 17, 1919), p. 3. The statement preferring Fordism to unionism is from *The Ford Man* (June 17, 1920), p. 4: Ford Archives.

69 The quotation is from "Assails the Closed Shop" *New York Times* (February 3, 1921), p. 14: The *Times* is paraphrasing a speech given by James Emery, former counsel to the National Association of Manufacturers, a major supporter of the open shop drive. See also Dunn, *Americanization of Labor*; and Heale, *American Anticommunism*, chapters 4–5.

70 Ford and Crowther, *My Life*, p. 174.

71 Klann quoted in Nevins and Hill, *Ford: Expansion and Challenge*, p. 354; also quoted is Ford and Crowther, *My Life*, p. 174. See also Sward, *Legend*, pp. 77–80.

72 Marquis, *Henry Ford*, p. 141.

73 "Less Ford Sociology" *New York Times* (February 3, 1921), p. 22. The reduced scope of Sociological Department activity is described in the company's publication *The Ford Industries*, 1926, pp. 48–49: Joe Brown Collection, Box 10, ALUA. For Marquis' perspective on the end of Ford paternalism, see his *Henry Ford*, pp. 141, 155; for Sorenson's see *Forty Years*, pp. 144–6; also Nevins and Hill, *Ford: Expansion and Challenge*, chapter 13; and Meyer, *Five Dollar Day*, chapter 9.

74 The various ways in which the Service Department was "a big help"

around the plant were explained to production workers in *The Ford Man* (May 3, 1918), pp. 1, 4; and then again in its successor publication, *Ford News* (August 1, 1925), pp. 3, 5.

75 On Bennett and Ford's Service Department, see Sward, *Legend*, chapters 22–28; and Lacey, *Ford*, chapters 21–22. For contemporary accounts, see Dunn, *Labor and Automobiles*, pp. 161–3, 169–70; John H. O'Brien, "Henry Ford's Commander in Chief" *Forum* 99 (February, 1938), pp. 67–72; John McCarten, "The Little Man in Henry Ford's Basement" *The American Mercury* 50 (May, 1940), pp. 7–15, and (June, 1940), pp. 200–8. For an account of Service Department coercion written by a Ford production worker, see Cruden, "Great Ford Myth," pp. 118–19.

76 The quotation of Henry Ford is from NLRB, *Decisions and Orders* vol. IV, p. 647. Sorenson quotes are from Victor Weybright, "Henry Ford at the Wheel" *Survey Graphic* (December, 1937), p. 688; and Sorenson, *Forty Years*, p. 261. Ford labor policy statement from *Ford Industries*, p. 46: Joe Brown Collection, Box 10, ALUA. On Ford's defiance of the NIRA, see "Ford vs. Blue Eagle" *News-Week* (September 9, 1933), pp. 3–4; and Sidney Fine, "The Ford Motor Company and the NRA" *Business History Review* 32 (1958), pp. 353–85.

77 This interpretation is based on a perusal of various issues of *Ford News* in the collection of the Ford Archives.

78 Quoted in Nevins and Hill, *Ford: Decline and Rebirth, 1933–1962* (New York: Charles Scribner's Sons, 1962), p. 48.

79 The UAW shop paper reported that in November, 1940, John Gallo had been fired for laughing and smiling while working on the River Rouge assembly line: *Ford Facts* (February 19, 1941), p. 4: ALUA. In 1940–41, reports of abusive supervisors and Service men were commonplace in the pages of *Ford Facts*. J. M. Wagoner is quoted in Babson, *Working Detroit*, p. 92.

80 C. Li, "A Summer in the Ford Works," *Personnel Journal* 7 (June, 1928), p. 24.

81 Tappes quoted in Babson, *Working Detroit*, p. 104. Babson reports on p. 92 that Ford's in-plant spy network employed between 8,000 and 9,000 Rouge workers as informers. On service department spying and powers of summary dismissal, see "Ex-Foreman Stirs Row in Ford Case" *New York Times* (July 15, 1937), p. 10.

82 Alex Baskin, "The Ford Hunger March – 1932" *Labor History* 13 (1972), pp. 331–60; Babson, *Working Detroit*, pp. 52–60; Keeran, *Communist Party*, pp. 71–5; and Peterson, *Automobile Workers*, pp. 136–9. Contemporary accounts include: "Four Killed in Riot at Main Ford Plant" *New York Times* (March 8, 1932), pp. 1, 10; "Reds are Sought in Fatal Ford Riot" *New York Times* (March 9, 1932), p. 3; "Ford Riot Inquiry Will Start Monday" *New York Times* (March 10, 1932), p. 12; Maurice Sugar, "Bullets – Not Food – for Ford Workers" *The Nation* (March 23, 1932), pp. 333–5; Oakley Johnson, "After the Dearborn Massacre" *The New Republic* (March 30, 1932), pp. 172–4.

83 Perhaps as many as fifteen or more people were beaten by Ford's Service men on that day. Of these, one unionist suffered a broken back and another

a fractured skull. As Dearborn police stood by, Ford's henchmen attacked the most prominent of the unionists in front of reporters and photographers, who were themselves harassed in an attempt to seize their notes, cameras and photographic plates. As a consequence, accounts of this incident – complete with surviving photographs – received widespread publicity in even the mainstream press. See "Battle at Ford Plant" *New York Times* (May 27, 1937), pp. 1, 3; "Ford: Frankensteen Gets a Beating ..." *News-Week* (June 5, 1937), pp. 7–8; and "On the Overpass" *Time* (June 7, 1937), pp. 13–15. Despite the national exposure of Ford's thuggery, Henry Ford's carefully cultivated image as an American folk hero and friend of labor was apparently not seriously eroded: see Lewis, *Public Image*, pp. 211, 251, 264. Incredibly, a survey of labor by Elmo Roper published in the June 1940 issue of *Fortune* (p. 163) reported that more than 73 percent of respondents named Henry Ford as "helpful to labor"; whereas only about 52 percent named Senator Robert Wagner, sponsor of the NLRA.

84 NLRB, *Decisions and Orders*, Vol. IV, pp. 621–78: passages quoted are from pp. 627, 648, 674–5. The Board's investigation of Ford was widely reported: see "NLRB Accuses Ford" *New York Times* (June 27, 1937), pp. 1–2; "Fordism vs. Unionism" *Time* (July 26, 1937), pp. 13–14; "Ford: The NLRB Tries a Case" *News-Week* (August 7, 1937), pp. 15–16; "NLRB Finds Ford Guilty of Violating Labor Law ..." *New York Times* (December 24, 1937), pp. 1–2; "Board on Ford" *Time* (January 3, 1938), p. 10; "Ford" *News-Week* (January 3, 1938), p. 40.

85 NLRB investigations of Ford branch plants did not receive the same publicity as did the original River Rouge case. On violence and intimidation at Ford branch plants, see Sward, *Legend*, pp. 398–400; Nevins and Hill, *Ford: Decline and Rebirth*, pp. 142–6; Bernstein, *Turbulent Years*, pp. 741–2; and Lewis, *Public Image*, pp. 251–2. The UAW's Ford shop paper carried a photograph of Herbert Harris, the union organizer who was tarred and feathered in Dallas: *Ford Facts* (January 8, 1941), p. 4: ALUA. On the depression era speed-up see Sward, *Legend*, pp. 358–61; Nevins and Hill, *Ford: Decline and Rebirth*, pp. 151–2; and Peterson, *Automobile Workers*, pp. 56, 132–3.

86 Auerbach, "La Follette Committee," pp. 435–59. On employers' hostility toward New Deal labor policy and especially the Wagner Act, see Harris, *Right to Manage*, chapter 1; and Vittoz, *New Deal Labor Policy*, chapter 7.

7 Unionism is Americanism: production politics and ideological struggle at Ford Motor Company, 1937–1952

1 "Why CIO Strives to Organize Ford: We Need You and You Need Us" by Michael Widman, Director of UAW–CIO Ford Drive, *Ford Facts* (October 23, 1940), p. 2. See also Irving Howe and B. J. Widick, *The UAW and Walter Reuther* (New York: Random House, 1949), chapter 2; Bernstein, *Turbulent Years*, chapter 11; Edsforth, *Class Conflict*, chapter 7.

2 V. Reuther, *Brothers Reuther*, p. 205. On the theme "unionism not Fordism" see "Union's Ford Drive Asks 6 Hour, $8 Day" *New York Times* (May 26, 1937), p. 13; and "Battle at Ford Plant" *New York Times* (May 27, 1937), pp. 1, 3. For different notions of "industrial democracy" circulating in socialist and labor communities during the interwar years, see Norman Thomas, "What is Industrial Democracy?" (1925), reprinted in B. K. Johnpoll and M. R. Yerburgh, eds., *The League for Industrial Democracy: A Documentary History* (Westport, CT: Greenwood, 1980), pp. 389–446 ; W. Jett Lauck, *Political and Industrial Democracy, 1776–1926* (New York: Funk and Wagnalls, 1926); and Clinton S. Golden and Harold J. Ruttenberg, *The Dynamics of Industrial Democracy* (New York: Harper and Brothers, 1942). On these themes of Americanism and industrial democracy I have benefited from reading Gary Gerstle, "The Politics of Patriotism." Gerstle (p. 91) emphasizes the basic ambiguity of these themes in the discourse of industrial unionists: "The central concepts of the CIO's Americanism were compatible with a variety of political alternatives, ranging from socialism to corporatism to business unionism." But he does not explain this ambiguity, or explore its potential implications, by relating it to structural tensions within liberal capitalism and its culture of abstract individualism.

3 "Ford's Idea of Democracy Illustrated by NLRB Report" *United Automobile Worker* (January 1, 1938); and "Ford Won't Admit Violation of Wagner Act" *United Automobile Worker* (January 15, 1938), p. 1; both at the Archive of Labor and Urban Affairs (ALUA), Wayne State University. Cameron quoted in Harvey Pinney, "The Radio Pastor of Dearborn" *The Nation* (October 9, 1937), p. 374. See also Lewis, *Public Image*, chapter 19.

4 Howe and Widick, *UAW*, chapters 3–4; Nevins and Hill, *Ford: Decline and Rebirth*, chapter 6; Bernstein, *Turbulent Years*, pp. 554–71, 734–51; V. Reuther, *Brothers Reuther*, chapters 15–16.

5 The first quotation is from "Dearborn Free Speech Fight Near Showdown in Courts" *Ford Facts* (October 23, 1940), p. 3; the Widman and Thomas quotes are from "Woman Judge Lays Down Law to Ford and Harry Bennett" *Ford Facts* (November 9, 1940), p. 2; the slogan "Americanize Ford" is from the first issue of *Ford Facts*, a mimeographed sheet dated May 20, 1940: all at ALUA.

6 R. J. Thomas, "The Ford Workers' Case" *United Automobile Worker* (March 15, 1941), p. 5; also "Thomas Nails Ford 'High Wages' Gag" *Voice of the Ford Worker* (February 26, 1940), p. 3. The slogan "winning an American deal" appeared in *Ford Facts* (December 4, 1940), p. 3. All are at ALUA.

7 "Ford Seven Times a Law-Breaker" *Ford Facts* (October 23, 1940), pp. 1–2: ALUA.

8 "CIO Convention Hits Communism, Nazism; UAW Does the Same" *Ford Facts* (December 4, 1940), p. 3; and "UAW–CIO Firmly Opposed to Communism, Nazism, Fascism" *Ford Facts* (March 19, 1941), p. 3: ALUA. See also Keeran, *Communist Party*, chapter 9.

9 "Lewis Vows CIO Will Stand on Guard to Protect our Basic American

Institutions" *Ford Facts* (October 23, 1940), p. 2: ALUA. The CIO had already declared its respect for the institution of the contract in order to establish itself as a responsible bargaining agent: "CIO Pledges to Respect Contracts" and "Resolution on Collective Bargaining Agreements" *United Automobile Worker* (October 18, 1937), p. 2: ALUA.

10 The handbill "Help Americanize Ford" is from the collection entitled "UAW Public Relations Department – Ford Motor Company," Box 2; Ford's refusal to return his Nazi medal even after World War II began is noted in *Ford Facts* (December 4, 1940), p. 3; the reference to "Fuehrer Ford" is from *Ford Facts* Number 1 (May 20, 1940), p. 2: all at ALUA. A photograph of UAW members with banners and signs proclaiming "Fordism is Fascism," etc. was taken in Monroe, Michigan in June, 1937 and is in the collection of the ALUA. On Ford's acceptance of the German medal, see Nevins and Hill, *Ford: Decline and Rebirth*, pp. 168–9; and Lewis, *Public Image*, p. 149.

11 "The Strength of 90,000" *Ford Facts* (March 19, 1941), p. 4. The following reported abuses of power by Ford supervisors or Service men: "Union Opposes Sharecropping for Jacketts" and "'Big-Feet' Street Trembles Before Union Gains" (October 23, 1940), p. 2; "Ford Workers Speak" (January 8, 1941), p. 3; "Ford Workers Speak Their Minds on Working Conditions in Plant" (March 5, 1941), p. 2; "Ford Workers Tell Why They are Joining CIO" (March 19, 1941), p. 3; "Servicemen's Brutality as Seen By Ford Worker" (April 23, 1941), p. 2; and "Sam Taylor ... Chief Thug at Rouge Plant" (April 23, 1941), p. 3: all in *Ford Facts*, ALUA.

12 "Shop Steward is the Man to Tame that Straw Boss" (March 19, 1941), p. 2; also "A Union at Ford's Will Mean Democracy Throughout Shop" (March 5, 1941), p. 3; "Take It or Leave It" and "USA + CIO = Industrial Democracy" (October 23, 1940), pp. 3, 4; "CIO Program for Ford Men" (October 23, 1940), p. 1: all in *Ford Facts*, ALUA.

13 "The Negro Ford Worker" *Voice of the Ford Worker* (April, 1940), p. 1; "Negro Workers Join CIO" *Ford Facts* (January 8, 1941), p. 3; "Ford Workers: Keep Faith With America!" *Ford Facts* (April 23, 1941), p. 4: ALUA. Of course, this is not to say that the CIO itself was free of racism: see Meier and Rudwick, *Black Detroit*; also Martin Halpern, *UAW Politics in the Cold War Era* (Albany: State University of New York Press, 1988), chapter 11.

14 "You Are Your Own Judge" *Ford Facts* (March 5, 1941), p. 2: ALUA.

15 Liberty Legion leaflet and letter to Ford workers are from Box 1 of the collection entitled "UAW Public Relations Department – Ford Motor Company," ALUA. The UAW debunked the Legion in *The United Automobile Worker* (August 21, 1937), pp. 1, 4: in the unbound newspaper collection of ALUA, Box 15, folder 15. The quotations are from the *Independent Ford Worker* (March 19, 1941), pp. 1, 2: also at ALUA. The *Independent Ford Worker* is denounced as a company sham in *Ford Facts* (March 19, 1941), p. 1: ALUA. Ford's full-page newspaper ads – "Does Ford Pay Good Wages? "and "What's This About Labor Trouble in Ford Plants?" – appeared in such papers as *The New York Times* (December 29, 1940) and *The Detroit Free Press*

(January 5, 1941). On Ford's propaganda campaign, see also Lewis, *Public Image*, pp. 261–5.

16 "22 Fired UAW–CIO Members Back at Ford: Union Buttons Are Worn By All …" (February 19, 1941), p. 2; "How Ford Empire Became Part of USA: Worker Describes Scene in Rouge as NLRB Order Went Up" (March 5, 1941), p. 3; "Rolling Mill Stoppage Brings Reinstatements" (March 19, 1941), p. 4: all in *Ford Facts*, ALUA.

17 Senator Diggs is quoted in Meier and Rudwick, *Black Detroit*, p. 96.

18 "Union Officers State Ford Strike Issues" *United Automobile Worker* (April 15, 1941), p. 2; "UAW–CIO Wins Union Shop, Top Auto Wages at Ford" *Ford Facts* (June 21, 1941), pp. 1, 4: ALUA; also Howe and Widick, *UAW*, pp. 97–106; Nevins and Hill, *Ford: Decline and Rebirth*, pp. 159–67; Bernstein, *Turbulent Years*, pp. 742–51; Meier and Rudwick, *Black Detroit*, chapter 2; and Nelson Lichtenstein, "Life at the Rouge" in C. Stephenson and R. Asher, eds., *Life and Labor* (Albany: State University of New York Press, 1986), pp. 242–3.

19 Lichtenstein, "Life at the Rouge," pp. 243–6. Henry Ford II reported that labor discipline and productivity declined markedly in Ford plants during World War II: *The Challenge of Human Engineering*, pp. 5–6: Accession 951, Box 5, Ford Archives. On communists in Local 600, see Marquart, *Journal*, pp. 97–8; also William D. Andrew, "Factionalism and Anti-Communism" *Labor History* 20 (1979), pp. 229–34; Keeran, *Communist Party*, pp. 218–20, 254, 259–60, 266; and Halpern, *UAW Politics*, pp. 110, 129.

20 Quotations are from Henry Ford II, *Human Engineering*, pp. 4, 7, 8: Accession 951, Box 5, Ford Archives. See also John Bugas, *Labor Relations and Productivity*: Vertical File: "Ford Motor Company – 1940s," ALUA.

21 The quotation is from an FMC letter to UAW, reprinted in *New York Times* (November 16, 1945), p. 11. On "company security," see Nevins and Hill, *Ford: Decline and Rebirth*, pp. 302–7; Lewis, *Public Image*, pp. 427–37; Harris, *Right to Manage*, pp. 143–9; Lichtenstein, "Life at the Rouge," pp. 248–51; and Halpern, *UAW Politics*, pp. 75–7. Ford explained the results of "company security" and increasing responsibility of labor in its shop paper: "Stoppages in '46 Drop 89 per cent" *The Rouge News* (February 4, 1947), pp. 1–2; and "Work Stoppages Continue to Decline" *The Rouge News* (January 31, 1948), p. 1: Ford Archives.

22 Nelson Lichtenstein, "Reutherism on the Shop Floor "in S. Tolliday and J. Zeitlin, eds., *The Automobile Industry and its Workers* (London: Polity, 1986), pp. 121–43; and "Walter Reuther and the Rise of Labor-Liberalism" in M. Dubofsky and W. Van Tine, eds., *Labor Leaders in America* (Urbana: University of Illinois Press, 1987), pp. 280–302. See also Howe and Widick, *UAW*, chapter 7; Keeran, *Communist Party*, chapter 11; and Halpern, *UAW Politics*, chapters 15–16. For an example of Walter Reuther's tripartist reformism, see his proposals for postwar reconversion in "Reuther Challenges 'Our Fear of Abundance'" *New York Times Magazine* (September 16, 1945), pp. 8, 32–3, 35.

23 Walter P. Reuther, "How to Beat the Communists" *Collier's* (February 28, 1948), p. 49.

24 The slogan "Teamwork in the Leadership, Solidarity in the Ranks" is from Victor Reuther's memoir, *Brothers Reuther*, p. 257.

25 Anti-wildcat and Bugas quotes are from "Ford Pact Makes History ..." *The Rouge News* (September 30, 1949), p. 1: Ford Archives. Reuther is quoted in Nevins and Hill, *Ford: Decline and Rebirth*, p. 338. See also "Ford and Union Settle Strike" *Ford Facts* (June 4, 1949), p. 1: ALUA. This and preceding paragraphs also draw upon Nevins and Hill (above), pp. 338–42; Flink, *Automobile Age*, pp. 246–7; Lichtenstein, "Life at the Rouge," pp. 253–5; and Halpern, *UAW Politics*, pp. 257–9.

26 Walter Reuther quoted in English translation of Henri Pierre, "Equal Sacrifices," *Le Monde* (September 21, 1951), p. 3: Walter P. Reuther Collection, Box 294, ALUA.

27 The Korean War endorsement, the loyalty oath policy, and Stellato's accusation of complicity are in *Ford Facts* (July 15, 1950), p. 1; see also "Ford Worker Dies in the Korean War" *Ford Facts* (August 19, 1950), p. 1; and "Latest List of Those Murdered by Stalin's Korean Storm-Troopers" (October 21, 1950), p. 4; "Five to Go On Trial: President Prefers Charges Against Suspected Commies" *Ford Facts* (August 19, 1950), p. 1. The *Ford Facts* "educational" series included: "Stalinism is a New Name for an Ancient Tyranny" (June 17, 1950), p. 4; "Russia Under the Red Terror" (June 24, 1950), p. 4; "Most Commies Are Simply Stupid" (July 1, 1950), p. 4; and "Local 600 is the Last Bastion of the Red Fascist Hopefuls" (July 8, 1950), p. 4. The ICFTU statement is reprinted in "World Union Group Blasts CP Aggression" *Ford Facts* (July 8, 1950), p. 1. All are from ALUA.

28 *Ford Facts* (July 15, 1950), p. 4: ALUA. The previous quote equating communism and Fordism is from a pamphlet signed by "The American Unionist Group," and entitled "Which Shall We Have?? UNIONISM, FORDISM, COMMUNISM": ALUA Vertical File: "Local 600."

29 Arblaster, *Western Liberalism*, chapter 18; Thomas G. Paterson, *Meeting the Communist Threat* (Oxford: Oxford University Press, 1988), chapter 1.

30 Andrew, "Factionalism," p. 232; also Halpern, *UAW Politics*, p. 130.

31 Andrew, "Factionalism"; Lichtenstein, "Life at the Rouge," pp. 255–9; Halpern, *UAW Politics*, pp. 259–63.

32 W. Reuther, "We Must Prove by Action that Bread and Freedom Can be Ours" *Ford Facts* (August 26, 1950), p. 4; and "A Total Peace Offensive to End Human Insecurity" *Ford Facts* (August 5, 1950), p. 4: ALUA.

33 Walter Reuther's vision for global peace and prosperity was presented to Local 600 in a six-part series in *Ford Facts*: (August 5, 1950), p. 4; (August 12, 1950), p. 4; (August 26, 1950), p. 4; (September 2, 1950), p. 4; (September 9, 1950), p. 4; and (September 16, 1950), p. 4: ALUA. The "positive program" quotation is from the second of these; and the counterexample to Soviet militarism is from the fourth. Reuther's general vision of liberal capitalism, producing peace and prosperity as the antidote to communism, is reaffirmed in an untitled column which he wrote for the ICFTU journal, *Free Labour World* (October 29, 1953): Walter P. Reuther Collection, Box 294, ALUA.

34 "Others Can Profit by Our Experience" *Ford Rouge News* (July 21, 1950), p. 2: Ford Archives. Empahasis added.

35 "Peoples of the World Looking to America" *Ford Rouge News* (July 14, 1950), p. 2: Ford Archives.

36 *Ford Facts* (April 1, 1950), p. 4: ALUA.

8 Fordism and neoliberal hegemony: tensions and possibilities

1 *Historical Statistics*: series D-804 (average weekly earnings of production workers in manufacturing), pp. 169–70; deflated with series E-2 (implicit price deflator for personal consumption expenditure, 1958 = 100), p. 197.

2 For evidence of labor market segmentation in which more strongly unionized workers in the corporate "primary" sector constituted a privileged group relative to workers in the more hardscrabble "secondary" sector, see Gordon, Edwards, and Reich, *Segmented Work*, pp. 192–200.

3 *Ford Facts*, 1949, various issues: ALUA.

4 "The Treaty of Detroit" *Fortune* (July, 1950), pp. 53–5.

5 *Historical Statistics*: series D-685 (manufacturing output per worker-hour, based on 1958 prices), p. 162; and series W-25 (real value-added per worker-hour, based on 1958 prices but indexed at 1967 = 100), p. 949; series D-802 (average hourly earnings for production workers in manufacturing), pp. 169–70, deflated with series E-2 (implicit price deflator for personal consumption expenditures, 1958 = 100), p. 197. The two years chosen for comparison were business cycle peaks. Note that this measure of hourly earnings excludes employer contributions to insurance and benefit plans: from a Marxian perspective, such payments might be viewed as contributions to interest-bearing money capital. While, at some point in their circulation, such funds make an important contribution to the reproduction of labor power (through the payment of various kinds of benefits), nonetheless their circulation as capital would distinguish them from wages: see Aglietta, *Capitalist Regulation*, pp. 179–86. Had such contributions been included in "wages," this measure would have grown by a greater magnitude and would appear not to lag behind productivity.

6 On the golden age of Fordism, see Aglietta, *Capitalist Regulation*, pp. 90–9, 152–61, 190–7, 203–8, 304–7, 349–51; for crises of disproportionality, see pp. 93–5, 284–7, 355–6. On the "socialization of the wage relation," see Davis, *Prisoners*, pp. 105–17.

7 On militarized containment as military Keynesianism, see Gaddis, *Strategies of Containment*, chapter 4; on American labor and the postwar boom, see Kim Moody, *An Injury to All* (London: Verso, 1988), pp. 41–5. The quotation emphasizing economic growth and democracy is from *The AFL–CIO's Foreign Policy*, AFL–CIO publication no. 181 (Washington, DC: AFL–CIO, 1987), p. 12. The AFL–CIO constitution is excerpted in John P. Windmuller, "Foreign Affairs and the AFL–CIO" *Industrial and Labor Relations Review* 9 (1956), pp. 422–3. For categorical statements which exemplify the anticommunist ideology of a global "free trade union" movement, see also

Gershman, *The Foreign Policy of American Labor*, pp. 2–7, 66–8. Gershman's characterizations of AFL–CIO foreign policy are all the more significant since he himself has been influential among those who shaped the policy: see Beth Sims, *Workers of the World Undermined* (Boston: South End Press, 1992), pp. 34, 46–50.

8 On the global activities of the AFL–CIO and its labor institutes see: *The AFL–CIO Abroad*, AFL–CIO publication no. 182 (Washington, DC: AFL–CIO, 1987); also Radosh, *American Labor*, chapters 13–14; V. Reuther, *Brothers Reuther*, pp. 377–8, 411–27, 488–9; Daniel Cantor and Juliet Schor, *Tunnel Vision* (Boston: South End Press, 1987), pp. 39–48; Moody, *Injury to All*, pp. 288–96; and Sims, *Workers of the World*, chapters 3–4. The Peter Grace quotation appears in Moody, p. 289; and the Reuther quotation is from *Brothers Reuther*, p. 418. On CIA links to AFL–CIO labor institutes, see Agee, *Inside the Company*, pp. 244–6, 620; and Sims (above), pp. 54–61.

9 See Cox, *Production*, chapter 8; B. Harrison and B. Bluestone, *The Great U-Turn* (New York: Basic Books, 1988), p. 22; S. Bowles, D. Gordon, and T. Weisskopf, *After the Waste Land* (Armonk, NY: Sharpe, 1990) pp. 36, 80–96; Block, *Origins*.

10 By 1983, the share of world manufactured exports among the developed market economies had declined to 64 percent; but this was still more than twice as great as it had been during the period preceding the establishment of the neoliberal order: Gordon, "Global Economy," table 7b, p. 47.

11 Bowles, Gordon, and Weisskopf, *Waste Land*, p. 76. Data on declining US share of world manufactured exports are from R. Lipsey and I. Kravis, "The Competitiveness and Comparative Advantage of US Multinationals, 1957–84" *Banca Nazionale del Lavoro Quarterly Review* 161 (1987), p. 151. On import penetration relative to manufacturing output, see Harrison and Bluestone, *U-Turn*, p. 9.

12 Harrison and Bluestone, *U-Turn*, p. 10. See also Bowles, Gordon, and Weisskopf, *Waste Land*, pp. 75–7; and "A Global Overcapacity Hurts Many Industries; No Easy Cure is Seen" *Wall Street Journal* (March 9, 1987), pp. 1, 14.

13 On the rank and file rebellion of the late 1960s and early 1970s, see Stanley Aronowitz, *False Promises* (New York: McGraw-Hill, 1973), pp. 21–50; Babson, *Working Detroit*, pp. 180–91; Zieger, *American Workers*, pp. 169–70; and Moody, *Injury to All*, pp. 83–94. In their account of the erosion of workforce discipline, the productivity slowdown and the emergence of a "profit squeeze," Bowles, Gordon, and Weisskopf place special emphasis on the declining coercive force of the threat of unemployment: see *Waste Land*, pp. 69–72, 77–9, 83–4.

14 Aglietta, *Capitalist Regulation*, pp. 90–100, 119–22, 162–9, 197–8, 285–7. Aglietta's interpretation of the crisis of Fordism also entails a financial aspect, with "creeping inflation" threatening to develop into a monetary crisis, and a crisis of "collective consumption" as the costs of social services increasingly burden the accumulation process: pp. 163–9, 350–1, 365–79.

15 For declining profitability, see Bowles, Gordon, and Weisskopf, *Waste Land*, figure 4.4, p. 45; and Harvey, *Postmodernity*, figure 2.4, p. 143.

16 Lipsey and Kravis, "Competitiveness," p. 151; also Gordon, "Global Economy," pp. 40–1; Moody, *Injury to All*, pp. 100–1; and Dicken, *Global Shift*, pp. 51–3, 59–67.

17 Moody, *Injury to All*, chapter 5; Harvey, *Postmodernity*, chapter 9.

18 On "flexible specialization," see Piore and Sabel, *Industrial Divide*. On Japanese "post-Fordism" see Martin Kenney and Richard Florida, "Beyond Mass Production" *Politics and Society* 16 (1988), pp. 121–58; and J. Womack, D. Jones, and D. Roos, *The Machine that Changed the World* (New York: Rawson Associates, 1990).

19 On the relationship between restructuring and unionism in the US auto industry, see Harry Katz, "Recent Developments in US Auto Labor Relations" in Tolliday and Zeitlin, eds., *Automobile Industry*, pp. 282–304; Stephen Wood, "Between Fordism and Flexibility?" in R. Hyman and W. Streek, eds., *New Technology and Industrial Relations* (Oxford: Basil Blackwell, 1988), pp. 101–27; and Stephen Herzenberg, "Whither Social Unionism?" in J. Jenson and R. Mahon, eds., *The Challenge of Restructuring* (Philadelphia: Temple University Press, 1993), pp. 314–36. For an example of the proponents' position, see Womack, Jones, and Roos, *Machine*, pp. 100–3. Among unionists, industrial relations reforms are highly controversial: see Katz, "Policy Debates over Work Reorganization in North American Unions" in Hyman and Streek, eds., *New Technology*, pp. 220–32.

20 Harley Shaiken, Stephen Herzenberg, and Sarah Kuhn, "The Work Process under More Flexible Production" *Industrial Relations* 25 (1986), p. 181.

21 Wood, "Between Fordism and Flexibility?" pp. 104–5, 110–11; Knuth Dohse, Ulrich Jurgens, and Thomas Malsch, "From 'Fordism' to 'Toyotism'?" *Politics and Society* 14 (1985), pp. 115–46; and Mike Parker, "Industrial Relations Myth and Shop-floor Reality" in N. Lichtenstein and H. Harris, eds., *Industrial Democracy in America* (Cambridge: Cambridge University Press, 1993), pp. 249–74, the quotation is from p. 250. Note that even such boosters as Womack, Jones, and Roos admit that management control of the pace and intensity of labor, and "removing all slack" from assembly line work in order to maintain continual pressure for improved performance, are crucial aspects of "lean production": *Machine*, pp. 80, 101, 154, 259.

22 Davis, *Prisoners*, pp. 151–3; Moody, *Injury to All*, p. 172; Harrison and Bluestone, *U-Turn*, pp. 42–7.

23 Davis, *Prisoners*, pp. 140–3; Moody, *Injury to All*, chapter 8. Quotations are from the latter: pp. 165, 166. See also Michael Goldfield, *The Decline of Organized Labor in the United States* (Chicago: University of Chicago Press, 1987), pp. 43–8; and Harrison and Bluestone, *U-Turn*, table 2.3, p. 41.

24 Robert Weissman, "Replacing the Union" *Multinational Monitor* (April, 1991), pp. 7–13; Viveca Novak, "Why Workers Can't Win" *Common Cause Magazine* (July–August, 1991), pp. 28–32; John B. Judis, "Permanently Replacing Labor's Stolen Rights" *In These Times* (August 7–20, 1991), p. 8;

Frank Swoboda, "Striking Out as a Weapon Against Management" *Washington Post Weekly Edition* (July 13–19, 1992), p. 20; and Jane Slaughter, "What Went Wrong at Caterpillar?" *Labor Notes* (May, 1992), pp. 1, 11–12. The GAO study on permanent replacements is reported in Weissman, "Replacing the Union," where the Lynn Williams quote appears on p. 12. Average numbers of major strikes are based on US Bureau of Labor Statistics, *Monthly Labor Review* (December, 1985), table 38, p. 94; and various subsequent issues; dating of business cycles is based on Bowles, Gordon, and Weisskopf, *Waste Land*, table 1.3, p. 11.

25 Data on average first year wage adjustments for contract settlements covering at least 1,000 workers are from US Bureau of Labor Statistics, *Monthly Labor Review*, various issues. For evidence that unionization contributes to economic equality and that vigorous unions generate "spill-over effects," see Richard Freeman and James Medoff, *What Do Unions Do?* (New York: Basic Books, 1984), chapters 5 and 10. On the decline of such "spill-over" effects in the 1980s, see also Moody, *Injury to All*, pp. 5–6.

26 Goldfield, *Decline*, table 1, p. 10; Novak, Workers Can't Win, p. 29.

27 Moody, *Injury to All*, pp. 119–20; for linearity of decline, see Goldfield, *Decline*, figure 4, p. 23.

28 Jim Sugarman, "Two Percent Justice for Workers" *Multinational Monitor* (April, 1991), p. 9. See also Davis, *Prisoners*, pp. 117–24, 138–40; Novak, Workers Can't Win; Goldfield, *Decline*, table 32, p. 196.

29 Davis, *Prisoners*, pp. 127–32; Goldfield, *Decline*, chapter 9; Moody, *Injury to All*, pp. 118–26, 193–219.

30 Bowles, Gordon, and Weisskopf, *Waste Land*, pp. 88–91, 121–69; Harrison and Bluestone, *U-Turn*, chapters 4–6.

31 Marc Baldwin, "Why So Few of the Unemployed Receive Benefits" *Dollars and Sense* (June, 1992), pp. 19–22; Bowles, Gordon, and Weisskopf, *Waste Land*, pp. 144–5. Baldwin (p. 21) presents somewhat different estimates of unemployment insurance coverage which show a marked decline through the 1980s, with a slight upturn in coverage at the end of the decade.

32 Lawrence Mishel and David Frankel, *The State of Working America, 1990–91* (Armonk, NY: Sharpe, 1991), tables 3.24 and 3.25, p. 104; Harrison and Bluestone, *U-Turn*, pp. ix, 122; US Bureau of the Census, *Workers With Low Earnings: 1964 to 1990*, series p-60, no. 178. (Washington, DC: Government Printing Office, 1992), table B, p. 3.

33 See Mishel and Frankel, *Working America*, pp. 25–7, especially table 1.11, p. 26.

34 Gramsci, *Prison Notebooks*, pp. 275–6.

35 Cantor and Schor, *Tunnel Vision*, chapter 4; Moody, *Injury to All*, pp. 294–5; and Sims, *Workers of the World*, pp. 91–2.

36 Dicken, *Global Shift*, pp. 51–3, 59–67. Dicken claims that intra-firm trade is increasingly common in the world economy as a whole, and now constitutes more than half of all US trade (pp. 48–9).

37 Joseph Grunwald and Kenneth Flamm, *The Global Factory* (Washington,

DC: Brookings Institution, 1985); but compare Gordon, "Global Economy," p. 49.

38 Grunwald and Flamm, *Global Factory*, pp. 137–79; Harley Shaiken, "High Tech Goes Third World" *Technology Review* (January, 1988), pp. 39–47, and "The Universal Motors Assembly and Stamping Plant" *Columbia Journal of World Business* (Summer, 1991), pp. 125–37; Kevin J. Middlebrook, "The Politics of Industrial Restructuring" *Comparative Politics* 23 (1991), pp. 275–97; "Detroit South" *Business Week* (March 16, 1992), pp. 98–103; Dan La Botz, *Mask of Democracy* (Boston: South End Press, 1992); and Jerome Levinson, "The Labor Side Accord to the North American Free Trade Agreement" (Washington, DC: Economic Policy Institute, 1993). Comparative wage levels are from Jeff Faux and Thea Lee, "The Effect of George Bush's NAFTA on American Workers" (Washington, DC: Economic Policy Institute, 1992), p. 11.

39 Robert A. Blecker and William E. Spriggs, "Manufacturing Employment in North America" (Washington, DC: Economic Policy Institute, 1992); Womack, Jones, and Roos, *Machine*, pp. 84–8; Shaiken, "High Tech Goes Third World" and "Universal Motors"; and Middlebrook, "Industrial Restructuring."

40 The auto worker is quoted in "Detroit South," p. 100 (see n. 38). Faux and Lee, "Bush's NAFTA"; Timothy Koechlin and Mehrene Larudee, "The High Cost of NAFTA" *Challenge* (September–October, 1992), pp. 19–26; Moody, "Free Trade Threatens Jobs and Income in US, Mexico, Canada" *Labor Notes* (July, 1991), pp. 8–10.

41 The quotation and its contextualizing argument are from *The AFL–CIO's Foreign Policy*, pp. 1–2; see also Lane Kirkland, *Toward a New Foreign Policy* (Washington, DC: AFL–CIO, 1989). On NAFTA and trade, see AFL–CIO, *Exploiting Both Sides* (Washington, DC: AFL–CIO, 1991); *International Trade* (Washington, DC: AFL–CIO, 1992); and United Automobile Workers, *Fast Track to Decline?* (Detroit: UAW, 1992).

42 The quotation is from AFL–CIO, *International Worker Rights* (Washington, DC: AFL–CIO, n.d.), p. 10. See also Kirkland, *New Foreign Policy*.

43 Sam Gindin, "Breaking Away" *Studies in Political Economy* 29 (1989), pp. 63–89.

44 Paul Garver, "Beyond the Cold War" *Labor Research Review* 13 (1989), p. 61.

45 Richard Feldman and Michael Betzold, eds., *The End of the Line* (Urbana: University of Illinois Press, 1990). Workers speak of their fears of job loss on pp. 9, 74, 147, 183, 201, 209, 210, 215, 216, 255, 266, 271. Expressions of dissatisfaction with the UAW appear on pp. 40, 45, 83, 88–9, 93, 188, 195, 209, 211, 225, 231, 245, 265, 273–5.

46 Auto workers quoted in Feldman and Betzold, *End of the Line*, pp. 22, 187, and 69; see also pp. 142, 242–3, and 276.

47 *Ibid.*, pp. 187, 38, 19.

48 Garver, "Beyond the Cold War," p. 61.

49 Feldman and Betzold, *End of the Line*, pp. 233, 259, 276.

50 Moody, *Injury to All*, pp. 298–302; and "Free Trade Threatens Jobs and Income," p. 10; also Laura McClure, "Workers of the World Unite!" *Dollars and Sense* (September, 1992), pp. 10–11, 19; Jeremy Brecher and Tim Costello, *Global Village vs. Global Pillage* (Washington, DC: International Labor Rights Education and Research Fund, 1991).

51 On labor and the Vietnam war, see Windmuller, "The Foreign Policy Conflict in American Labor" *Political Science Quarterly* 82 (1967), pp. 205–34; Zieger, *American Workers*, pp. 170–4; and Philip Foner, *US Labor and the Vietnam War* (New York: International Publishers, 1989).

52 Cantor and Schor, *Tunnel Vision*; Moody, *Injury to All*, pp. 290–4; and Sims, *Workers of the World*, pp. 94–7. Blaylock quoted in Cantor and Schor, p. 3. Insofar as they have been written by labor activists for an audience of unionists and sympathizers, even if considered apart from the documentation they contain, these books are themselves evidence of the currents of dissent within the American labor movement. See also the exchange between Paul Garver, a critic of AFL–CIO foreign policy, and Tom Kahn, director of the AFL–CIO's Department of International Affairs, in *Labor Research Review* 13 (1989), pp. 61–79. Note that Kahn (p. 76) was still invoking anticommunism as the primary rationale of labor's foreign policy as late as 1989.

53 Camille Colatosi, "Eleven Unions Oppose Gulf War" *Labor Notes* (February, 1991), pp. 1, 15 and "Union Attitudes Split on War" *Labor Notes* (March, 1991), pp. 3, 12; Marty Rosenbluth, "AFL–CIO Debates War, Decides Little" *Labor Notes* (April, 1991), p. 3. The Oregon unionists are quoted on p. 15 of Colatosi, "Eleven Unions."

54 John Cavanagh, "Free Trade as Opportunity" in J. Cavanagh *et al.*, eds., *Trading Freedom* (San Francisco: Institute For Food and Development Policy, 1992), pp. 6–7.; William Greider, "The Global Marketplace: A Closet Dictator" in Ralph Nader *et al.*, *The Case Against Free Trade* (San Francisco: Earth Island Press, 1993), p. 196. For further discussion, see Mark Rupert "(Re)Politicizing the Global Economy: Liberal Common Sense and Ideological Struggle in the NAFTA Debate." Paper prepared for the annual meeting of the International Studies Association, Washington, DC, April 1, 1994.

55 I must count myself among those who have written of American national decline: Mark Rupert and David Rapkin, "The Erosion of US Leadership Capabilities" in P. Johnson and W. Thompson, eds., *Rhythms in Politics and Economics* (New York: Praeger, 1985), pp. 155–80.

Bibliography

Archive sources

Ford Archive: Research Department, Henry Ford Museum and Greenfield Village, Dearborn, Michigan.

ALUA: Archive of Labor and Urban Affairs, Reuther Library, Wayne State University, Detroit, Michigan

Published sources

Adamson, W., *Hegemony and Revolution* (Berkeley: University of California Press, 1980)

AFL–CIO, *The AFL–CIO's Foreign Policy* (Washington, DC: AFL–CIO, 1987)
  The AFL–CIO Abroad (Washington, DC: AFL–CIO, 1987)
  International Worker Rights (Washington, DC: AFL–CIO, n.d.)
  Exploiting Both Sides (Washington, DC: AFL–CIO, 1991)
  International Trade (Washington, DC: AFL–CIO, 1992)

Agee, P., *Inside the Company* (New York: Bantam Books, 1976)

Aglietta, M., *A Theory of Capitalist Regulation* (London: Verso, 1987)

Alker, H., "The Presumption of Anarchy in World Politics," manuscript, Massachusetts Institute of Technology, 1986

Amberg, S., "Democratic Producerism" *Economy and Society* 20 (1991), pp. 57–78

Andrew, W. D., "Factionalism and Anti-Communism" *Labor History* 20 (1979), pp. 227–55

Arblaster, A., *The Rise and Decline of Western Liberalism* (Oxford: Blackwell, 1984)

Armstrong, P., A. Glyn, and J. Harrison, *Capitalism Since 1945* (Oxford: Blackwell, 1991)

Arnold, H. L. , and F. L. Faurote, *Ford Methods and the Ford Shops* (New York: The Engineering Magazine Company, 1915)

Aronowitz, S., *False Promises* (New York: McGraw-Hill, 1973)

Arthur, C. J., *Dialectics of Labor* (Oxford: Blackwell, 1986)

Ashley, R., "Three Modes of Economism" *International Studies Quarterly* 27 (1983), pp. 463–96

242

"The Poverty of Neorealism" *International Organization* 38 (1984), pp. 225–86

Auerbach, J., "The La Follette Committee" *Journal of American History* 51 (December, 1964), pp. 435–59

Augelli E., and C. Murphy, *America's Quest For Supremacy and the Third World* (London: Pinter, 1988)

Babson, S., *Working Detroit* (Detroit: Wayne State University Press, 1986)

Baldwin, M., "Why So Few of the Unemployed Receive Benefits" *Dollars and Sense* (June, 1992), pp. 19–22

Bardou, J.-P., J.-J. Chanaron, P. Fridenson, and J. M. Laux, *The Automobile Revolution* (Chapel Hill: University of North Carolina Press, 1982)

Baskin, A., "The Ford Hunger March – 1932" *Labor History* 13 (1972), pp. 331–60

Becker, W. H., "1899–1920, America Adjusts to World Power" in Becker and Wells, eds., *Economics and World Power*, pp. 173–223

Becker, W. H., and S. F. Wells, Jr., eds., *Economics and World Power* (New York: Columbia University Press, 1984)

Berki, R., "On Marxian Thought and the Problem of International Relations" in R. Walker, ed., *Culture, Ideology, and World Order* (Boulder: Westview, 1984), pp. 217–42

Bernstein, I., *The Lean Years* (Boston: Houghton Mifflin, 1960)

Turbulent Years (Boston: Houghton Mifflin, 1970)

Blecker, R. A., and W. E. Spriggs, "Manufacturing Employment in North America" (Washington, DC: Economic Policy Institute, 1992)

Block, F., *The Origins of International Economic Disorder* (Berkeley: University of California Press, 1977)

Blum, J. M., *V Was for Victory* (New York: Harcourt Brace, 1976)

Bowles, S., and H. Gintis, "The Crisis of Liberal Democratic Capitalism" *Politics and Society* 11 (1982), pp. 51–93

Democracy and Capitalism (New York: Basic Books, 1986)

Bowles, S., D. Gordon, and T. Weisskopf, *After the Waste Land* (Armonk, NY: Sharpe, 1990)

Boyer, R. O., and H. M. Morais, *Labor's Untold Story* (Pittsburgh: United Electrical, Radio and Machine Workers of America, 1955)

Braverman, H., *Labor and Monopoly Capital* (New York: Monthly Review Press, 1974)

Brecher, J., *Strike!* (Boston: South End Press, 1972)

Brecher, J., and T. Costello, *Global Village vs. Global Pillage* (Washington, DC: International Labor Rights Education and Research Fund, 1991)

Brenner, R., "The Origins of Capitalist Development: A Critique of Neo-Smithian Marxism" *New Left Review* 104 (1977), pp. 25–92

"The Social Basis of Economic Development" in J. Roemer, ed., *Analytical Marxism* (Cambridge: Cambridge University Press, 1986), pp. 23–53

Brody, D., "The Expansion of the American Labor Movement" in S. Ambrose, ed., *Institutions in Modern America* (Baltimore: Johns Hopkins University Press, 1967), pp. 11–36

Workers in Industrial America (Oxford: Oxford University Press, 1980)

Bibliography

Burawoy, M., *The Politics of Production* (London: Verso, 1985)

Cantor, D., and J. Schor, *Tunnel Vision* (Boston: South End Press, 1987)

Carew, A. *Labor under the Marshall Plan* (Detroit: Wayne State University Press, 1987)

Carnoy, M., *The State and Political Theory* (Princeton: Princeton University Press, 1984)

Caute, D., *The Great Fear* (New York: Simon and Schuster, 1978)

Cavanagh, J., "Free Trade as Opportunity" in J. Cavanagh *et al.*, eds., *Trading Freedom* (San Francisco: Institute For Food and Development Policy, 1992), pp. 1–11

Chandler, A. D. "The American System and Modern Management" in Mayr and Post, eds., *Yankee Enterprise*, pp. 153–70

Cochran, B., *Labor and Communism* (Princeton: Princeton University Press, 1977)

Cohen, L., *Making a New Deal* (Cambridge: Cambridge University Press, 1990)

Colatosi, C., "Eleven Unions Oppose Gulf War" *Labor Notes* (February, 1991), pp. 1, 15

"Union Attitudes Split on War" *Labor Notes* (March, 1991), pp. 3, 12

Commager, H. S., ed., *Documents of American History*, 6th. edn. (New York: Appleton Century Crofts, 1958)

Conybeare, J., "Public Goods, Prisoners' Dilemmas, and the International Political Economy" *International Studies Quarterly* 28 (1984), pp. 5–22

Council of Economic Advisors, *Economic Report of the President, 1991* (Washington, DC: Government Printing Office, 1991)

Cox, R., "Social Forces, States, and World Orders" *Millennium* 10 (1981), pp. 126–55

"Gramsci, Hegemony, and International Relations" *Millennium* 12 (1983), pp. 162–75

Production, Power and World Order (New York: Columbia University Press, 1987)

Cruden, R., "The Worker Looks at Ford" *Labor Age* (June, 1928), p. 2

"The Great Ford Myth" *The New Republic* (March 16, 1932), pp. 116–19

Davis, M., *Prisoners of the American Dream* (London: Verso, 1986)

Der Derian, J., "Mediating Estrangement: A Theory for Diplomacy" *Review of International Studies* 13 (1987), pp. 91–110

"Detroit South" *Business Week* (March 16, 1992), pp. 98–103

Devinat, P., *Scientific Management in Europe*, International Labor Office Studies and Reports, series B, no. 17 (Geneva, 1927)

Devine, J. N., "Underconsumption, Over-Investment and the Origins of the Great Depression" *Review of Radical Political Economics* 15 (Summer, 1983), pp. 1–28

Dicken, P., *Global Shift* 2nd. edn. (New York: Guilford Press, 1992)

Dohse, K., U. Jurgens, and T. Malsch, "From 'Fordism' to 'Toyotism'?" *Politics and Society* 14 (1985), pp. 115–46

Donohue, P., "'Free Trade' Unions and the State" *Research in Political Economy* vol. XIII (Greenwich, CT: JAI Press, 1992), pp. 1–73

Dubofsky, M., "Not So 'Turbulent Years'" in C. Stephenson and R. Asher, eds., *Life and Labor* (Albany: State University of New York Press, 1986), pp. 205–23

Dunn, R. W., *The Americanization of Labor* (New York: International Publishers, 1927)

  Labor and Automobiles (New York: International Publishers, 1929)

Edsforth, R., *Class Conflict and Cultural Consensus* (New Brunswick, NJ: Rutgers University Press, 1987)

Faux, J., and T. Lee, "The Effect of George Bush's NAFTA on American Workers" (Washington, DC: Economic Policy Institute, 1992)

Feldman, R., and M. Betzold, eds., *The End of the Line* (Urbana: University of Illinois Press, 1990)

Ferguson, T., "From Normalcy to New Deal" *International Organization* 38 (1984), pp. 41–94

Fine, S., "The Ford Motor Company and the NRA" *Business History Review* 32 (1958), pp. 353–385

Flink, J. J., *The Automobile Age* (Cambridge, MA: MIT Press, 1988)

Foner, P., *US Labor and the Vietnam War* (New York: International Publishers, 1989)

Ford, H., and S. Crowther, *My Life and Work* (Garden City, NY: Doubleday, 1922)

  Today and Tomorrow (Garden City, NY: Doubleday, 1926)

Foreman-Peck, J., "The American Challenge of the Twenties" *Journal of Economic History* 42 (1982), pp. 865–81

Freeland, R. M., *The Truman Doctrine and the Origins of McCarthyism* (New York: Schocken Books, 1974)

Freeman, J., "Delivering the Goods" *Labor History* 19 (1978), pp. 570–93

Freeman, R., and J. Medoff, *What Do Unions Do?* (New York: Basic Books, 1984)

Fridenson, P., "The Coming of the Assembly Line to Europe" in W. Krohn et al., eds., *The Dynamics of Science and Technology* (Dordrecht: Reidel, 1978)

Frieden, J. A., *Banking on the World* (Oxford: Blackwell, 1987)

  "Sectoral Conflict and US Foreign Economic Policy, 1914–1940" *International Organization* 42 (1988), pp. 59–90

Gaddis, J. L., *Strategies of Containment* (Oxford: Oxford University Press, 1982)

Gartman, D., *Auto Slavery* (New Brunswick, NJ: Rutgers University Press, 1986)

Garver, P., "Beyond the Cold War" *Labor Research Review* 13 (1989), pp. 61–71

Gershman, C., *The Foreign Policy of American Labor* (Beverly Hills: Sage, 1975)

Gerstle, G., "The Politics of Patriotism" *Dissent* 33 (1986), pp. 84–92

  Working-Class Americanism (Cambridge: Cambridge University Press, 1989)

Giddens, A., *The Nation-State and Violence* (Berkeley: University of California Press, 1985)

Gill, S., "American Hegemony: Its Limits and Prospects in the Reagan Era" *Millennium* 15 (1986), pp. 311–39

  American Hegemony and the Trilateral Commission (Cambridge: Cambridge University Press, 1990)

Gilpin, R., *US Power and the Multinational Corporation* (New York: Basic Books, 1975)
  The Political Economy of International Relations (Princeton: Princeton University Press, 1987)
Gindin, S., "Breaking Away" *Studies in Political Economy* 29 (1989), pp. 63–89
Golden, C. S., and H. J. Ruttenberg, *The Dynamics of Industrial Democracy* (New York: Harper and Brothers, 1942)
Goldfield, M., *The Decline of Organized Labor in the United States* (Chicago: University of Chicago Press, 1987)
Gordon, D. M., "The Global Economy" *New Left Review* 168 (1988), pp. 24–64
Gordon, D. M., R. Edwards, and M. Reich, *Segmented Work, Divided Workers* (Cambridge: Cambridge University Press, 1982)
Gould, C., *Marx's Social Ontology* (Cambridge, MA: MIT Press, 1978)
Gramsci, A., *Selections from the Prison Notebooks* Q. Hoare and G. Smith, eds. (New York: International Publishers, 1971)
Green, J. R., "Working Class Militancy in the Depression" *Radical America* 6 (1972), pp. 1–35
  The World of the Worker (New York: Hill and Wang, 1980)
Greider, W., "The Global Marketplace: A Closet Dictator" in Ralph Nader *et al.*, *The Case Against Free Trade* (San Francisco: Earth Island Press, 1993), pp. 195–217
Grunwald J., and K. Flamm, *The Global Factory* (Washington, DC: Brookings Institution, 1985)
Halpern, M., *UAW Politics in the Cold War Era* (Albany: State University of New York Press, 1988)
Harris, H. J., *The Right to Manage* (Madison: University of Wisconsin Press, 1982)
  "The Snares of Liberalism?" in S. Tolliday and J. Zeitlin, eds., *Shop Floor Bargaining and the State* (Cambridge: Cambridge University Press, 1985), pp. 148–91
Harrison, B., and B. Bluestone, *The Great U-Turn* (New York: Basic Books, 1988)
Hartz, L., *The Liberal Tradition in America* (New York: Harcourt Brace and World, 1955)
Harvey, D., *The Condition of Postmodernity* (Oxford: Blackwell, 1989)
Haydu, J., *Between Craft and Class* (Berkeley: University of California Press, 1988)
Heale, M. J., *American Anticommunism* (Baltimore: Johns Hopkins University Press, 1990)
Herzenberg, S., "Whither Social Unionism?" in Jenson and Mahon, eds., *The Challenge of Restructuring*, pp. 314–36
Hogan, M., *The Marshall Plan* (Cambridge: Cambridge University Press, 1987)
Horowitz, R. L., *Political Ideologies of Organized Labor* (New Brunswick, NJ: Transaction Books, 1978)
Hounshell, D. A., "The System" in Mayr and Post, eds., *Yankee Enterprise*, pp. 127–52
  From the American System to Mass Production, 1800–1932 (Baltimore: Johns Hopkins University Press, 1984)

Howe, I., and B. J. Widick, *The UAW and Walter Reuther* (New York: Random House, 1949)

Hughes, T. P., *American Genesis* (New York: Viking, 1989)

Hyman, R., and W. Streek, eds., *New Technology and Industrial Relations* (Oxford: Basil Blackwell, 1988)

Isaac, J., *Power and Marxist Theory* (Ithaca: Cornell University Press, 1987)

Jacoby, S., *Employing Bureaucracy* (New York: Columbia University Press, 1985)

Jay, M., *Marxism and Totality* (Cambridge: Polity Press, 1984)

Jeffreys-Jones, R., *The CIA and American Democracy* (New Haven: Yale University Press, 1989)

Jenson, J., and R. Mahon, eds., *The Challenge of Restructuring* (Philadelphia: Temple University Press, 1993)

Jessop, B., *The Capitalist State* (New York: New York University Press, 1982)

Johnson, O., "After the Dearborn Massacre" *The New Republic* (March 30, 1932), pp. 172–4

Judis, J. B., "Permanently Replacing Labor's Stolen Rights" *In These Times* (August 7–20, 1991)

Katz, H., "Recent Developments in US Auto Labor Relations" in Tolliday and Zeitlin, eds., *The Automobile Industry and its Workers*, pp. 282–304

"Policy Debates over Work Reorganization in North American Unions" in Hyman and Streek, eds., *New Technology and Industrial Relations*, pp. 220–32

Katzenstein, P. J., ed., *Between Power and Plenty* (Madison: University of Wisconsin Press, 1978)

Keeran, R., *The Communist Party and the Auto Workers' Unions* (New York: International Publishers, 1986)

Kennedy, D. M., *Over Here* (New York: Oxford University Press, 1980)

Kenney, M., and R. Florida, "Beyond Mass Production" *Politics and Society* 16 (1988), pp. 121–58

Kenwood, A., and A. Lougheed, *The Growth of the International Economy, 1820–1980* (London: George Allen and Unwin, 1983)

Keohane, R., "The Theory of Hegemonic Stability and Changes in International Economic Regimes, 1967–77" in O. Holsti, R. Siverson, and A. George, eds., *Change in the International System* (Boulder: Westview, 1980), pp. 131–62

"Hegemonic Leadership and US Foreign Economic Policy in the 'Long Decade' of the 1950s" in W. Avery and D. Rapkin, eds., *America in a Changing World Political Economy* (New York: Longman, 1982), pp. 49–76

"The Demand for International Regimes" in S. Krasner, ed., *International Regimes* (Ithaca: Cornell University Press, 1983), pp. 141–71

After Hegemony (Princeton: Princeton University Press, 1984)

"Theory of World Politics" in R. Keohane, ed., *Neorealism and its Critics* (New York: Columbia University Press, 1986), pp. 158–203

Keohane, R., and J. Nye, *Power and Interdependence* (Boston: Little, Brown, 1977)

Keeran, R., *The Communist Party and the Auto Workers' Unions* (New York: International Publishers, 1986)

Kindleberger, C., *The World in Depression, 1929–1939* (Berkeley: University of California Press, 1973)

"Dominance and Leadership in the International Economy" *International Studies Quarterly* 25 (1981), pp. 242–54

Kirkland, L., *Toward a New Foreign Policy* (Washington, DC: AFL–CIO, 1989)

Koechlin, T., and M. Larudee, "The High Cost of NAFTA" *Challenge* (September–October, 1992), pp. 19–26

Krasner, S., "State Power and the Structure of International Trade" *World Politics* 28 (1976), pp. 317–47

Kraus, H., *The Many and the Few* 2nd. edn. (Urbana: University of Illinois Press, 1985)

Kurth, J. R., "The Political Consequences of the Product Cycle" *International Organization* 33 (1979), pp. 1–34

La Botz, D., *Mask of Democracy* (Boston: South End Press, 1992)

Lacey, R., *Ford: The Man and the Machine* (New York: Ballentine, 1986)

LaFeber, W., *The American Age* (New York: Norton, 1989)

Lauck, W. J., *Political and Industrial Democracy, 1776–1926* (New York: Funk and Wagnalls, 1926)

Lee, J. R., "The So-Called Profit Sharing System in the Ford Plant" *Annals of the American Academy of Political and Social Science* 65 (May, 1916), pp. 297–310

Leffler, M. P., "1921–1932, Expansionist Impulses and Domestic Constraints" in Becker and Wells, eds., *Economics and World Power*, pp. 225–75

Levin, S. M., "Ford Profit Sharing, 1914–1920" *Personnel Journal* 6 (August, 1927), pp. 75–86

"The End of Ford Profit Sharing" *Personnel Journal* 6 (October, 1927), pp. 161–70

Levine, R., *Class Struggle and the New Deal* (Lawrence: University Press of Kansas, 1988)

Levinson, J., "The Labor Side Accord to the North American Free Trade Agreement" (Washington, DC: Economic Policy Institute, 1993)

Lewchuk, W., "Fordism and the Moving Assembly Line" in Lichtenstein and Meyer, eds., *On the Line*, pp. 17–41

Lewis, D. L., *The Public Image of Henry Ford* (Detroit: Wayne State University Press, 1976)

Li, C., "A Summer in the Ford Works" *Personnel Journal* 7 (June, 1928), pp. 18–32

Lichtenstein, N., "Auto Worker Militancy and the Structure of Factory Life, 1937–1955" *Journal of American History* 67 (1980), pp. 335–53

Labor's War at Home (Cambridge: Cambridge University Press, 1982)

"Conflict over Workers' Control" in M. Frisch and D. Walkowitz, eds., *Working Class America* (Urbana: University of Illinois Press, 1983), pp. 284–311

"Life at the Rouge" in C. Stephenson and R. Asher, eds., *Life and Labor* (Albany: State University of New York Press, 1986), pp. 237–59

"Reutherism on the Shop Floor" in Tolliday and Zeitlin, eds., *The Automobile Industry and its Workers*, pp. 121–43

"Walter Reuther and the Rise of Labor-Liberalism" in M. Dubofsky and W. Van Tine, eds., *Labor Leaders in America* (Urbana: University of Illinois Press, 1987), pp. 280–302

Lichtenstein, N., and S. Meyer, eds., *On The Line* (Urbana: University of Illinois Press, 1989)

Linklater, A., "Realism, Marxism and Critical International Theory" *Review of International Studies* 12 (1986), pp. 301–12

Lipsey, R., and I. Kravis, "The Competitiveness and Comparative Advantage of US Multinationals, 1957–84" *Banca Nazionale del Lavoro Quarterly Review* 161 (1987), pp. 147–65

Locke, J., *Two Treatises of Government* (Cambridge: Cambridge University Press, 1988)

Lukes, S., *Individualism* (Oxford: Blackwell, 1973)

Macshane, Denis, *International Labor and the Origins of the Cold War* (Oxford: Oxford university Press, 1992)

Maddison, A., *Phases of Capitalist Development* (Oxford: Oxford University Press, 1982)

Maier, C., *In Search of Stability* (Cambridge: Cambridge University Press, 1987)

"The Politics of Productivity" in *In Search of Stability* pp. 121–52

"The Two Postwar Eras and The Conditions for Stability in Twentieth-Century Western Europe" in *In Search of Stability*, pp. 153–84

Marquart, F., *An Auto Worker's Journal* (University Park: The Pennsylvania State University Press, 1975)

Marquis, S. S., "The Ford Idea in Education" *National Education Association: Addresses and Proceedings* 54 (1916), pp. 910–17

Henry Ford (Boston: Little, Brown, 1923)

Marx, K., *Early Writings* (New York: Vintage Books, 1975)

"Critique of Hegel's Doctrine of the State" in *Early Writings* pp. 57–198

"On the Jewish Question" in *Early Writings*, pp. 211–41

"Economic and Philosophical Manuscripts" in *Early Writings*, pp. 279–400

"Theses on Feurbach" in *Early Writings*, pp. 421–3

Capital, Volume I (New York: Vintage Books, 1977)

"Appendix: Results of the Immediate Process of Production" in *Capital, Volume I* pp. 948–1084

Karl Marx: Selected Writings, D. McLellan, ed. (Oxford: Oxford University Press, 1977)

Marx, K., and F. Engels, *The German Ideology* C. J. Arthur, ed. (New York: International Publishers, 1970)

May, M., "The Historical Problem of the Family Wage" in E. C. DuBois and V. L. Ruiz, eds., *Unequal Sisters* (New York: Routledge, 1990), pp. 275–91

Mayr, O., and R. Post, eds., *Yankee Enterprise* (Washington, DC: Smithsonian Institution Press, 1981)

McCarten, J., "The Little Man in Henry Ford's Basement" *The American Mercury* 50 (May, 1940), pp. 7–15, and (June, 1940), pp. 200–8

McClure, L., "Workers of the World Unite!" *Dollars and Sense* (September, 1992), pp. 10–11, 19

McKeown, T., "Hegemonic Stability Theory and Nineteenth Century Tariff Levels in Europe" *International Organization* 37 (1983), pp. 73–92

Meeker, R., "What is the American Standard of Living?" *Monthly Labor Review* 9 (July, 1919), pp. 1–13

Meier, A., and E. Rudwick, *Black Detroit and the Rise of the UAW* (New York: Oxford University Press, 1979)

Merkle, J., *Management and Ideology* (Berkeley: University of California Press, 1980)

Meszaros, I., *Marx's Theory of Alienation* 4th. edn. (London: Merlin Press, 1975)

Meyer, S., III, *The Five Dollar Day* (Albany: State University of New York Press, 1981)

  "The Persistence of Fordism" in Lichtenstein and Meyer, eds., *On The Line*, pp. 73–99

Middlebrook, K. J., "The Politics of Industrial Restructuring" *Comparative Politics* 23 (1991), pp. 275–97

Milton, D., *The Politics of US Labor* (New York: Monthly Review Press, 1982)

Mishel, L., and D. Frankel, *The State of Working America, 1990–91* (Armonk, NY: Sharpe, 1991)

Montgomery, D., *Workers' Control in America* (Cambridge: Cambridge University Press, 1979)

  The Fall of the House of Labor (Cambridge: Cambridge University Press, 1987)

Moody, K., *An Injury to All* (London: Verso, 1988)

  "Free Trade Threatens Jobs and Income in US, Mexico, Canada" *Labor Notes* (July, 1991), pp. 8–10

Motor Vehicle Manufacturers Association, *World Motor Vehicle Data* (Detroit: MVMA, 1991)

National Labor Relations Board, *Decisions and Orders*, vol. IV, November, 1937–February, 1938 (Washington, DC: Government Printing Office, 1938)

Nelson, D., *Managers and Workers* (Madison: University of Wisconsin Press, 1975)

Nevins A., and F. E. Hill, *Ford: The Times, the Man, the Company* (New York: Charles Scribner's Sons, 1954)

  Ford: Expansion and Challenge, 1915–1933 (New York: Charles Scribner's Sons, 1957)

  Ford: Decline and Rebirth, 1933–1962 (New York: Charles Scribner's Sons, 1962)

Noble, D. F., *America by Design.* (Oxford: Oxford University Press, 1977)

Novak, V., "Why Workers Can't Win" *Common Cause Magazine* (July–August, 1991), pp. 28–32

O'Brien, J. H., "Henry Ford's Commander in Chief" *Forum* 99 (February, 1938), pp. 67–72

Ollman, B., *Alienation* 2nd. edn. (Cambridge: Cambridge University Press, 1976)

Palmer, B., "Class, Conception and Conflict" *Review of Radical Political Economics* 7 (1975), pp. 31–49

Parker, M., "Industrial Relations Myth and Shop-floor Reality" in N. Lichtenstein and H. Harris, eds., *Industrial Democracy in America* (Cambridge: Cambridge University Press, 1993), pp. 249–74

Paterson, T. G., *Meeting the Communist Threat* (Oxford: Oxford University Press, 1988)

Peterson, J. S., *American Automobile Workers, 1900–1933* (Albany: State University of New York Press, 1987)

Pinney, H., "The Radio Pastor of Dearborn" *The Nation* (October 9, 1937), pp. 374–6

Piore, M. J., and Sabel, C. F., *The Second Industrial Divide* (New York: Basic Books, 1984)

Pisani, S., *The CIA and the Marshall Plan* (Lawrence: University Press of Kansas, 1991)

Polenberg, R., *War and Society* (New York: Lippincott, 1972)

Pollard, R., *Economic Security and the Origins of the Cold War, 1945–1950* (New York: Columbia University Press, 1985)

Radosh, R., *American Labor and United States Foreign Policy* (New York: Random House, 1969)

Reuther, V., *The Brothers Reuther and the Story of the UAW* (Boston: Houghton Mifflin, 1976)

Reuther, W. P., "Reuther Challenges 'Our Fear of Abundance'" *New York Times Magazine* (September 16, 1945), pp. 8, 32–3, 35

"How to Beat the Communists" *Collier's* (February 28, 1948), pp. 11, 44–9

Richard, G., "On the Assembly Line" *Atlantic Monthly* 159 (April, 1937), pp. 424–8

Roberts, P., *English for Coming Americans* (New York: Association Press, 1912)

Rosenberg, N., "Why in America?" in Mayr and Post, eds., *Yankee Enterprise*, pp. 49–61

Rosenbluth, M., "AFL–CIO Debates War, Decides Little" *Labor Notes* (April, 1991), p. 3

Ruggie, J., "International Regimes, Transactions, and Change" in S. Krasner, ed., *International Regimes* (Ithaca: Cornell University Press, 1983), pp. 195–231

Rupert, M. "(Re)Politicizing the Global Economy: Liberal Common Sense and Ideological Struggle in the NAFTA Debate." Paper prepared for the annual meeting of the International Studies Association, Washington, DC, April 1, 1994

Rupert, M., and D. Rapkin, "The Erosion of US Leadership Capabilities" in P. Johnson and W. Thompson, eds., *Rhythms in Politics and Economics* (New York: Praeger, 1985), pp. 155–80

Russell, J., "The Coming of the Line" *Radical America* 12 (1978), pp. 28–45

Russett, B., "The Mysterious Case of Vanishing Hegemony or Is Mark Twain Really Dead?" *International Organization* 39 (1985), pp. 202–31

Sassoon, A. S., *Gramsci's Politics* 2nd. edn. (Minneapolis: University of Minnesota Press, 1987)

Sayer, D., *Marx's Method* 2nd. edn. (Atlantic Highlands: Humanities Press, 1983)

"The Critique of Politics and Political Economy" *Sociological Review* 33 (1985), pp. 221–53

Schaffer, R., *America in the Great War* (Oxford: Oxford University Press, 1991)

Shaiken, H., "High Tech Goes Third World" *Technology Review* (January, 1988), pp. 39–47

"The Universal Motors Assembly and Stamping Plant" *Columbia Journal of World Business* (Summer, 1991), pp. 125–37

Shaiken, H., S. Herzenberg, and S. Kuhn, "The Work Process under More Flexible Production" *Industrial Relations* 25 (1986), pp. 167–83

Sims, B., *Workers of the World Undermined* (Boston: South End Press, 1992)

Skocpol, T., "Wallerstein's World Capitalist System" *American Journal of Sociology* 82 (1977), pp. 1075–90

States and Social Revolutions (Cambridge: Cambridge University Press, 1979)

Slaughter, J., "What Went Wrong at Caterpillar?" *Labor Notes* (May, 1992), pp. 1, 11–12

Snidal, D., "The Limits of Hegemonic Stability Theory" *International Organization* 39 (1985), pp. 579–614

Sorenson, C., *My Forty Years With Ford* (New York: W. W. Norton, 1956)

Stein, A., "The Hegemon's Dilemma" *International Organization* 38 (1984), pp. 355–86

Strange, S., "The Persistent Myth of Lost Hegemony" *International Organization* 41 (1987), pp. 551–74

Stricker, F., "Affluence for Whom?" *Labor History* 24 (1983), pp. 5–33

Sugar, M., "Bullets – Not Food – for Ford Workers" *The Nation* (March 23, 1932), pp. 333–5

Sugarman, J., "Two Percent Justice for Workers" *Multinational Monitor* (April 1991), p. 9

Sward, K., *The Legend of Henry Ford* (New York: Rinehart, 1948)

Swoboda, F., "Striking Out as a Weapon Against Management" *Washington Post Weekly Edition* (July 13–19, 1992), p. 20

Taylor, F. W., *Scientific Management* (New York: Harper and Brothers, 1947)

Thomas, N., "What is Industrial Democracy?" in B. Johnpoll and M. Yerburgh, eds., *The League for Industrial Democracy: A Documentary History* (Westport, CT: Greenwood, 1980), pp. 389–446

Tolliday, S., and J. Zeitlin, eds., *The Automobile Industry and its Workers* (London: Polity, 1986)

United Automobile Workers, *Fast Track to Decline?* (Detroit: UAW, 1992)

US Bureau of the Census, *Historical Statistics of the United States* (Washington, DC: Government Printing Office, 1975)

Workers With Low Earnings series p-60, no. 178 (Washington, DC: Government Printing Office, 1992)

US Bureau of Labor Statistics, *Handbook of Labor Statistics* (Washington, DC: Government Printing Office, 1989)

van der Pijl, K., *The Making of an Atlantic Ruling Class* (London: Verso, 1984)

Viner, J., "Power versus Plenty as Objectives of Foreign Policy in the Seventeenth and Eighteenth Centuries" *World Politics* 1 (1948), pp. 1–29

Vittoz, S., "The Economic Foundations of Industrial Politics in the United States and the Emerging Structural Theory of the State in Capitalist Society" *Amerikastudien* 27 (1982), pp. 365–412

New Deal Labor Policy and the American Industrial Economy (Chapel Hill: University of North Carolina Press, 1987)

Walker, R. B. J., "Realism, Change, and International Political Theory," *International Studies Quarterly* 31 (1987), pp. 65–86

Wallerstein, I., *The Modern World-System I* (New York: Academic Press, 1974)

The Capitalist World-Economy (Cambridge: Cambridge University Press, 1979)

The Modern World-System II (New York: Academic Press, 1980)

"Crisis as Transition" in Samir Amin *et. al.*, *Dynamics of Global Crisis* (New York: Monthly Review Press, 1982), pp. 11–54

The Politics of the World-Economy (Cambridge: Cambridge University Press, 1984)

Weissman, R., "Replacing the Union" *Multinational Monitor* (April, 1991), pp. 7–13

Wendt, A., "The Agent-Structure Problem in International Relations Theory" *International Organization* 41 (1987), pp. 335–70

Weybright, V., "Henry Ford at the Wheel" *Survey Graphic* (December, 1937), pp. 686–8, 717–23

Windmuller, J. P., "Foreign Affairs and the AFL–CIO" *Industrial and Labor Relations Review* 9 (1956), pp. 419–32

"The Foreign Policy Conflict in American Labor" *Political Science Quarterly* 82 (1967), pp. 205–34

Womack, J., D. Jones, and D. Roos, *The Machine that Changed the World* (New York: Rawson Associates, 1990)

Wood, S., "Between Fordism and Flexibility?" in Hyman and Streek, eds., *New Technology and Industrial Relations*, pp. 101–27

Zieger, R. H., *American Workers, American Unions, 1920–1985* (Baltimore: Johns Hopkins University Press, 1986)

Index

254

Garver, Paul 198, 200
General Motors
  model of mass production 64
Gill, Stephen 1
Gilpin, Robert 1, 4–5, 8, 31
Gintis, Herbert 84–5
global competition
  intensification 176–7
global division of labor
  American position 67–72, 177
global hegemony
  American 43–5, 72, 85, 103
  organized labor 49
global political economy
  1930s–1940s 81–2
Gramsci, Antonio 10–11, 14–17, 25–31, 33, 35–7, 109, 191
  hegemony 41
  world politics 34
Gramscian IPE 10–11, 14–15
Greider, William 205–6

Harris, Howell 96
Hartz, Louis 83–4
hegemonic factory regimes 86
hegemonic stability theory 5
hegemony
  Americanism 65
  bourgeois 30–1
  crisis 191
  Gramsci 29, 34
  liberalism 42
  neoliberalism 54–5, 57, 59, 78, 83, 87, 92
  politics of productivity 61
  theories 1–2, 41
  transnational 36
  Wallerstein 9
  working class 30–1
heterogeneous workforce
  integration 117
historic bloc 2
  Gramsci's concept 55
  hegemony 29–30, 34
  neoliberal 57, 171, 191
  organized labor 50
  transnational 36
Hogan, Michael 44–5
Homestead strike of 1892 88
Hounshell, David 62, 66, 72
House Un-American Activities
  Committee (HUAC) 99, 158
human engineering 151

ideology
  Gramsci 27

immigrant workforce
  Americanization 119–20, 122–3, 129, 164
  integration 112
immigrants
  Americanization 132
imperialism 42
income inequality
  1920s 79–80
  1980s 190–1
industrial conflict
  World War I 89
industrial democracy
  capitalism 162, 164
  company unions 79
  liberalism 159
  unionism 146
industrial discipline
  Depression era 80, 92
industrial productivity
  American 67, 172, 179
  comparative levels 68
industrial unionism
  Americanism 144–6
  conservative backlash 99
  Depression era 81, 92
  establishment 94
  liberal capitalism 102
  mass production 56
  World War II 95
industrial unions
  bureaucratization 97
  emergence 93–4
  stabilizing force 150–2, 162
industrial workers
  as consumers 170
  wage levels 80, 86, 169–71, 190
internal relation 17, 21, 210 n.3
International Confederation of Free
  Trade Unions (ICFTU) 49, 156
  see also free trade unions
international economic institutions
  post-World War II 59
international labor solidarity 197–8, 200–1, 205
International Political Economy see
  IPE
international trade
  AFL and CIO 46
International UAW 198
International Workers of the World 112
internationalism
  organized labor 49
internationalization of production 192–5, 200–1

257